Promoting Racial Literacy in Schools

Differences That Make a *Difference*

Howard C. Stevenson

TEACHERS COLLEGE PRESS

TEACHERS COLLEGE | COLUMBIA UNIVERSITY

NEW YORK AND LONDON

Promoting Racial Literacy in Schools

Differences That Make a Difference

Howard C. Stevenson

TEACHERS COLLEGE PRESS

TEACHERS COLLEGE | COLUMBIA UNIVERSITY

NEW YORK AND LONDON

Published by Teachers College Press, 1234 Amsterdam Avenue, New York, NY
10027

Copyright © 2014 by Teachers College, Columbia University

Library of Congress Cataloging-in-Publication Data

Stevenson, Howard C., 1958–
Promoting racial literacy in schools : differences that make a difference / Howard
Carlton Stevenson, Jr.
  pages cm
  Includes bibliographical references and index.
  ISBN 978-0-8077-5504-4 (pbk.)—ISBN 978-0-8077-5505-1 (hardcover)
  1. Multicultural education—United States. 2. Discrimination in education—
United States. 3. Educational equalization--United States. 4. United States—
Race relations. I. Title.
  LC1099.3.S894 2014
  370.1170973—dc23

2013029279

ISBN 978-0-8077-5504-4 (paper)
ISBN 978-0-8077-5557-0 (hardcover)
eISBN 978-0-8077-7254-6 (ebook)

Printed on acid-free paper

Manufactured in the United States of America

21 20 19 18 17 16 15   8 7 6 5 4 3

Contents

Acknowledgments

In pulling together this book, I have tried to integrate humorous storytelling, research, metaphor, and practical learning strategies. I want to thank the people who have been supportive of me being odd and in applying racial literacy in classrooms, neighborhood community centers, playgrounds, and barbershops. Thanks go first to my family. Gwendolyn Davis, thank you for being supportive and patient with my quirkiness, irritability, and need for room to complete this work. Through your powerful work of educating parents to care for themselves despite harsh life circumstances, you have given me new ways of thinking about racial matters. Julian, thank you for keeping me focused on how children think and feel and come to learn about racial stuff by asking a thousand questions. Also thanks for spontaneously hugging me for no reason. Bryan, thank you for pushing me to cultural, fatherly, worldly places that I hadn't been because of your commitment to follow your dreams and your creative style. I'm amazed at your courage to step out on faith to be your own person. Playing soccer with you, though, keeps me smiling ear to ear and is priceless.

I'd like to thank my father, Howard "Hobby" Stevenson, for reminding his children to take care of ourselves, relax more, and not forget to thank the Lord for every brand-new day. To the memory of my mother, Alice Golden Stevenson; I'm grateful for her kisses and her brilliance under a bushel that she modeled for us to practice, shine, and speak loudly in the presence of friend and foe. To my sister, Christy, whose love for music is a testament to never giving up what you love to do, thank you. To my brother, Bryan, as always, you remain the angel from my childhood, reminiscing on our playful times and giving feedback and love at my most desperate times. Thank you for being there for me emotionally and making me laugh beyond and above despair. Thank you, family.

To my Penn students over the last 2½ decades, I thank you for the questions and banter back and forth to help forge these ideas. I am particularly thankful for the most insightful question you often asked me: "Isn't it educational malpractice and a violation of our commitment to all children not to practice racial literacy?" The answer is still yes.

To my colleagues at the Philadelphia Child Guidance Clinic in the 1980s, where I got to practice my "therapeutic styling," you will see elements of Structural Family Therapy in this book. To my colleagues at the Jewish Board of Family and Children's Services in New York City, thank you for letting me teach the odd combination of racial stress management and family therapy in my training of your staff and supervisors. Trying out these ideas of racial literacy, stress reduction, and family communication in domestic violence shelters, residential treatment centers, conference rooms, and outpatient clinics across the five boroughs for 3 years was amazing and lots of fun. To the JBFCS staff, like a bunny rabbit loves carrots, your hunger for learning was remarkably contagious and energized me to pursue the family racial literacy project, called ViRUS (Villages Raising Us).

To my "When Keepin'-It-Real Goes Right" brothers, Brother Robb, Eric, and Russell: Thanks for your encouragement during knock-down drag-out debating/therapy sessions to keep pursuing ideas on Black folks and to not give up despite the multiple barriers in our way. We have much more writing and fighting to do and many more arguments to have.

To my teammates on the many soccer teams, it has been an honor to play with you and for learning that I will never be too old to play. The element of play can be found throughout this book when encouraging individuals to take risks with stressful moments and to try racial literacy as a powerful opportunity for relational depth and not simply a game.

Racial Illiteracy

...tion of Racial Stress and Resilience Through Storytelling

> Race prejudice in the United States today is such that most Negroes cannot receive proper education in white institutions . . . many public school systems in the North where Negroes are admitted and tolerated but they are not educated; they are crucified . . . certain Northern universities where Negro students . . . cannot get fair recognition, either in classroom or on the campus, in dining hall or student activities, or in human common courtesy.
>
> —DuBois, 1935

> She read me the riot act every other day.
> Not because I was the calamity.
> But so I wouldn't forget the riots about the civil rights.
> This mommy didn't make the bed every day or look for best buys.
> She wasn't like the mommies who held the pain back from their eyes.
> No slack she'd cut for me.
> No making a snack for afterschool mommy.
> Just flack about anything holding me back.
> She did the casting and the molding
> of our consciousness—to prevent unconscious hostage holding
> She was blessed with the best
> that God could invest in the mind
> and she was just as kind
> as the other mommies, just not blind to the politics of her time.
>
> —Excerpt from *Mommy Knew You When*, Stevenson

Overcoming racism in schools requires more than rhetoric. It requires a willingness to fight against a special kind of ignorance and to fight for a different kind of literacy. Battling racial stereotypes that attack intellectual potential and motivation has to be one of the most stressful psychological challenges facing Black students in a society that is afraid to discuss or resolve racial matters (Purdie-Vaughns et al., 2009). As the efforts to close the achievement gap and leave no child behind in receiving high-quality education have not been matched in financial resources, there is a surreal hollowness to the social justice claims from political and educational leaders advocating school reform and choice (Slaughter-Defoe, Stevenson, Arrington, & Johnson, 2012). The emptiness of these claims is surpassed only by the failure of numerous programs to address directly the racism and prejudice that underlie the resource and achievement gaps.

GENTLY APPROACHING RACISM AND WHITENESS THROUGH METAPHOR AND STORYTELLING

To match this social justice irony, I assert that a racial stress–focused approach to overcoming racism to reduce Black academic underachievement and rejection must begin with metaphor. The direct focus on racism in American discourse and schooling has drawbacks. Reform strategies to identify racism in schooling are so stressful that American educators have often employed a Teflon–bulletproof-vestment level of engagement. Racial discourse is stressful emotionally, physiologically, as well as intellectually, leading some educators to absurd levels of avoidance—like running from a herd of stampeding elephants. Hence, part of my justification for using the metaphor of elephants in this book is to reflect the tension or anxiety that remains unspoken but foundationally frightening in American education. A herd of elephants that are peacefully grazing one moment and raging in a stampede the next fits quite well. This anxiety or conflict is racial and is framed very similarly to the way I've described the Ellisonian experience of Black boys and manhood as a kind of "conspicuous invisibility" (Stevenson, Davis, Carter & Elliott, 2003, p. 86). Racial conflict is experienced by many as grazing elephants that could at any moment run rampant over them, their identities, reputations, and social capital. I will try not to overuse these metaphors, but I confess to an uneasy addiction in this area. If these tensions could be revealed, discovered, or listened to, perhaps we might see this stampede as a force of nature and a wake-up call for viewing racial conflicts in school as opportunities for meaningful reform instead of fate-ridden natural disasters of certain annihilation. Metaphors are extremely helpful in sidestepping or skirting around defensive postures, particularly those ignited by racial tension. Through metaphor, I hope to bring pause to the initial resistance of educator leaders, parents, teachers, and even students to embrace school reform that directly faces racial conflicts instead of evading them.

Only three metaphors are used throughout the book for reducing racial defensiveness on three core dynamics that prevent the development of positive race relations in schools (racial denial, racial role-playing, and racial stress). The first is meant to challenge the huge but hidden denial of racial dilemmas (raging elephants in the classroom obvious to few), the second for highlighting America's obsession with racial hierarchy where Black inferiority and White supremacy exist in mutual reciprocity (scripted roles and dancing around racial tension), and the third for explaining personal and group stress reactions to racial conflict (tsunamis, mountains, and anthills as levels of racial stress). Using metaphor eases acceptance of the need for a deeper understanding of racial politics in school reform that uncovers stereotypical thinking, reduces the fear and stress of racialized social interactions, and resolves racial conflicts in schools to improve the academic performance of all students, particularly students of color in Predominantly White Schools (PWS).

While racial stereotypes haunt American societal politics and undermine race relations, they haunt American education and the quality of relationships in schools as well. In maintaining the structural power of racial hierarchy and Whiteness through unconscious bias (Hughey, 2010; Lewis, 2004), some educators and advocates of social reform can't or won't even bother to see, let alone battle these stereotypes—these powerful elephants in the classroom (Guinier, 2004; Macedo, 1995). The politics of maintaining the privilege of Whiteness supports blindness toward racial dilemmas in and out of schools (Fine, Weis, Powell, & Wong, 1997; Frankenberg, 1993; Katznelson, 2005; Lewis, 2004; Perry, 2001). Other reformers attack racial matters with extreme prejudice. Either method of avoidance or embattlement is stressful. Without a set of coping responses to the ideologies of racial inferiority that intentionally and unintentionally contribute to racially inequitable practices in schools, students, parents, and educators will be overwhelmed by racial matters. Moreover, they will rarely view them as resolvable, will learn few tangible racial conflict resolutions skills, and will act out this incompetence in daily relationships.

The problem of American race relations is not simply rooted in our failure as a society to have an in-depth, meaningful conversation about race. The problem rests in our denial and refusal to admit to our fears of what such a conversation will ignite. Without admitting to and managing our fears, we remain unprepared for racial conversations, encounters, or conflicts. Trying to improve race relations and combat racial stereotypes without addressing the stress that is generated by these endeavors is like trying to solve algebraic equations without understanding multiplication or learning to drive a car without lessons. The fear of the unknown usually undermines the completion of the task at hand. This can lead some (Huber, 2013) to explain and problem-solve racial politics in fear-ridden, unsophisticated, stereotypical, and ineffective ways.

The negative health, academic, and social effects of unresolved racially stressful social interactions on an individual's emotional and academic well-being are significant (Mattison & Aber, 2007). But these negative effects are not completely invisible. Stress reactions to racial rejection can be observed. Although the eradication of racism in the United States is a murky social venture, reducing racial stress is less unwieldy. There is a boundary to the concept of stress that doesn't seem to accompany the concept of "race relations." Stress affects thoughts, feelings, body reactions, relationships, and actions. I am hopeful about improving race relations in schools but not without an appreciation and management of the stress that accompanies America's historical and contemporary circumvention of racial politics.

While racial conflicts can be resolved, they cannot be resolved without knowledge or skill. The skill sets to resolve these conflicts are complex and constitute a literacy level of practice, but they can be taught within school curricula and family conversation. Conversely, public, private, charter, and independent schools resist teaching this literacy daily. Most families struggle at teaching these skills daily. Mostly, schools and families fail at teaching racial coping because teachers, administrators, parents, and students are not trained to do so, do not approach it as a competency topic, nor do they have a rationale for engaging in such a "risky" practice. I would argue that families and schools are more likely to be skilled on how to evade racial conflicts than teach how to resolve them.

This talent or skill set of "how not to talk about race" is a form of literacy and also constitutes an "elephant in the room." Finally, the stark absence of racial literacy and competence to process and resolve these issues is also a missing element in strategies to close the achievement gap. It is a problem ably and partially identified in Gary R. Howard's (2006) book *We Can't Teach What We Don't Know*. Still, what I am suggesting regarding racial literacy is that despite our ignorance about racial matters, educators and schools continue to "teach what we don't know or are afraid to know about racial matters"—every day. So, what is there to know about racial literacy?

Racial literacy is the ability to read, recast, and resolve racially stressful social interactions. The teaching of racial literacy skills protects students from the threat of internalizing negative stereotypes that undermine academic critical thinking, engagement, identity, and achievement. Can schools and families prevent the internalization of racial inferiority that contributes to academic disengagement in underachieving Black students in PWS by teaching them to become emotionally, intellectually, and socially literate in the negotiation of racial politics? This is a key subtext question of the book. "How do educators and parents develop racial literacy?" In much the same way that internalization of racial inferiority occurs through exposure, so too does racial literacy occur through racial socialization or a set of child-rearing practices during childhood (Hughes et al., 2006; Rockquemore, Laszloffy, & Noveske, 2006).

DISCOVERING RACIAL STRESS AND RESILIENCE IN A STORY

Putting on 10-minute variety shows for our parents was a common pastime for my brother Bryan, sister Christy, and me in our home when we were growing up—mostly endless performances of corny comedy skits and singing anything from gospel to Broadway musical theme songs. Although I had no idea at the time, these were early practices of racial socialization. Perhaps the most influential and racially socializing music we listened to and acted out was the music of Stevie Wonder. In so many songs, Stevie paid tribute to the beauty of Brown and Black skin color, especially in women; to the power in remembering one's racial history; to the importance of cultural style in communication; to the historical and contemporary tragedy of and triumph over racial discrimination; and to the healing of painful racial conflicts in relationships. Resolving racial conundrums has been an interest of mine since childhood.

Stevie's *Songs in the Key of Life* album was masterful. Memorizing the words and dancing to the music, my brother and sister and I learned more about Black history, racism, racial awareness, cultural pride, colorism, skin color appreciation, and racial justice than from any lesson in 12 years of predominantly White public schooling. The music kept our interest and the rhythm allowed the words to sink into our minds and hearts ever so smoothly and with minimal resistance. Music was and remains one of the most efficient methods of racial socialization. If I had my wish, everyone would be racially socialized in this way. Like metaphor, music tames the initial resistance to reject emotionally disturbing information.

My parents racially socialized very differently. My mother was very direct and self-affirming about what to say and do in the presence of White people. My father would rarely talk about race. Watching their behaviors while they were in the presence of Whites was interesting in that my mother was less trusting, while my father was more open. They presented contrasting styles of how to engage White people in social spaces. My father was conversational and my mother was confrontational. Both got stressed from the encounters with White people but managed that stress in different ways. My father might be unhappy with how he might be treated by others in the workplace or public thoroughfare, but you wouldn't know it until he got in the car or was at home angrily muttering to himself. Mother was not afraid to share her political or personal emotions about racial discrimination in the moment, in the presence or in the face of White people, particularly in stores, but also at work. She would tell stories of racial microaggressions from her work as a civilian in the military, but there would be very little muttering. She was conversational and confrontational. Sue et al. (2007) define *racial microaggressions* as "brief and commonplace daily verbal, behavioral, or environmental indignities, whether intentional or unintentional, that communicate hostile, derogatory, or negative racial slights and insults toward people of color" (p. 271). Speaking assertively about racial injustice requires using political navigation at times and at other times requires a direct challenge of a person's ignorance or unethical behavior. So too is my theory about racial socialization a combination of confrontation and empathy. It consists of engaging and resolving racial encounters with both passive reflection and disruptive action.

Getting along with White colleagues, White classmates, and predominantly White ecologies has been a journey that I believe warrants reflection about the ideology more than the people. I think it is better to evaluate the social and cultural worldviews of schools and public spaces according to whether or not they endorse the importance and supremacy of Whiteness rather than if there happen to be a majority of White people or students in the setting (Hughey, 2010; Martinot & Sexton, 2003). As a quiet boy in a religiously and behaviorally strict household, I spent much time listening to and watching people talk, argue, and avoid racial matters. I took many mental notes on human attitudes and body movements. Throughout graduate school I remained quiet, often fearing my opinions and thoughts would not be appreciated because I was the fifth Black student ever admitted in the psychology program's history and the only or one of two Black students among mostly White classmates in my cohort. Some of this was my fear rooted in a lack of assertiveness, and a desire to avoid violating unspoken rules. Some of this was related to the subtle and blatant disregard of racial inequity in my coursework. Most of my fear was related to the continuous exposure to racial microaggressions that challenged my sense of potential until I developed a useful set of comeback lines and coping strategies. It was my contention early on that racial conflicts could be resolved if individuals could move their worst fears out of the way, but that meant first moving a few of my own.

SHOPPING WHILE BLACK: A CHILD'S-EYE VIEW OF RACIAL STRESS AND RESILIENCE IN THE GROCERY STORE

I have always been struck by the awesome smoothness and dent of will with which my mother would "handle" White people who disrespected us in the public thoroughfares of rural commerce and social interaction. She taught us to be defiant to racial injustice through her protective actions and yet cautious not to be victimized by the petty indignities of arrogant men and women. I am empowered by remembering how she engaged each racial encounter with a sense of resolve. Memories and mannerisms of her resolve remain with me today for better or worse as menu options of racial coping that I use to manage racial microaggressions and insults to my intelligence or being.

I noticed often that many, not all, of the White people my family engaged with in public looked at our Blackness with disdain. Unable to withhold their anxiety, they reminded us of our smallish place in the world. My brother and sister and I were trained to see these tics and spastic involuntary movements, and once bitten, we couldn't really turn those spider senses off. Over time we could see that Black and White folks expressed these stress reactions, albeit in different ways. There was a time in the 1960s where it was commonplace for some to hold public disdain for Black folks in rural southern surroundings without fear of reprisal. As if they had a drug addiction, some were incapable of restraining their disgust by making a public challenge to our movement or voice or property.

When South Carolina Republican congressman Joe Wilson yelled out "You lie!" at President Obama during his presidential address on health care to a joint session of Congress in 2009, it was described as a "breach of decorum." While I was hurt and ashamed by Wilson's lack of impulse control toward the president of the United States, I was not surprised. This simply represented the kind of nervous, involuntary, and spastic disgust reaction to Blacks I was accustomed to seeing and feeling from growing up in southern Delaware. In his political incontinence or racial Tourette's, Wilson appeared to be as incapable of politically managing his anger at his Black president as some would be swallowing sour milk. Although painful, this public racial disgust was not new to me. It is not new to me now as civil rights leaders and parents from poor, Black, and urban neighborhoods beg for more financial resources from state legislatures to keep their children's schools open or get them better resources and receive the same type of sour disrespect. Debates on the racial inequity of resources or revisiting desegregation for predominantly Black schools are barely possible under these racially hostile conditions. Still, while not all Whites we encountered were racially antagonistic, there was no place more political to view the national social battle with race relations than the local grocery store.

I grew up in a multicultural family household. Both of my parents were African American, but both were as different from each other culturally as the East is from the West, as African is from African American, as New York City is from Montgomery, Alabama. Southern Delaware was the birthplace of my father and embodied in this rural Sussex County climate was a host of historical and tragic but mostly suppressed stories of racial animosity and tension. The Black folk there rarely left the area, and the poverty in our neighborhood was intense and evident in our schooling. The climate was that of the caricatured "Deep South" as clear demarcations of White versus Black were visible and invisible. The power differences were stark in wealth and opportunity for youth of color compared with their White counterparts, by way of access to summer jobs in the local establishments, some of which extended to the more progressive areas of the beach area most famously known as Rehoboth. In Delaware's history, there is evidence of both the worst and best of racial progress, but mostly by not talking about these tensions, race relations remained stagnant and segregated in the 1960s, if not by law, then by history and culture.

My father was the youngest of four children and very religious. My father took us to church with the regularity with which most folks would go to the bathroom. Between choir practice, serving as ushers and willing workers, or the perpetual building fund meetings, it seemed we were in church 24 hours a day, 7 days a week. Because God was discussed in our household, music, social network and peer relationships, and worship in an African Methodist Episcopal church, the connection between civil rights, African American heritage, and religious justice was integrated within daily living, singing, and play.

Rarely were racial tensions discussed openly on my father's side of the family. They often practiced the southern hospitalities and southern avoidance of racial segregation. It was just the way life was. Anyone who didn't understand that was just "not from here." My father's approach to racial conflict was spiritual. In essence, he would take a caricatured Martin Luther King Jr. religious nonviolent Christian, surviving through oppression, "climbing up the mountain" approach. When we were mistreated by virtue of our racial difference in public spaces, my father's strategy would be to pray for the assailants with the faith that God would punish them in the end. We talked a lot in church about "end times" because "today" often had more "troubles" than "triumphs" but at least we would win in the end. Nobody really knew when the end was going to be, but there would be "an end." The problem is that despite living in "these last and evil days," the end didn't come yet and so justice sometimes seemed an intangible, silenced, and distant concept while White people were kicking our butts.

In contrast, my mother's approach to racial injustice was relationally assertive and confrontational, more Malcolm X–like. Rather than my father's gospel choir, Mahalia Jackson "How I Got Over" song-singing coping strategy, my mother was interested in not letting White folks get over on us—today and now ("How We Get Over") or like Stevie Wonder's "I Ain't Gonna Stand for It," "Contusion," and "Knocks Me Off My Feet" or just her own rendition of "I Wish a M-F Would." She grew up in north Philadelphia, where neighborhood blocks defined racial segregation. If you walked through a neighborhood where your racial group was not the majority, you would have to run because you would be chased, harassed, or beaten by the youth on the block. Conversely, she and her family and friends were used to rumbling with and chasing out any unwanted racial group from her neighborhood. It was the "way it was" and fighting racial hostility directly was the order of the day—as long as it was in your neighborhood.

Is MLK, Malcolm, or Elvis in the Room?

On some matters, my parents' racial coping feedback was synchronized. I remember being cautioned by them both not to look at White girls directly in the eye. As racial coping strategies go, this admonition was designed to protect us from disrupting that serene southern decorum that lasted as long as people knew their place on the social hierarchy. Ironically, a marathon of Elvis Presley movies on late-night TV undermined that parental feedback. If Elvis could impress White girls with a wink, a sultry voice, and a smile, why couldn't I? This line of misguided racial reasoning also neglected any number of the invisible southern Delaware racial interaction laws like "Don't talk to White girls" or "Don't stand your ground around White girls" or "See Jane, run." My neglect culminated in an embarrassing incident in which I tried to seduce Janet Winsome, a red-headed White girl seated behind me in Mrs. Smith's 1st-grade classroom. As weakened and spellbound by my Elvis impersonation as she was, her daze of shock and awe did not quite satisfy my ego. I decided to push the envelope and risk racial life and limb and jump the racial chasm between us. The problem was that I misinterpreted her daze as being starstruck instead of her being actually paralyzed in fear after I spilled her strawberry milk from snack time all over her new dress. As I was applying my best suave and debonair turnaround move, my incredibly skinny and gangly arm knocked over her box of milk. My life flashed before me—all 5 years of it. As my classmates were laughing (and some guffawing) loudly, and with the shame of the incident so thick in the room and in my mouth, I could barely swallow. I can still remember being so choked up with fear and shame that the whole situation seemed to turn into a slow-motion Neo from the *Matrix* moment—except without escape routes and without me dodging any of the bullets. The consequence was that it took 10 years before I would look at White girls directly in the eye. The moral of that incident for me was that my parents might have been right.

My father worked for General Foods in Dover, an hour's ride by car, while my mother worked for the Dover Air Force Base. In their commute to Dover, "the big city," my parents would travel through rural settlements and neighborhoods of seasonal migrant workers as well as decades of generations of poor Black, Brown, and White families, the children of which were my friends and "enemies" in school. They drove through enclaves that represented years of racial segregation that haunted the race relations of our childhood, and remains to this day in the ways different school systems inland versus closer to the beach vary in their opportunities for students to pursue higher education—the kind of education that potentially gets you economic and social mobility away from southern Delaware poverty. Each of my parents had lessons to teach us about race.

I learned from my mother's way of racial coping that it is okay to (1) identify and face oppression when you see it (translated, "Don't let nobody racially disrespect you without retaliation"), and (2) you have a choice in how to respond when others dismiss you. The consequence of not responding may be that you will be defined by their dismissal. My father's way also represented a form of racial coping. His Christian walk focused on realizing that the pain of this world is sometimes incomprehensible, illogical, spiritual, and beyond human control, and that perhaps only a just God could resolve an unjust but surreal situation. Both ways have benefits and blind spots that influenced our emotional, economic, and physical well-being.

Despite my parents' rare synchronized racial coping socialization, my mother's feedback was more influential in recognizing the vaguely visible racial enmity within our daily comings and goings. As a result, no lesson or socialization was as influential in navigating that segregation as "The Talk."

The Talk

When we went to the grocery store with my mother, it sometimes would feel like we were going to the front lines of a war zone. Because it was the biggest establishment I had been to, it seemed huge in our youth. But so were the tensions. My mother would prepare us for the ensuing battle by giving us "The Talk" and usually just outside the store or in the car on the way. You know, "The You Better Not Act a Fool in Public Talk," the one where your parent makes you responsible for race relations since 1865, through Reconstruction, lynching, and the Harlem Renaissance? Because so few Black people did anything respectable in the eyes of Whites, the fear was that one wrong move from Black children could end in imprisonment or render their parents helpless, publicly confessing their failure as parents in how to control, raise, or civilize their dark offspring. My mother would occasionally remind us, with her most stern look and clenched teeth intonation, not to act up, because there would be no confessions or temper tantrums in any public place.

"When we go into this store, let's get one thing straight. You better not act up because there will be hell to pay. Do you understand what I'm talking about?" ("Yes, Mom.")

"Don't ask for nothing. Don't touch nothing [something about the two negatives in a sentence seemed to solidify the importance of the thing being said]. Stay behind me at all times and don't stray. If I look around, you better be there." ("Yes, Mom.")

"I don't care if every other child in this place is climbing all over the stacks in the store, they are not my child. You're my child, do you understand what I'm saying to you?" ("Yes, Mom.")

"Do you think I come here for my benefit to deal with these crazy folks; for my health? ("No, Mom.") No! I want to get in and get out and you betta not slow me down." [I have often thought that my brother and sister and I began our accomplishment of three-part harmony from the sing-songy way we responded "Yes and No, Mom" in such perfect unison]

The Olympic Trials of Racial Competition:
A Race, a Battle, or a Game?

So "The Talk" was like a pep talk that coaches give before a sporting contest, or a general gives before a crusade, except it had a lot more cultural flair, cultural legacy, and cultural retribution to it. Going to the store was like fighting a battle in a war where we couldn't tell whether we were winning or losing, but one that we had to fight or else. No one ever explained the "else" (just like they never explained "in the end"), and we really didn't want to know. Basically, as children my younger brother and sister and I had little desire to fight. We just wanted to get our food, go home, and eat. The larger racial politics of the time had escaped us as preteens, but that didn't mean we didn't get a training lesson every time we went to the grocery store. The lesson was stark, swift, and on some days there was no conflict at all. But on other days, there would be this clashing. We hated those moments as children, or at least I did. Not because they were embarrassing. (Those embarrassing moments came later, when I realized that not all of the Black mothers would come to the school and argue with the White teachers to stop messing with their child.) I can't speak for my brother or sister, but for me, these encounters were scary because I was afraid someone would harm my mother.

So as we walked into the supermarket after getting our mission briefing, we would do so with a sense of both trepidation and circumspection. As children we didn't really get the larger picture of race relations in southern Delaware, but we could read nonverbal language and physical movement quite well. Anthropologists suggest that about 70% of our communication is nonverbal. If that is the case, then my brother Bryan and sister Christy and I were experts in nonverbal bilinguality, because there was a whole lot of "talking" going on when my mother and the "three live crew" walked into the store.

I observed that many of us as Black folks in our southern Delawarean wooded neighborhoods were much more deferential (physically and verbally) or stoic toward Whites as we passed them on the street or encountered them in public spaces, careful not to raise any ruckus, much more apologetic and ready to avoid direct confrontation or unwanted attention. My mother was not deferential. Polite? Yes. Deferential? No. So when she walked into the supermarket, she was strident. She affected air and space and moved with the grace and force of an Olympic ice-skater in the lead on the last two laps of the race toward the finish line and the gold-medal ceremony. As she moved with purpose and with each foot sure, we three siblings had to keep up or risk the failure of the mission, the wrath of Khan, the loss of the gold, and the demise of the Race. Oh, the shame of it all.

Any serious Olympic skater knows that reducing drag force by drafting behind the lead skater is a key way to win the race. So we drafted behind our mother's speedy entry into the supermarket, being careful to stay behind her in tune, speed, and motion. So as our little legs kept up, we could see in slow motion the hostile nonverbal looks and grunts, eye-rolling, and teeth-sucking gestures of the White salespeople watching my mother and her three ducklings skate into the store. Since as children we were smaller, we hadn't yet learned to look away from the negativity and tension around us, mostly directed toward my mother's walk, style, and way. As children, we didn't just feel the tension; we saw body movements of knees, elbows, and feet all giving off messages of apprehension and disdain.

Some days the tension was so thick in the place you could scoop it with a spoon and it was on sale. As we watched this impending drama unfold and it became increasingly stressful, I remember distinctly giving and getting a look from my brother and sister to go to plan B. Plan B was a primitive, unspoken, eye-contact-gesturing, and stress-reduction dance that my siblings and I engaged in whenever we felt that "shit was gonna happen" or a racial volcanic eruption event was imminent. As children, we decided to distract our mother while skating from aisle to aisle by demonstrating our smarts, something she was proud of no matter what time of day it was.

So in unison and on cue, we all began to talk to each other and add up the cumulative cost of the food in the shopping cart to see who would come the closest to the actual final cost at the register. The register was the last stop on this climactic and icy roller-coaster ride through race relations hell. The key to our synchronized, updated-in-real-time arithmetic exercises was to be verbal, not loud, but loud enough to distract our mother from the hostile stares and attitudes of the White shoppers and market workers. White people just scared us with their looks, but if we could get through the register safely, we could complete our mission, go home alive, and eat.

Somedays, shopping cart math worked. Our mother would be distracted. But on days where the counting had absolutely no effect on my mother's hypervigilance in seeing the store employees' enmity, we continued skating from aisle to aisle in a unified string, hopelessly imagining the hell waiting at the end of the shopping visit, at the finish line, at the register. On those days when creative and rhythmic arithmetic would fail, we did what our father taught us to do. Pray.

So we prayed in silence, while skating, to a God who sat high and we hoped was looking low—low enough to see that hell was just about to break loose up in this M—F— unless He or She did something special, and quick. On some days, our prayers were answered and we skated through the register without a whimper or a cry or a fight, taking the gold without dispute. But on those days when the White salesperson behind the register counter would have a Joe Wilson meltdown moment and feel compelled to insult my mother with some nonverbal statement or behavior of derision, it was time to run for cover. But given the lessons of "The Talk," we could not run. We had to stay behind our mother. It was during these times in my small-child mind that I believed God was sleeping or busy helping another group of poor Black children shop under the siege of White people stares.

And so it was. The "evil" register person would do or say something to my mother as if to remind her of her lower social station. Sometimes it would be a look or a comment about who she thought she was. The worst, though, was when they would throw our food into the bag. If that happened, it was on! My mother would begin and we would stop praying and step back. She would address the salesperson directly by cursing him or her out (communication). My mother would tell the person who he or she was (identity), who his or her family was (history or genealogy), where they could go (direction), how fast to get there (speed), which train to take (transportation), and where the train ticket office was (information or mapping). Before the minute of rapid-fire cursing was over, the salesperson would be disheveled and shaking on the supermarket floor behind the register counter, whimpering in a pool of racial shame (therapy). Now I may not have mentioned that my parents were both Christians. But what this usually meant in southern Black Delaware was that they both believed in the "worth of prayer." One major cultural difference between my parents, though, is that my father would pray before the racial conflict and my mother would pray after. The moral of the story for me as I skate through or navigate racial conflict today is that sometimes you have to pray and sometimes you have to push.

Praying for and Pushing Over Angels of Racial Illiteracy

I repeat this story during public speaking engagements on racial tension and resolution to encourage others to tell their stories and analyze the stress and resilience of their childhood experiences. (I must apologize for the added Olympic Games metaphor, but I told you I have a mild addiction to this stuff.) It illustrates several elements of how I've come to believe racial stress is palpable and racial negotiation is possible—but not by hoping and wishing we could all postracially "just get along." I have often forgotten I was not the only one stressed by these racialized social interactions. Each of the players in the grocery store story was stressed too. When my brother and I speak about my mother, we tend to share different pictures of her. My brother Bryan, an amazing civil rights lawyer in challenging the nation's laws on the disproportionate use of the death penalty on the poor and underaged, has a wonderful TED talk about our family and his work (www.ted.com/talks/bryan_stevenson_we_need_to_talk_about_an_injustice.html). Bryan will often tell stories of my mother as a kind and sweet and gentle woman while I portray her as the radical racial activist who would cry out often and without warning Malcolm X's retort that "we didn't land on Plymouth Rock, Plymouth Rock landed on us." But she was both incredibly affectionate and protective. I just like the fiery aspects of her personality because they communicate how standing up for yourself and family is often a battle. Much like Frederick Douglass's quotes on "there is no progress without struggle," my mother's way would often remind us that proactive racial coping is a necessary step toward progress.

What I also remember when considering my childhood is that racial stress was present for all of my family members, and in different ways. As children we were worried about how others would respond to us as Black people. My parents were worried that we as children would be misunderstood or mistreated and they would be left helpless to protect us. Thus, the reason for that "Talk" (which can be clumsy to give or hear) before going into the store was not simply my mother "wanting to hear herself talk" or some strange "paranoia." She was schooling us to the illiterate way the world thought of us and that our behavior was on trial, every day, even in the grocery store. Praying for and pushing over the angels of racial illiteracy were not acts to prove our humanity; they were acts to reassert it for the clueless, the forgetful, and the ignorant. We were "Black while shopping," and as tragic as that might seem, we had better understand it, prepare for it, and respond to it.

LOOKING FOR THE "LOOKS": META-OBSERVATION OF THE RACIAL STRESS OF WHITE PEOPLE

One benefit of racial storytelling is the development of metacognitive skills to observe the self and others in social interactions. It is a sort of "Otherizing Racial Consciousness," which involves figuring out how other people view you. Robert Sellers at the University of Michigan has coined a term close to but not similar to this concept—"public racial regard"—which reflects how much an individual believes others (the public) favorably view his or her racial group. The more you believe the public views your racial group positively, the less threatened you are and the safer is the climate of the context you inhabit. I would adjust this definition slightly toward a skill rather than a belief, an ability to discern accurately how others might perceive an individual's Blackness. This accuracy comes through the skillful accumulation and analysis of intrapersonal and interpersonal information from multiple incidents of racial conflict rather than simply a belief about how others perceive your Blackness. I would think of it as *public racial discernment*. How well can we identify the intensity of emotional threat from the people in the grocery store and shield and counter their negative reactions to our presence as Black people?

"The Talk" included behavioral skills instructions on how to self-regulate, inhibit impulsive reactions, maintain social vigilance, and exercise public racial discernment. These are invaluable skills in cross- and same-racial social gatherings. They include famous Black racial coping strategies such as the "Never Let Them See You Sweat" technique or the "Why are the White children misbehaving and cursing their mothers out in the supermarket, Mommy?" query or the famous "Always Keep Your Receipt in Case You Get Accused of Stealing the Groceries You Just Bought" maneuver. In essence, that talk and other lessons from our parents developed the most useful racial coping skill of all—seeing how people see you. This is a psychological strategy to interpret the other's fears, the other's lens for viewing racial conflict. Now, if I were to say that this kind of psychological training has no negative consequences, I would be mistaken. Without other types of compassion and support and explanation, simply teaching youth to "look out" for racist behavior can lead to a form of racial paranoia. But we will talk about these other skills later. Suffice it to say, there was more in my mother's "outside the store talk" than protecting her parental image.

I could also observe racial stress for the store clerk or register person. I could see that when my mother began to challenge the person's history and family background, that person's eyes would get really big. His or her mouth would open wide in shock and horror, and speech would stutter. I knew "shock and awe" long before American political spin artists coined it. These were powerful reactions that as children we witnessed on multiple occasions. My mother had power using her voice and her style, all meant to protect us. Despite our pleas to God, "Please Lord, whatever happens, please don't let that man behind the register throw my mother's food into the bag," it was still amazing to watch how my mother stood up when all around us were fearful; arrogant eyes and stares demanding that we lie down. But her lesson was that we cannot lie down. We should not lie down, not in the face of racial fear or racial hostility or racial stress.

There was racial stress in my mother as well. While I often tell this story with a sense of humor and affection, I remember my mother's frequent pacing at home before going to the store, muttering to herself, "These White folks better not mess with me today. I'm sick and tired of this, every time we . . ." This pacing and muttering revealed her own worry at having to face resistant salespeople who lose the "service" part of their job when Black people are the recipients. She was both preparing herself and practicing comeback lines should a volcanic eruption present itself. But as life goes, it also took its toll on her.

It is stressful to prepare for racial antagonism from others. Its occurrence is random and not always predictable. It is subtle in ways that one may be hard-pressed to acknowledge, let alone tell a friend or loved one about. These slights of racial antagonism or racial microaggressions are detrimental, like the multiple stabbings of tiny daggers that steal our energy, self-efficacy, self-worth, self-control, self-care, and focus (Sue, Lin, Torino, Capodilupo, & Rivera, 2009).

It may appear odd to raise issues of racial microaggressions in a public space like a grocery store in a book about schools. My motivation is not tangential. In our research on PWS, my colleagues and I found the most significant predictor of Black students' psychological sense of membership and belonging in their school was the frequency of racial discrimination they experienced in public settings (Arrington, Hall, & Stevenson, 2003; Stevenson & Arrington, 2009). The more discrimination experienced in public, the less belonging the students felt in school. The consequences of racial injustice are not about slogans, dreams, paranoia, or sermons. Those events occur after injustice has happened. Failing to see that racism in daily face-to-face activities contributes to the disparities we see in justice, health, wealth, and education systems is unfortunate as it explains the failure of systemic change initiatives (Massey, 2007). More important, these public experiences affect individuals' well-being.

Storytelling Is Seeing Is Believing

Through storytelling, we can see ourselves differently, assess our emotions, and find the capacity to change. We can change our responses to the plot, the background, the punch line, and reduce the power of the oppression. In storytelling, individuals can ease into self-reflection and become self-critical without public scrutiny. With practice, one can learn to forgive mistakes and see how context and history matter in racial decisionmaking and action. In storytelling, individuals and systems can rethink past decisions and take responsibility for their actions. They can also forgive others for being wrong or just confused. Storytelling is like practice for the next time you run into a herd of racial elephants or just one.

Racial literacy as the ability to read, recast, and resolve racial stress in social encounters is necessary not only in the context of school classrooms, political debates, and supermarket politics. It is necessary in the various ways social contexts demand competence, skills, and psychological and social functioning. While telling a story about race is not a substitute for engaging race relations ("I walked 5 miles in the storm barefoot to fight racism" or "Some of my best friends are Black militants"), it can prepare us to tackle difficult racial encounters. Storytelling helps individuals believe they can resolve racial tensions that arise within five cultural psychosocial ecologies to be discussed later: information dissemination, relationship-building, identity development, ✓ style management, and stereotype reproduction. Racial literacy goals differ across these five contexts and over time demand the procurement and exercise of advanced skills, including the *strategic deconstruction of racial information and knowledge, the building of healthy cross- and same-racial relationships, the flexible reconstruction of racial identity, the willful choosing of racial styles and self-expression, and the assertive countering of racial stereotypes.*

In stories, we can reexamine our roles, the information we were given, and question or research its authenticity. We can examine how we shied away from the relationships where racial stress was present. In storytelling, we can recollect memories about our behaviors, legacy communications from family, and our responses to those interactions and rituals. Through memory, we can also reconstruct and connect our intersecting racial, gender, sexual orientation, age, and personal identities. In storytelling, we are able to observe the styles we used during moments of indecision, inaction, or agency in the context of racial matters. Through story, we can also begin to see patterns of racial discrimination and injustice and our emotional and behavioral reactions to these negative experiences. Through this discovery of patterns, we can better prepare for future racial microaggressions and develop healthy and stylistic comeback lines to racial insults or hostilities. These are strategies for becoming aware of racial stereotypes in everyday life, seeing their detriment to achievement and healing, and countering stereotypes as they crop up—in school, in neighborhoods, in families, and in relationships with people in those contexts.

While mastering the basic literacy skills of racial self-observation could take a lifetime, another benefit of storytelling is seeing racial stress in others. Becoming facile at appraising one's stress reactions during racial encounters teaches individuals to notice the stress reactions of other people. More important, one can become competent at choosing to respond to those reactions differently. Seeing racial stress in others makes them more predictable and perhaps less threatening.

As storytelling helps individuals and systems accomplish the first racial literacy objective of racial stress awareness of self and others through observation, repressed experiences of racial interactions may resurface. Remembering and reexamining past racial experiences is essential to healing. Although they may bring distress, they will also enhance one's competence during racially stressful interactions. To process these racial stories and experiences or keep them repressed is not an easy choice. The biggest tragedy of repressed racial encounters is that their lessons cannot be integrated into one's craft—whether that is learning, teaching, counseling, leading, or parenting. Without processing, we remain uncertain about why racial conflicts are so distressing to us, if they are. So storytelling about racial encounters from family and daily life experiences is a form of social justice risk taking. What risks are educators willing to take to become competent to protect and affirm racially different students in schools where racial stress undermines their achievement?

Risky Racial Business: Storytelling Is Racial Socialization

Storytelling has become a form of therapy in my work. Racial socialization has been my research interest for over 2 decades. As a therapist and researcher, I often find it difficult to reconcile the expectations, rules, values, and methods of research and therapy to support well-being in the lives of youth and families. Such is the case with investigating racial processes in others and experiencing racial microaggressions for myself. Sometimes my clients, students, colleagues, and I needed knowledge and action steps to cope with racism, and sometimes we needed therapy to navigate the trauma. My definition of racial socialization that follows reflects the need for both knowledge and therapy. Racial socialization *is the transmission and acquisition of intellectual, emotional, and behavioral skills to protect and affirm racial self-efficacy by recasting and reducing the stress that occurs during racial conflicts with the goal of successfully resolving those conflicts.*

Mostly, those who are confronted with racial microaggressions daily need a buffer against racial insult and support to develop healthy racial coping strategies. This, to me, represents the importance and role of racial socialization—to buffer and to inspire; to protect and affirm; to defend and support so that youth and adults can speak and act assertively in social interactions, especially where learning and academic progress are expected. It is the role of mediation between a stimulus and a response, between stress and coping.

In my research and therapy projects, I teach youth and families how to use a variety of intellectual, affective, and behavioral skills to protect and affirm the racial self-efficacy and coping of their children. Self-efficacy is believing "I can" accomplish a task and reach a goal. Racial self-efficacy is the belief that one can successfully meet racial demands and accomplish racial tasks. I teach folks how to see, survive, and transcend racial hardship, not by hiding from the stress of racial interactions but by identifying, reducing, and assertively communicating their thoughts and feelings about that stress. While racial socialization is occurring in media, family conversation, music, and pop culture continuously, rarely is it employed to manage racial conflict. That's what I confidently expect to accomplish—teaching individuals and groups through stress reduction and mindfulness to resolve racial conflicts in adult authority and peer relationships, particularly in schools, for youth. It seems daunting, I know, but my confidence in building racial literacy within schools begins with storytelling.

Promoting Racial Literacy in Schools is a book about noticing and lessening the racial fears and the stressful reactions that teachers, parents, and students experience when they face racial conflicts. These reactions include eye-blinks, hesitation, stuttering, uncomfortable pauses, linguistic gaffs, frequently avoidant eye contact, excessive excuse-making, excessive probing for approval, inappropriate redirection of conversation, and the use of silence by one, some, or many individuals who perceive a racial matter will surface and lead to unresolvable tension. For many, negotiating racial conversation and discourse is like walking circumspectly through a dense forest or jungle or being thrown into a pool and expected to swim without lessons. If individuals are able to reduce their stress during racial conflicts, resolving them will be easier.

Given that racial interactions engender anxiety for educational leaders, teachers, parents, and students, this book will include stories, strategies, and recommendations to explain how racial stress underlies many underachievement outcomes and to successfully negotiate racial conflicts in schooling relationships. As these reactions are observable and negotiable, the integrated set of skills required to successfully navigate racial conflicts that arise during information and knowledge processing, relationship-building, identity development, style expression, and stereotype deconstruction constitute a form of literacy. As racial self-efficacy and literacy in this book are defined as the belief in and ability to read, recast, and resolve racially stressful encounters, it makes sense why schools and families might be reluctant to change racial inequities in learning. Yet because of this crisis in quality of leadership, knowledge, and climate, schools are best suited for that change.

Racial Literacy for Educators and Families

Racial literacy was notably coined by France Winddance Twine (2003) and Lani Guinier in 2004. Although my definition of racial literacy is similar to Guinier's (2004) focus on balancing individual and systemic racial politics that intersect with other diversity politics, it is more similar to Twine's (2011) definition as focused on relational dynamics where skills sets are taught. Twine suggests that racial literacy involves

(1) the definition of racism as a contemporary problem rather than a historical legacy; (2) an understanding of the ways that experiences of racism and racialization are mediated by class, gender inequality, and heterosexuality; (3) a recognition of the cultural and symbolic value of whiteness; (4) an understanding that racial identities are learned and an outcome of social practices; (5) the possession of a racial grammar and vocabulary to discuss race, racism, and antiracism; and (6) the ability to interpret racial codes and racialized practices. (p. 92)

Twine (2003) had previously identified racial literacy as transracial parenting by White parents, a minority of whom learned to teach children of African and Caribbean background to identify racism in "ideologies, semiotics, and practices"; use knowledge and strategies to combat that racism; and make available resources of art, toys, books, and music to increase a positive connection to Black legacies, people, and history. While Twine's racial literacy is derived from her ethnographic investigations into the multiracial family processes and practices of White parents of Black children in Britain, my research has sought to understand more deeply the multidimensionality of racial socialization practices of African American parents of Black children and the context within which parents find this socialization necessary for their children's success.

Racial literacy in this book is derived from my research on racial socialization, which frames parenting practices and processes as a skills-building endeavor. I have encouraged the field of racial socialization research to shift its focus away from only what parents intentionally communicate to children about race and move toward an integration of what parents teach and youth internalize through intentional, nonverbal, and unintentional messages from their actions. Moreover, I've been more interested in the functions of racial socialization. So the ways in which Black families prepare their children and themselves for racial hostility in everyday social interactions fuel how and why racial literacy is necessary. These daily social interactions or racial encounters are frequent and unpredictable but occur with individuals, institutions, and authority figures in health, educational, and justice systems. Racial socialization is generated by these systems and figures and is not simply family-based or solely the purview of Black families or parents of Black children (Twine, 2011). Preliminary research on racial socialization in White families with White parents and children has revealed very little by way of racial literacy, although a race avoidance coping strategy appears to be the most salient strategy (Bartoli et al., 2013).

Although my research focuses on racial literacy within Black families, the concept is functionally useful in response to racial conflict and competence in public racial discourse that occurs in schools and classrooms for anyone. Families and school personnel are equally culpable for delivering these skills too, whether or not they are conscious of racial politics. Racial literacy assumes there is a gap in the ways authority figures relate to students and parents of color. One thrust of a racial literacy agenda for reforming education rests in evaluating not if but how well individuals, families, and systems navigate racial discourses in the multiple worlds in which children learn. A second thrust of this agenda is recognizing that for racial literacy to influence how families and youth engage the social and academic world, it takes practice.

Racial Literacy to Change Racism or Racial Stress?

While changing racism at the macro level of systems like desegregation, racial profiling, and racial redistricting to benefit wealthy White communities is important, attending to the effects of racism at the face-to-face encounter level of relational thoughts and feelings is equally important. The major example of systemic racial progress is the election of the first Black president of the United States. It ranks highest among a long list of "Racial Firsts" that assume that the symbolic nature of these monumental events creates changes in the way racism influences equity at the micro level of individual and family functioning. While these "firsts" reform American societal functioning, I believe that the social and economic benefits of the symbolism of "Racial Firsts" can be exaggerated. The benefits are not always far-reaching. Trickle-down symbols of racial progress may not effectively change racially stereotypical fears before and during social interactions as Americans would hope. Instead, I see stress as a better way than symbolic "Racial Firsts" to frame racial conflict resolution or social reform, as it is observable, modifiable, and usable in relationships within and across racial groups. Racial fears and conflict avoidance are also often predictable, even if they are manifested in extreme reactions. So, it's the effects of racism at the relationship level that are most likely to be the targets of a racial literacy agenda in schools.

In the following chapters, I will make the argument, using Black students and parents as the identified population and school as the identified context, that racial politics or the processes and effects of racism can be observed. These politics are prevalent in the racially stressful social interactions between all youth and parents, teachers, or other authority figures in schools, and students from different racial backgrounds, within neighborhoods, and in classroom learning processes. Everyone experiences some level of racial stress, but the experiences range from low to high. A key theme of the book will be that racial stress is remediable if we practice stress-reduction skills (through racial socialization and racial mindfulness) that are specific to racial conflicts.

Fortunately and unfortunately, since the 1960s, many of our approaches to antiracist teaching in relationships has involved denouncing blatant racist acts and attacking individuals who use politically incorrect language. In schools, similar failed strategies abound and include planning but failing to increase the numerical diversity of a teacher or student cohort or conducting diversity training that provides details on information and knowledge without teaching skills to advocate for racial equity. These strategies acknowledge that a racial problem exists (history, prevalence, and frequency) but find going further than this acknowledgment to be too costly, as it requires greater expertise in healing the racial antagonism. These strategies fail in schools and society, in part because for many leaders, facing racial conflict is too anxiety-producing and the risk of public humiliation and stigma for saying or doing the wrong racial thing is too high.

Viewing racism as a daily face-to-face test that is fueled by macrosystemic forces without considering the daily struggle individuals experience as a result is unethical. Individuals muddle through messy issues like trying not to think or say "racist" thoughts or fears and avoiding making awkward statements. Given this inner turmoil, it is easier to see how educational, political, and intellectual leaders rarely make substantive proclamations on racial topics. Many have insufficient knowledge, words, or remedies for the specific burden that racial stress places on the lives of Black and Brown families and children. This ignorance or incompetence about culturally specific emotional burdens is cumulative, as are the effects of those burdens. Eventually, the failure of schools and families to address racial stress can create a dangerous "jungle" or climate for students, teachers, and parents of color who need safety in order to learn, teach, and achieve.

In predominantly White public and independent schools, the mission statement's clarity on diversity matters in schooling becomes a recipe for chaos or competence in creating a climate of safety for students of diverse backgrounds (Datnow & Cooper, 2000; Hall & Stevenson, 2007; Linn & Welner, 2007). Educational leaders who cannot articulate a vision, plan, and educational curricular goal for diversity may be setting up their schools for failure in race relations. The use of avoidance and obfuscation are tools of leaders who want to become politicians rather than educators. The stress of racial interactions in the classroom must be acknowledged and confronted. Unfortunately, it has been my experience that students, parents, and faculty who hold worldviews with strong racial equity principles fueled by explicit racial socialization will see more racial conflicts and carry this burden of racial stress more than others. Those who consciously or unconsciously endorse Whiteness as the primary lens to interpret educational outcomes will find it harder to see or reduce racial stress for themselves or others (Twine & Gallagher, 2008). Still, it is my contention that without an explicit racial socialization strategy, avoidance will remain the default and most practiced coping option.

In this Introduction, I have shared a personal story to demonstrate that racial storytelling is the first step toward racial literacy, that racial socialization should be explicit, and that racial stress in public spaces affects a student's experience of schooling. As each person shares his or her own story of racial microaggressions, he or she can begin to *recast* the meaning and stressfulness of racial politics from his or her childhood. These memories can serve as triggers for developing awareness of racial politics in one's current context. Storytelling of racial experiences, small and large, makes room for one to see the television, neighborhood, street corner, supermarket, and classroom as different contexts of racialized social interactions.

In Chapter 1, I will argue that taking a large-systems approach to combating racism is insufficient. Although racial progress in the courts influences the daily functioning of teachers, students, and parents, these advances are not powerful enough to change the management of racial stress at the level of relationships between teachers, students, and parents. In Chapter 2, I will explore how being the "Racial First" and symbolic representations of racial progress are different and perhaps less powerful than social interaction acuity in resolving racial conflict. In Chapter 3, I briefly review the literature on racial fear and the relevance of fear to coping effectively in predominantly White academic contexts. Facing our racial fears is the only way to improve race relations and reduce the detrimental psychological effects of racial discrimination or microaggressions. In Chapter 4, I explain recast theory as a way to illustrate how healthy racial socialization practices can reduce the negative effects of racial stress on ineffective social problem solving. Using recast theory, I present a training model for teachers, students, educational leaders, and parents with examples of racially stressful classroom and school interactions that can increase teachers', parents', and students' racial literacy. In Chapter 5, I try to examine how parents and educators can use racial literacy to reduce racial threat and shame that undermines coping in social interactions. Not only must students muddle through racial ambivalence in schools, but so must adults. Parents and educators are given suggestions about how to talk to youth about racial discrimination in order to protect and affirm their children's racial identities and well-being. The final chapter, Chapter 6, includes exercises and examples that can be used to teach racial assertiveness skills to resolve racially stressful encounters.

Schooling Whiteness: Resistance to Racial Literacy is Institutional

I realize that those who hold either opposing pessimistic or optimistic views of racial progress may find this book troublesome. Particularly troublesome could be the focus on individual and dyadic psychological experiences as a route to address systemic racism. Some may see this volume as changing deck chairs on the *Titanic* and question why we aren't directly challenging rather than negotiating racist practices in the classroom. For these folks, negotiation is a pipe dream. The optimistic racial progressives, whom I call postracialists, may view racial literacy as too depressing, because it fails to recognize social and systemic advances that have occurred, that it requires too much work, and that this work will make Whites uncomfortable and therefore is destined to fail. Other critics may suggest that

I'm essentializing Blackness, ignoring intersectionality, and ascribing too much order to a racial process that is chaotic and fraught with unaccounted-for diversity.

Still, the ways in which racial interactions are hidden in schools of Whiteness begs the question of how healthy racial interaction can occur in these contexts. Having conversations about resolving racial matters is easier said than done. Whether progress in schools is likely may depend on a courageous someone to risk ridicule, burden, and faith to raise racially contentious issues. Hence, the notion of "If": If educational leaders, teachers, and parents could see the racial conflicts, then perhaps they could be resolved. If educators could admit to their fears, then perhaps students could feel safe to admit their fears. If fears were acknowledged, then perhaps school climates would improve and schools could become safer places to speak outwardly on a diversity of racial and nonracial matters, in and outside of the classroom.

By "schools" I don't just mean educational institutions, but also business, sports, political, health, justice, and societal institutions that reward, punish, privilege, and hide avoidant racial interactions daily. By "schooling" I don't just mean getting a formal education. I also mean schooling to reflect learning life lessons despite school curricula and policies that teach students, parents, and leaders to see and resolve racial elephants or conflicts in the curriculum and the polities. One hope I have is that all schools will take off the racial blinders and give students, parents, teachers, colleagues, and patrons safe opportunities to express their voices about racial conflict; to tell stories and to sing and dance to a different racial rhythm than avoidance and denial. My greatest hope is that these schools become courageous hubs of relational learning that teach racial literacy to educators, students, and families as clearly and efficiently as they teach how a cell works, how to do subtraction and addition, how to make smart financial investments, or how to shoot a basketball. The goal of this racial literacy could be as important and creative as teaching students how to become self-confident as learners about these traditional topics as they learn about their racial heritage while imitating a Stevie Wonder riff.

CHAPTER 1

If Elephants Could Talk

Stress and Incompetence in the Politics of American Race Relations

It's not about the blame.
Not trying to make you feel guilty.
It's not just about you.
It's the filthy way
we both ignore the elephant in the room.
I deplore the card games, the slurred names, and the
fanning of the politically correct flames.
It's not even about the shames that we can't mention,
'cause the silencer on the racial tension is the doom,
that we presume.

—Howard C. Stevenson, *Elephant Attention* (2012)

Yes: we lived through avalanches of tokens and concessions but white power remains white. And what it appears to surrender with one hand it obsessively clutches in the other.

—James Baldwin, *The Price of the Ticket* (1985)

Hidden in America's classrooms lurks the fear that racial tension will show itself in the most unpredictable fashion. Yet, like a nagging pain, we ignore that tension. In this chapter, I use the metaphor of an "elephant in the classroom" to signify the hidden but troublesome presence of racial conflicts in society and schools that go unaddressed. The relational dynamics that surround the tension reveal pretense, denial, silence, and shock as the common coping strategies to manage this huge but unveiled tension. The goal of this metaphor is to provide a context for examining attempts at reform of academic achievement disparities that are racial in outcomes and process.

THE RACIAL STRESS OF AMERICAN SCHOOLING

Under the pressure to provide the best education for America's children and youth and simultaneously promote racial and economic progress, independent, private, and public schools have jockeyed for decades to emerge as the best option. The charter school movement has arisen amid this effort to save the scholastic day only to come up short as evidence mounts that these alternatives represent choices not solely, but mostly, for wealthier families and business marketers (Slaughter-Defoe et al., 2012). The sporadic failure of many public schools to complete this mission leads many to conclude that perhaps the war on the achievement gap is lost and the racial divides will remain indefinitely (Hacker, 1995).

The achievement gap concerns have increased and Black and Brown children are at risk of graduating from many urban public high schools at lower rates and, as graduates, of making no appreciable headway in finding gainful employment. The changing face of the workplace requires more creative thinking and technological skills not taught in most traditional school curricula. The more standardized these curricula become, addressing the unique challenges for students of color and poor Whites is seen as unnecessary, unproven, time-consuming, and perhaps divisive to American education reform. It is troublesome that as new ideas for educational accountability emerge, a vision of creativity and critical thinking about negotiating the racial politics of schooling is not only missing but seen as irrelevant in addressing a racialized achievement gap.

Racial segregation of America's schools remains a problem as the expansion of "double segregation" of race and poverty affects Latinos and Blacks primarily. "Intensely segregated schools" means concentrated poverty and apartheid status (schools with less than 1% Whites) collide to result in poorer-quality teachers, administrators, and resources (Orfield, Kucsera, & Siegel-Hawley, 2012) for Latino and Black students. Conversely, White students are becoming more isolated, spending time in schools where most of their classmates are White, which increasingly creates PWS where students of color make up a stable but small minority. As such, White students, parents, and teachers have limited exposure to students and families of color and the development of racial negotiation skills is likely to be compromised, especially if PWS are racially avoidant in their curricular approaches to diversity matters. The politics of race and racism within these schools is not fully understood but constitutes an arena of social interaction unlike predominantly Black or Latino schools.

For some millions of Americans who pay enormous emotional and economic costs at the hands of racism, negotiating the politics of racial discourse is more complex than a numerical gap debate. Although there exists a game of school choice, access, and equity, there is no race card to be played here. The larger game is that many schools serving Black and Brown students do not offer a viable education for future social mobility. Now, *that* is a game. Raising issues of racial disparity in schooling is not. This illumination of injustice is not a game designed to fool America's White majority group into giving up its heritage, dignity, resources, school enrollment spaces, or power. Racial injustice in schools is about demanding equity in the basic provision of good schooling. Racial injustice is about the tragic misuse of suspensions and expulsions to cover up the absence of competent teaching and classroom management—conditions that disproportionately affect youth of color. It cannot be understood through the comparison of test scores, but through an in-depth look at the resource and relationship differences that Black, Brown, and poor White students experience from educators, schooling materials, barriers, and access to future employment.

While the achievement gap debate highlights the differences between White children and Black and Brown children, its greatest flaw is the inordinate emphasis on race status differences rather than the differences in racial dynamics and lived experiences that contribute to this gap. In the classroom, this racial gap is not so visible, not so statistical or quantifiable. It is relational and therefore reflected in the distancing between achievers and underachievers. But while these relational processes may be invisible and subtle, they are mostly stressful. Stress regarding self-doubt about one's racial positioning can be reduced. Self-affirmation strategies targeting Black students have proved successful at narrowing achievement differences (Cohen, Garcia, Apfel, & Master, 2006; Cohen, Garcia, Purdie-Vaughns, Apfel, & Brzustoski, 2009). I intend to suggest how individuals can learn to stop avoiding racial interactions and develop a self-affirming literacy that engages and resolves racial stress and conflicts in schooling at the level of relationships.

To successfully engage a competent dialogue on racial politics in the schools among educators will require relational engagement that is supported by an array of cognitive, behavioral, and emotional intelligence skill sets. Although easier said than done, racial dialogue is impossible without the skills to navigate the jungle of diverse racial stress reactions. In furthering the work of Twine (2011) and Guinier (2004), I am calling the development, practice, and internalization of these skill sets *racial literacy*. Racial literacy is the ability to read, recast, and resolve racially stressful encounters. That is, *learning to see and resolve racial stress and conflict in relationships involves explicit teaching and practice of racial literacy skills in how not to get "played" by the larger stressful game of racial inferiority.*

Promoting Racial Literacy in Schools proposes assumptions, guidelines, and strategies to examine and develop successful racial communications and interactions between individuals generally, and between teachers, students, and parents in schools specifically. My goal is to illuminate the dynamics of racial conflict avoidance and postracial reactions such that healthy racial dialogue and literacy can flourish. The relationship between societal/systemic and interpersonal racial politics deserves illumination. I seek to distinguish racial dreams from racial interactions; macroracial systems from microracial situations; racial rhetoric from racial dialogue; racial wishes from racial accomplishments; racial solutions from racial skills; moral antiracist character from racial competence; and race status from racialized lived experiences. Because of the obfuscation that surrounds racial conversations and politics, I use the metaphor of "elephant in the room" to isolate the frustrating "both-and" nature of how schools are so proximal to resolving these politics, but so overwhelmingly phobic in facing them.

What is the elephant? The elephant is the "obvious, yet denied" tension of negotiating racial interactions in schools and classrooms. That tension can be seen in how two or more actors hover around it. It is a dance of sorts. The elephant can be seen in hesitation, distancing, halting speech, distraction, changing of subject, lack of eye contact, nervous laughter in both interpersonal interactions and intrapersonal emotions, and thoughts of children, teens, and adults when racial conflicts are at issue. It most certainly influences the relationships within schools, namely parent-child, teacher-student, administrator-staff, and parent-teacher relationships. There are many elephants. The elephants of racial stress loom large when individuals are especially fearful of being discovered as illiterate about racial conflicts in schools.

ENCOUNTERING RACIAL STRESS IN SOCIAL INTERACTION

What is *racial stress*? Dr. Shelly Harrell from Pepperdine University defines racial stress as "race-related transactions between individuals or groups and their environment that emerge from the dynamics of racism, and that are perceived to tax or exceed existing individual and collective resources or threaten well-being" (Harrell, 2000). Thus, racial stress is the emotional overload or shock to an individual's coping system before, during, and after racial interactions.

I would modify Harrell's focus on transactions and propose the concept of *encounter*. This word was coined in the literature on the psychology of race by the noted psychologist William Cross (1991). An *encounter* is defined as a racial conflict that challenges one's previous naïve "deracinated" view of race relations and pushes one to adopt a naïve worldview of racial immersion. A deracinated worldview is a perception that racial matters are not relevant to daily social living or in the construction of one's identity. I define *encounter* slightly differently from how Cross meant it. Stress is ignited through perceived and actual interactions that individuals experience as threatening. So I see *racial encounters* as stressful intra- or interpersonal interactions that tax individual self-regulation of emotions, physiology, cognitions, and voice. How stressful remains a matter of individual coping. An example is when an individual is struggling with whether to use the term *Black* or *African American* during a conversation. The conversation can start out benignly casual and humorous but once an individual has to use language that might be perceived as racialized and open to interpretation by others, one's speech may become halting and stinted, followed by a barrage of apologies for one's missteps of speech, thought, or deed. The best comedic example of this is the *Saturday Night Live* skit of "MacGruber," when former pro basketball player Charles Barkley was the guest host. MacGruber is so anxious about how to speak to Charles Barkley, one of his Black employees, that his misuse of racial language leads to an explosive disaster and MacGruber's discipline referral to ridiculously ineffective diversity training. The point is that racial stress can be quite debilitating to one's speech, thinking, and movement.

A key distinction from my modification (racial encounter stress) and Harrell's definition of *racial stress* and Cross's definition of *encounter* is the perceived interactions that individuals anticipate, not just engage. Fear of a stressful racial interaction with a parent of color who might challenge an educator's racial competence, for example, can be as stressful as or even more stressful than the actual conversation. The practical implications of the concept of racial encounter stress is that it (1) explains how individuals are worried by racial interactions before and during their occurrence; (2) can be appraised at different levels (from minimal to severe) and across emotions, cognitions, physiology, and voice; (3) can arise from vicarious interaction (witnessing others who experience racial insult) and be just as debilitating as direct experiences; and (4) can be reappraised (recasting) and reduced if practiced.

Framing or reframing race relations as a series of racially stressful encounters raises several questions: How do individuals make meaning of racial interactions or encounters if they are overwhelmed by them? How do they manage the stress of these encounters and stay focused on the interaction? First, let's examine the ways Americans perceive and misperceive racial matters.

NATIONAL RACIAL POLITICS AFFECT RACE RELATIONS AND EDUCATION REFORM

Given current educational and health-based racial disparities, talking frankly about racial tension should be embraced, not shunned. Liberals and conservatives agree that the election and reelection of the first Black president were watershed historical moments that revised our meaning-making of the civil rights movement. The advances in civil rights prior to the claims of a postracial America should not be minimized. Still, racial disparities in health and education remain and in many states have worsened over the past 6 decades (Davis & Bangs, 2010; Orfield, 2009; Skiba et al., 2011). Those solutions of integration and middle-class advancement for families of color were powerful but not as far-reaching as expected for low-income families. One wonders if any connection exists between the national racial politics surrounding the president and the politics of racial tension in face-to-face relationships in schools.

The metaphors of politicians to highlight educational, race, and class inequity while championing a policy agenda for social justice are flawed in their meaning and scope. It is time to change the way educators and politicians lift up those who come behind, who walk behind, who are left behind, or who fall behind those who have "made it." Not all boats (like poor communities) rise with the tide, because some have holes or need repair and sink in the wake of the advancement of other boats or yachts. The waves of social progress are higher in some communities. For neighboring impoverished communities without economic, political, and institutional affection, correction, and protection, these waves of economic wealth flood potential and hope. This poverty of resources reflects a dance between colorblindness as a sign of racial progress and denial of racial hierarchy, disparity, and supremacy as a method of racial coping. While liberal and conservative politicians and educators tout postracial victory, it is the colorblindness policies about poor schooling since the 1960s for Black, Brown, and poor White children that remain outdated. One connection between national racial politics and local school racial politics is how misguided national optimism prevents the seeing of local racial disparity.

Postracial Progress Masks Racial Casualties

Tragically, states and local governments spend less money on teachers' salaries in public schools serving low-income students than in schools serving high-income students (Heuer & Stullich, 2011). Given this, the postracial America claims look eerily like the "Mission Accomplished" mantra of the Iraq War: that we can win wars without daily battles and before they are over and without bringing attention to the carnage and casualties of war. Moreover, "Mission Accomplished Schooling" assumes educators can reform schools and teachers through rote testing and market competition, teach children in poverty with fewer resources, and improve race relations without relationship-building skills.

Currently, the political climate in American race relations is particularly contentious and the first Black president is often at the center of the firestorm

(Aleman, Salazar, Rorrer, & Parker, 2011). Although President Obama has worked hard to appear neutral on matters of racial conflict, with a few incidental exceptions (Trayvon Martin and Professor Henry Louis Gates Jr.), he has withstood an incomparable amount of racialized subtle and blatant criticism, innuendo, and caricature about his political actions, legislation, and motivations. These racialized critiques have come as much from elected officials as from pundits and as such, represent a form of socialization. Some of us emotionally experience this unjust racialized commentary like an oncoming tsunami while others are unafraid of these types of racial conflicts and respond as if they are momentary gusts of wind. For some of us, it is so stressful to hear bad news about the first Black president, we turn off television pundits and talking heads without thinking about ways to counter what is said. It is stressful because many of us identify with Obama racially or politically or civil rights–wise as the first Black president and the first biracial president. He embodies and reflects our collective racial identity and posterity. Obama's representation is not simply a skin color identification symbol. He is like a brother or family member who has experienced life like those of us who are Black. At least, we assume so. And if we project onto Obama our racial hopes and fears, we become racially stressed when he is attacked. For others who see Obama's racial background as inferior or a reflection of a challenge to one's racial identity and status, hearing such racial derision fuels their conspiracy about the demise of our democracy and world that only a Black president could destroy.

Postracial Advocates Protest Too Much

When Obama became president, racial political discourse morphed into claims that racism no longer exists and a new postracial age had begun. The backlash seemed primitive and terrifying to many. The racialized epithets increased and the resistance to anything Obama proposed seemed to concretize this backlash. It wasn't just a few crazy nut jobs. This racialized hostility was integrated in the way some Americans legislate their power, view their country, and define their American-ness even as it overshadowed nonracialized and appropriate criticism and debate of the president's policies. As Congress stubbornly refused to support some of President Obama's policies even at the risk of government shutdown behind earlier mandates from Mitch McConnell, a major party leader, in both a *National Journal* interview (Garrett, 2010) on October 23, 2010 and in a speech to the Heritage Foundation in 2010 (www.youtube.com/watch?v=W-A09a_gHJc). When he stated in the speech that "our top political priority over the next two years should be to deny President Obama a second term," many of us questioned our country's history, ideas, and practices of egalitarianism. Comparisons of national polls taken during the elections of Barack Obama found that over half of Whites (51%) held strongly anti-Black sentiments in 2012 while 48% held anti-Black attitudes in 2008 (USA Today, 2012). For some these are political retorts, but for others of us these are racialized retorts as well. What's stressful behind all of these racial politics is the nagging, persistent fear that racism will never fully be over, only undercover, and that as much progress that America makes, Black humanity will remain expendable and appear inferior in the eyes of key powerbrokers.

To manage the stress that accompanies these hostile racial politics surrounding Obama, most mainstream and liberal American commentators have taken the low road to deny that racial angst, let alone enmity, has anything to do with these politics. Any denial of racial processes at the national level makes difficult any real change in race relations at the local community level or in the quality of our face-to-face racial conversations. Why change or try to have a racial conversation when we've accomplished the dream? But despite the distraction of postracial progress, national racial politics seems to consistently obscure and omit the effects of racism on mainstream America, poor families, and children in schools.

Upon Obama's reelection, the postracial claims remained without attention to the persistence of extreme racial threat from a divided populace and despite intransigent racialized inequality in the quality of life (education, health, and justice) between poor and wealthy families. Despite Obama's reelection, liberal and conservative pundits readily identify how interest groups of White males overwhelmingly (62%) voted against the president without discussing the racial threat reasons that might explain this phenomenon. Again, "the silencer on the racial tension is the doom."

Although new racial conversations and relations are in order, educational leaders must address our collective racial amnesia and challenge the assumption that a preracial America was mature enough to usher in an Obama presidency and create a postracial America. Not only are the claims of a postracial America false and premature, but they are greatly exaggerated. These claims are buttressed by an ignorance of history and a shallow thinking that reduces centuries of racial antagonism, struggle, sacrifice, and progress to one symbolic feel-good election. Still, this kind of shallow thinking deserves psychological analysis. This postracial reaction belies more doubt than assertion and mimics a racialized form of what psychoanalysts label in some personality coping stances to stress as *reaction formation*. Reaction formation is a psychological defense in which stressful or undesirable emotions and impulses are controlled by overindulging and expressing the opposite feeling or behavior. Postracial America declarations reflect a blindness and overreaction to the widening gap in race relations. This gap is not hidden, but what fuels the failure to see it is the growing sophistication in America's traditional race relations coping strategy—racial conflict avoidance. Nowhere is the practice of avoidant coping more prevalent than in public and private schooling.

CAN EDUCATION REFORM RACIAL DISPARITIES IN A POSTRACIALLY REACTIVE AMERICA?

The state of American public schooling has been deteriorating for youth who live in the least advantaged and resourced neighborhoods where schools have been underresourced for two or more generations (Slaughter-Defoe, Stevenson, Arrington, & Johnson, 2012; Heuer & Stullich, 2011). Amid middle-class Black youth, achievement gaps with Whites persist despite improved economic access, suggesting that wealth alone does not explain racial disparities (Education Week, 2011).

It would be myopic to blame the disparities on the talent of the youth, the competency of the teachers, or racial profiling in health, justice, and educational systems. Achievement gaps are generated by an interaction among these and other factors. Recent systemic school reform efforts have shown that once students are motivated to achieve success and racially disproportionate discipline approaches are reduced, achievement outcomes become more manageable and predictable (Gregory, Cornell, & Fan, 2011; Mattison & Aber, 2007). Still, there are relational factors that are proximal to, not distal from, a child's learning, and they have unique influence on achievement outcomes. Factors such as climate safety, diversity of the teacher corps, teacher-student bonding, preservice teacher competence, school support, sense of belonging, self-efficacy, coping skills, and agency all constitute "free agent" phenomena that can change the momentum and trajectory of student academic engagement and well-being.

Schooling for Black youth is a less positive experience than for other youth, as evidenced by lower teacher-student closeness, school belonging, and academic expectations (Casteel, 1998; Weinstein, 2002). Unfortunately, we spend more money and energy on the distal achievement gaps than we do the proximal emotional challenges that youth face. The racial politics of expecting low performance and fearing Black cultural styles that Black students and parents face within key schooling relationships can be debilitating to achievement motivation (Neal, McCray, Webb-Johnson, & Bridgest, 2003; Parsons, 2005; Webb-Johnson, 2002). These politics often remain invisible to educational leaders who, while progressive in disaggregating achievement data according to race, class, and gender categories, remain racially blind to the emotional trauma these politics bring to students in those categories. Unfortunately, disaggregated racial and gender status information reveals a lot of racial trauma, but the postracial reaction formations of leaders prevent the amelioration of that trauma. By communicating a willingness to identify and resolve the racialized achievement gap without a theory of resolving stressful racial social interaction, these achievement gap politics reflect a familiar rhythmic dance that masks a stable and foundational racial hierarchy. Without directly identifying and negotiating the racial stressors in classrooms, education reform efforts will not improve the emotional and relational factors known to enhance academic achievement for children of color, despite the claims of postracial progress.

ELEPHANTS AS METAPHOR FOR THE POLITICS OF RACIAL STRESS AND LITERACY IN SCHOOLS

Let's ponder the image of an elephant surrounded by blind scientists inspecting different body parts. As a metaphor, this famous cartoon shows how different perspectives can be derived from investigating the uncertainty of life's mysteries. As you investigate this image, try using a "both-and" lens in which discovery and uncertainty are co-occurring. By "both-and," I mean (1) view the various and opposing perspectives or investigator "finds" of the image as true and false and (2) view the condition of being blindfolded as both a barrier and a benefit. Not only does the blindfold reflect a failure to see, but each scientist is forced to use this blindness to make sense of the uncertainty before him or her and develop a unique view or conclusion. Each scientist's perspective reveals a debilitating blindness and a creative sight. At best, this image informs us of the necessity of sharing information and discoveries across investigators in order to reach understanding and meaning of uncertainty (Figure 1.1)

The image of the elephant is an efficient way to explain how complex it is to problem-solve conflict or mysterious interactions. With only the tools of feeling and touch, the inspectors are unable to know that they are studying an elephant. Emotionally speaking, you can imagine how these "ologists" might not only assert what they know the "thing" to be, but distrust their colleagues' inspection conclusions and methods. Concluding this "elephant" to be "a fan" or "a wall," "a snake" or "a rope" shows how individuals can be both informed and clueless. Each "ologist" has conducted a thorough inspection that reveals a worldview that is both narrow and full. It is full because of the time, energy, and diligence expended and it is narrow due to the inaccessibility of the data. Their findings are relevant and irrelevant, narrow and deep. Understanding these industrious investigations in a "both-and" manner can explain why some investigators, even in the face of uncertainty, remain belligerent about their discovery and wrong in their assumptions.

FIGURE 1.1. Discovering Elephant as Scientific Mystery

Still, there is more complexity to this elephant metaphor than the uniqueness and narrowness of discovery. Let's call the elephant *The Stress of Racial Politics* (Figure 1.2). That an individual discovers the presence of racial politics is interesting but the more important dimension is the level of stressfulness of that discovery. Each discovery is unique in the degree of fear that it might stimulate. To discover a wall is less stressful than discovering a snake. To find oneself suddenly in the middle of a racial interaction and judge it to be as stressful as finding a snake would be far more stressful than surmising it to be a wall. So the stress appraisal of the individual matters. Stress appraisal could ultimately influence future discoveries and interpretations of racial interactions as well as consequential coping responses, including running away, asking for help, giving up, or simply remaining paralyzed in a zombie-like state.

The Continuum of Racial Stress

Now, let's say the each person's stress appraisal of "the racial thing" can be judged using a scale from 1 to 10, with 10 being "very stressful" and 1 being "not stressful at all." If the racial interaction is experienced as facing a venomous snake or tsunami, paralysis may be the primary coping strategy

FIGURE 1.2. Discovering Elephant as Stressful Mystery

and a score from 8 to 10 would reflect the intensity of that paralysis. An example is being asked by the teacher to go to the blackboard and explain the quadratic equation in front of the whole class when you not only hate math, but you failed to do the homework lesson about the quadratic formula. A tsunami moment triggers coping strategies such as calling on or praying to the deity of one's affection or childhood and/or giving up and accepting failure or death. If the discovery was experienced as stressful but not unbearable, the example of climbing a steep mountain or discovering a wall might best be rated between 5 and 7. One's fear could be intense without being futile, despite the dangers of mountain or wall climbing. It would be like being asked to solve the quadratic equation on a test, and despite your diligent studying habits, you still get nervous. This anxiety could potentially undermine your performance because you know part of the answer but you can't retrieve from memory the rest of the answer. With the appropriate weather protection gear, mountain boots, training, and relaxation, climbing a mountain or solving the quadratic equation on a test may be difficult but not impossible (a score from 5 to 7). If the discovery of racial politics is experienced as witnessing an "anthill" or finding a rope, the stressfulness is unlikely to debilitate one's coping and is best rated with a score from 1 to 4. An equivalent classroom anthill-like experience is being asked by the teacher to erase and clean off the blackboard.

The diversity of racial stress. The fear of discovering that a racial interaction could become life-threatening is sometimes too much to bear and from this fear comes a host of cognitive, behavioral, and emotional stress reactions resident in individuals *and* systems. Since one's level of stressfulness can vary, our exposure, education, and experience in inspecting and problem-solving racial mysteries might prepare us not to panic when stressed and cope accordingly. If you have seen many racial conflicts before, have made multiple accurate and inaccurate interpretations, and have practiced your coping responses, you are probably less blind, less clueless, and perhaps less stressed. Experience and exposure to uncertainty matters.

So racial interactions represent a confluence of limited and essential truth. Not only do racial encounters engender a diversity of discovery interpretations and methods, a confirmation and invalidation of the truth of the discoveries, and a range of emotionally stressful reactions, but also these reactions reveal one's degree of exposure and experience with a breadth of racial interactions. If you are on your first elephant safari, everything is unfamiliar. Educated guessing won't help, and a perceived racial conflict is more likely to be overwhelming.

Still, to perceive a racial encounter as a tsunami rather than a mountain can reveal how much threat and self-efficacy one has available to resolve the conflict. We mustn't forget that it is not the conflict or stressful discovery that is the most essential element of the mystery. It's the panic, the meaning (or the level of the panic) we ascribe to the racial conflict that determines how debilitating the discovery is or becomes and how many resources we have available to address its stressfulness. This does not solely apply to individuals. Racial groups can also have collective stress reactions. Without some form of wise leadership, overarching ground rules, collective bargaining, communal sharing, data collaboration, and interpersonal communication, it is difficult to engage in racial dialogue and decisionmaking about educational reform, whether it occurs with a school board or within a school classroom. Moreover, although exposure and experience to racial matters is fundamental to racial stress reduction, neither will be as beneficial without supportive socialization, mentoring, or instruction.

I have written elsewhere that this type of racial socialization and training for racially stressful encounters works best if it includes affection, correction, and protection as demonstrated in physically, emotionally, and culturally relevant ways (Stevenson, 2003; Stevenson, Davis, & Abdul-Kabir, 2001). Wise and racially competent educational reform starts with assumptions that undergird a racial stress and literacy focus in schools. This frame of elephant as racial stress is fueled by theories of stress and coping (Lazarus & Folkman, 1984) and racial socialization (Adams & Stevenson, 2012; Coleman & Stevenson, 2013; Stevenson & Arrington, 2009, 2012).

SEEING RACIAL POLITICS IN SCHOOLS:
ASSUMPTIONS OF RACIAL STRESS AND LITERACY

My assumptions behind the importance of taking a racial stress and literacy focus toward youth development and schooling include the following:

1. Racial stress and coping reactions are different from general stress/coping reactions.
2. The politics of race versus the politics of racial interaction represent different perspectives and approaches to problem-solving race relations dilemmas.
3. When the meaningfulness of racial hierarchy is challenged, the experiences, perspectives, and lives of Black and Brown people become expendable.
4. Schools are places where avoidant racial socialization, politics, and skills are taught.

Reactions to Racial Stressors Are Different from Reactions to Other Stressors

The tenets that undergird the assertion that racial and general stressors yield different coping reactions tend to rely on the notion that racial stressors are more collectively avoided and experienced as terrifying (like snakes) by most Americans than other types of stressors.

Consequently, while one's biological expressions of threats to one's self-esteem and ability are similar across conflicts, the emotional and behavioral reactions to racial conflicts are different than, say, the stress of getting married. Because of different socialization, teaching, and skill sets, each conflict reveals breadth of exposure as well as maturity in one's coping with the conflict. How one navigates the stress of teaching for the first time is not the same as how one navigates the stress of teaching Black students for the first time if one's concerns about racial matters preoccupy the teacher-student relationship or the teacher's perception of his or her abilities. Similarly, knowing how to swing a baseball bat does not prepare an athlete to play tennis or that being proficient at swimming does not automatically equip one to become a star at water polo. Although the knowledge of swinging or swimming is a component of the other sport, without specific preparation, training, and practice of the unique skills of that sport, individuals will not become competent. Though teachers may receive instruction in classroom management, very few teachers receive training in managing the stress of racial conflicts with Black students while they are managing wayward or different behaviors in the classroom.

The implications of this assumption is enormous in that (1) universal stress management or reform approaches are viewed as ineffective for addressing racial conflicts of interaction and achievement; (2) preparation is required of educators, students, and families in specific training in identifying and practicing racial conflict resolution; and (3) reducing initial racial threat reactions must be addressed first before any learning of racial literacy skills can begin. Two issues that are key to appreciating the fear factor of racial threat in social interaction and the specific amelioration of racial stress include the developmental immaturity of racial coping in American race relations and how that immaturity interferes with understanding racial stress and coping as learned and observable rather than lofty, philosophical, idealistic, and rooted in a collective sense of social justice protest.

As such, colorblindness and avoidance are primitive, developmentally nascent, but learned and observable coping reactions to stressful racial encounters in individuals and systems. The lack of sophistication in American coping in race relations endangers the resolution of racial conflicts by encouraging disengagement from the smallest of racial matters instead of resolution.

Racial stress and coping reactions to racially stressful encounters tend to be developmentally immature due to the limited exposure to and experience with those encounters. Racial stressors are different from other stressors because racial blindness, avoidance, and hostility represent limited experience with successful outcomes to racial conflict. What if our cumulative knowledge and coping skills with race relations are underdeveloped? Perhaps the postracial reaction formation that "racism is over" and the reassertion of colorblindness reveal that America's progress on civil rights matters was less advanced as once believed. Perhaps our failure to address the interpersonal challenges of this "progress" has left us confusing legal progress with emotional progress. Perhaps the civil rights movement in the 1960s was politically, ethically, and emotionally essential, to yet developmentally nascent America's growth in race relations. If true, the civil rights movement is to race relations what toddlerhood is to child development. It was essentially cataclysmic and crucial in its contribution toward healthy maturation, but it requires much more nurturance and forging.

Although walking into the sunshine or sunset of racial harmony is a common civil rights image and the call for a national conversation on race is every presidential administration's default position, we have yet as a country to acquire the skills of competently talking to each other while we are walking into the sunset or starting the conversation. As a country we have yet to acquire developmentally mature racial literacy skills that include other-perspective-taking, cooperative play, and "both-and" comprehension, which is the ability to entertain two opposing ideas and realities at the same time. These skills are essential in confronting racial stereotypes and the concrete thinking of ideologies that turn situations into "either-or" life-and-death decisions will not work. Still, these racial developmental milestones of identifying "good and bad" racial encounters are foundational skills, like walking is to mobility or saying "da-da" is to acquiring language. They are necessary but they remain unsophisticated and insufficient for carrying on in-depth dialogue.

By resting on the laurels of the 1960s as crises America should never repeat, many of us are willing to accept a developmentally immature avoidance coping position. Using Piagetian cognitive developmental theory as a frame, America race relations are stuck in the developmental equivalent of a preoperational stage. If I can take the preoperational (between ages 2 and 7) frame a little further, American racial progress would match the developmental equivalent of cruising or duck-walking, using 3-word sentences from a 50-word vocabulary and putting both feet in our mouths. The good news is that for most of us, we've advanced beyond drooling. Still, we have yet to move beyond the egocentric, incessant others-pleasing, and magical thinking of preschoolers when it comes to race relations. This developmental stuckness is partially why racial stress is different from other stressors.

It's hard to know if the "racial magical thinking" inherent in postracial rhetoric is related to the systemic but invisible nature of racism in the air. Perhaps it's the lack of knowledgeable and caring role models who can teach gross- and fine-motor racial negotiation skills within a safe and supportive context. The pressure to navigate the daily stress of racial decisionmaking can be overwhelming. Fear shouldn't drive foreign policy, race relations policy, or educational policy, yet we approach racial interactions in public and private spaces as reminders of our guilt and victimization. Without guidance, teaching, or healthy modeling it will be hard for individuals to move beyond magical thinking, guilt, or shame regarding racial matters. Over time, many of us get tired of feeling guilty and become angry at anything or anyone who reminds us of that guilt. We confuse guilt with trauma, and instead of seeing racial politics as an internal process, we respond to it as abuse and are often threatened by any presence of racial matters wherever we might see them, smell them, or anticipate them.

Although reaction formation and preoperational thinking are two ways to temporarily explain undesirable impulses about racial matters, extremely hostile temper tantrumming is another. Some of this can be seen in the outrageous anger at a Black president from Americans who blamed him for everything from endangering children with his political speeches to murdering seniors through universal health care. This hostility can also be seen as an unintentional defense against racial shame or a reaction to the threat of annihilation or inferiority; so too is colorblindness an immature reaction to the stress of racial inferiority (Cress Welsing, 1990). Still, as conscious and unconscious biases that are not easily acknowledged, their negative effects on well-being are numerous even as they remain invisible.

Racial blindness, avoidance, and hostility are learned and observable threat reactions. Avoidance, denial, and even hostility are coping strategies that must be taught or practiced. As theoretical frames for resolving racial conflict, racial stress and socialization explain how much individuals have received reinforcement for avoidance coping. These behaviors are reinforced in school classrooms daily as well as in television shows, in political entertainment news, or during public and private conversations with friends and family at home. Often, avoidance and denial are triggered by fears or intentions of confirming negative and scary stereotypes of self and others.

Although racial stress avoidance is more often nonverbal, it is not imperceptible. It can be seen in body movements, hesitation, eyesight aversions, stuttering, and a host of body, mind, and heart reactions. Instead of a thing to be feared, I see racial stress as a signal or alarm that presents a unique wake-up opportunity to problem-solve racial conflict. Facing and embracing one's racial stress reactions are essential steps toward developing healthy within- and cross-racial relationships and schools, but only if parents, teachers, and students see, hear, or feel them. Facing and embracing these conflicts is extremely difficult for most Americans because there have been few opportunities to learn how to do so.

Teachers can't teach what they don't know about racial politics (Howard, 2006). But we can't know about any topic if we don't start at the most basic level of self-knowledge—or *self-observation*. Not to know how one reacts when stressed in moments of racial conflict is an efficient description of being "colorblind." To not see how the body, feelings, and thoughts react when individuals become overwhelmed in racial encounters is the first problem that needs intervention.

Colorblindness is traditionally defined as the way individuals are blind to the cultural and racial experiences of others. I see it differently. Colorblindness is more about blindness to one's own cultural and racial dynamics, experiences, and reactions that occur in real time, in the moment of the conflict. An alarm is of no use if you either don't hear it or train yourself not to hear it. The mindlessness of colorblindness is as blissful to some as it is convenient, since it not only encourages but also activates a host of avoidance coping strategies.

In addition to preventing observation and correction of one's reaction to racial conflicts, colorblindness impairs the recognition of power differences between racial groups. Colorblindness egalitarianism may reflect what Cross and Vandiver (2001) calls a *Preencounter, Miseducated Identity* stance. It is an identity orientation that does not find relevant the salience of racial matters or chooses not to. In a colorblind world, to see and expose the larger narrative of intransigent racism in one's social interaction is anxiety-producing. Seeing racial elephants disturbs a "just world" worldview.

Because colorblindness prevents healing from the trauma of racial conflict by not recognizing early warning symptoms of racial stress, it *becomes* a racial elephant in the classroom. In the many years my colleagues and I have conducted research in PWS, one of the most troubling responses I've heard from students of color is how painful it is to watch classmates and teachers pretend to not see a racial conflict that arose in a class lesson or comment, and have no one acknowledge that the conflict happened. Watching others remain colorblind in the face of racial disparity is surreal and stressful. To the degree that this blindness exists in the classroom, its traumatic effects will target mostly racially aware youth and families of any background who can't avoid seeing these politics (Mattison & Aber, 2007; Stevenson & Arrington, 2009; Sue, 2010; Sue et al., 2009).

Colorblind approaches to racial conflicts influence decisionmaking processes. Through colorblindness, educators forget or fail to include their own goals for diversity in the basic decisionmaking required in hiring, curriculum development, and professional training of their organizations. It stands to reason that if racial matters are wrong or contentious, or that seeing color is unfair, educators would consistently "miss" the meaning of racial politics in school teaching, administration, leadership, pioneering, and entrepreneurship.

Taking a colorblind position excuses educators who lead urban educational institutions in poor and Black and Brown communities from having to mention, plan, or integrate racial matters in their curricula, teaching strategies and styles, climate and morale assessments, or relationships with students. *Racial afterthought planning* is the absence of integration of race and cultural knowledge in the core of one's institution or mission at the planning stages and its inclusion only after protest from oppressed groups. What I've learned through our research is that if challenged, educators will often discount the relevance of these matters or integrate them in the most superficial ways. These compromises inadvertently highlight the supremacy of racial hierarchy and reinforce avoidant coping responses to racial conflict. Several examples come to mind. One is failing to include research literature that examines the influence that racial/gender and social justice play in learning and achievement. Another example would be to define diversity so broadly that it carries no specific plan of action. Such vague plans tend to fuel resistance to diversity initiatives within the school. Additionally, these plans blur distinctions between diversity agendas (age versus gender versus sexual orientation versus race). In some ways, the proof of incompetence may reside in the missing link between the diversity definition and the mission and practices of the school.

The problem of racial equity in education is not just pointing out that leaders forget that racial matters influence learning and achievement, but that educators and schools *consistently* forget that racial and diversity matters matter. It's the habitus of forgetting racial matters that matters. Racial justice as afterthought is the habitus. The afterthought is a process, not an event. It is not a momentary memory lapse or a "mistake." It is the first "oops" or "my bad" step in a dance—a predictable and spastic dance with the racial elephants in classrooms across America. That first step of racial amnesia is part of a larger story that is historical and current between students and teachers, parents and schools, education and societal politics. The interactive rhythm of racial stress and avoidance moves back and forth within the hidden curriculum of America's schools, all for the sake of reducing stress.

Still, some might argue that with respect to racial insult, illiteracy, avoidance, or cluelessness, doesn't intentionality matter?

To Derald Sue (2010), the question of intentionality is moot. Still, the interaction of race and racism dynamics in one's social context, or from micro- to macrosystems, redefines what "colorblindness" may mean. Whether intentional or not, constructing a race-less (Fordham, 1988; 1991) identity within a racialized context has implications for how individuals approach or avoid the acquisition of knowledge, the building of relationships, the reconstruction of identity, the expression of personal styles, and the deconstruction of stereotypes.

Recent neuroscience research (discussed in Chapter 3) has found that the fear of being labeled as racially incompetent or as a stereotype is so overwhelming that one's body reactions are visible and access to knowledge and competence is thwarted. Moreover, individuals can become exhausted physically and blame the entire experience on unnecessary racial dynamics. Racial stress affects physiological functioning so much that it can lead to phobic-like mannerisms and spastic movements. Between teachers and students, these reactions are rarely addressed as part of the discipline injustice that affects Brown and Black students. Denying that the doorbell is ringing or an elephant is in the room takes practice. Even as racial conflicts bring distress, denial reduces stress in the short term in ways that are underreported and unconscious. But there is hope. Managing racial stress and coping is more hopeful a reality than eradicating racism. That is, *while negative and unhealthy reactions to racial stress can affect one's body like other stressors, the academic, emotional, intellectual, and relational stress and coping reactions are unique to racial politics; moreover, socialized avoidant coping strategies can be unlearned, modified, and mature beyond preoperational cognitions.*

Race Relations as the Politics of Racial Interaction, Not Race Status

The second assumption I propose is that the politics of race and the politics of racial interaction represent different ways of framing, engaging, and negotiating race relations.

Simply put, racial relations are best framed as what occurs in social interactions and how individuals and groups experience and differentially interpret racial triumphs and conflicts. Racial politics are here defined as what occurs within the lived experiences of racial interactions for individuals and groups.

Too often, doing the "right thing" is the theme behind racially equitable practices. Morality is less relevant to racial politics but if at all, it is relevant insomuch as the outcomes of those relations prove beneficial to groups, not only individuals. Healthy race relations should rest on what happened successfully in our social interaction, not our moral visions.

Race politics focus on framing race relations as consisting of status comparisons or differences found in numerical gaps, card games, dreams that represent disengagement from the messiness of racial interaction. Race politics serve to frame the discussion and problem solving of race relations from a distance. Criticizing the morality and character of individuals is too often the substance of unhealthy racial politics, while understanding racial politics as stressful relationships requires individuals to competently negotiate interpersonal conflict despite their personality characteristics. Race politics are evident within a worldview keen to demonstrate that a moral antiracist character that emphasizes the innocence of the intention of an individual's actions is a superior criterion for evaluating racial equity. The goal of these principles is to reduce blame for race relations that fail.

Racial politics reflect a "getting hands dirty" approach that belies a deeper curiosity for and engagement with racial conflicts than a hands-off race status political approach. It includes coping with racially stressful moments. Racial politics are more concerned about illuminating the ecological, social, and psychological processes that undermine face-to-face race relations. Framing race relations as racial emphasizes the need for and use of racial competence and skills-building to resolve these conflicts.

This differentiation of race and racial politics belies differences in coping with the negative effects of racial stress. How individuals negotiate the politics of racial experiences rather than the discourse of race status defines the teachings and recommendations of this book. Daniels and Schulz (2006) remark about the use of racial status to frame racial disparities in health research:

> The use of racial categories and comparisons with no consistent foundation for theorizing, understanding, or interpreting observed racial differences (or

their absence) in health outcomes provides space for a wide range of potential explanations. Each of these "explanations" implicitly or explicitly constructs both race and Whiteness. . . . In the absence of an explicitly social theory of race, analyses explaining racial disparities in cardiovascular disease in terms of biological, "lifestyle," or "cultural" factors can reify racial differences and obscure connections to socially structured inequalities. In other words, explaining racial differences in health in terms of individual biology, genes, or behavior can locate health problems in the bodies of those most negatively affected by social inequalities. . . . In the process, they also take out of the equation—and thus make invisible—the processes through which Whites maintain positions of relative advantage or privilege within racial hierarchies. In this sense, such explanations are consistent with the "colorblind" strategies of neoconservative and neoliberal Whiteness projects described above, in that they explain racial disparities in health in nonracial terms. (p. 2)

When researchers and educators question whether racial dynamics play a bigger role in academic differences between racial groups, rarely do they make the distinction between racial interactions and race status. Policies or intellectual arguments that are based on race status differences are simplistic because they frequently involve comparing differences in the color of the students' skins rather than differences in what it means to be a member of those racial groups. The number comparisons tell you little as to why those differences matter. Race is a biological concept that is primarily defined by differences in physical characteristics (skin color) and race conflicts often reflect politics about the meaning of phenotypic differences in presentation and expression. Race status cannot explain the meaning or influence of racial tension that occurs within relationships. Racial politics focuses on the challenges in different life experiences of people from different races.

Although I believe that the conversation of racial tension is more necessary now than ever before in schools, no such conversation is attainable without first addressing why and how people get anxious. Without a focus on the lived experiences that are different for youth and families of color, it is easy to stereotype and attribute deficits or potential to one's own or someone else's race group status. A more ecological-interactional approach suggests that it is the relational experiences of racial rejection, affection, protection, and correction that individuals and groups experience consistently over the developmental lifespan that more powerfully explain racial disparities in behavioral, academic, and economic outcomes (Stevenson, 2003).

Numerical Diversity Is Insufficient to Resolve Racial Illiteracy. Often, the race status debate focuses on numerical and percentage differences of status, and many are eager to report on these differences without hesitation. Conversely, most educators and politicians dodge a conversation about racial conflict like feudal villagers running from dragons. Numbers often define the conversations we can have about racial politics. In many PWS, an important strategic planning goal is to increase the numbers of diverse students and/or faculty. Although noble and necessary, this strategy is insufficient to fully understand and resolve racial disparities (Parker & Villalpando, 2007). Increasing numerical diversity (the number of people of color) may reflect some level of progress for schools that have not historically been diverse, but it is a smaller win than schools teaching students how to identify and overcome unseen racial tensions in the classroom.

Although it reduces the degree of isolation for the students of color, numerical diversity is only a first step within a school's nascent equity endeavor. How the fears of the many through hierarchy and blindness drive the way we view or engage the challenging experiences of the few is a better way to understand race relations in a schooling context than how many Black and Brown students or faculty there are. Numbers growth may become a failure if it doesn't result in school climate safety and optimal academic functioning for the few.

Recruiting more students of color is important insomuch as schools are competent to create a diversity-safe climate for learning. The challenging issues of survival and success are bracketed more by the harshness of the desert conditions than the largeness of one's only canteen having a few more drops of water. In schools of Whiteness, the safety of the climate should define diversity success as much as, if not more than, the numbers of students of color. Without a strategy or plan to keep students of color from experiencing disaffection, biased punishment, and little to no emotional protection, what purpose does it serve to increase the number of diverse students?

Racial politics rejects the framing of race relations as gamesmanship. Despite claims that racial politics represent a card to be played to avoid facing meritocracy, it's really the reframing of racial politics as a game that undermines meaningful and equitable racial conversation. This reframing serves the purpose of ignoring fact-based racial disparities in the daily lives of people of color across the economic spectrum and poor Whites as well. By remaining colorblind, educators facilitate the tragic outcomes of racial disparities by blocking their resolution. Fueled by racial blindness, a common hindrance to racial dialogue is the gamesmanship of dodging the appearance or practice of making racial mistakes.

Sometimes, educators focus less on the navigation of racism politics and more on the failure of individuals to demonstrate a public flawlessness regarding racial matters. Unfortunately, most public racial political conversation has been whittled down to a game of sorts in the public eye. Americans are more focused on the racial gaffes and botched commentary of leaders, politicians, judges, or pastors rather than on the competence to rise above or block the negative effects of the politics of racism. American journalism has become like a game show, one we might call "Find the Racists" or "Play the Race Card." For instance, the "Name That Racist" game involves categorizing people's potential and character based on their latest gaffe. This search for failure and what "not to do or be" distracts from the more meaningful search for successful approaches and social justice endeavors to end racial oppression. Because there are certainly skills to be had and students and educators need to know what to do when faced with oppression that occurs from within and outside of schools.

There is a game being played regarding race, but it's a relational game of racial supremacy versus inferiority, not of race status. The search for political correctness behaviors and statements across our current landscape of racial conversations is another testament to racial illiteracy in schools, but also in the political discourse within many American public institutions. With a ferocious anxiety of sorts, conservative and liberal pundits work together to find the "racists" or "bad people" who play the "race card." As such, these "opponents" collude to be silent on the racial conflicts or dynamics that reflect processes of coping rather than evidence of racism. "Find the Bad Guy" is a childish approach to resolving racial conflicts. Race relations have been reduced to identifying which leader has said the wrong racial thing rather than identifying the negative effects of their policy decisions on oppressed groups of color. It's a political game show that tends to reward those who uncover racial injustice as a hoax in a "bad guy," rather than actually stopping racial injustice as a virus in the water supply.

Navigating racial politics requires competence more than moral character. The beauty of Martin Luther King's "I Have a Dream" speech is in the way it provides a vision of what democracy can become. But as dreams go, the walk into the sunsets of harmonic race relations involves tripping over molten lava rocks of racial supremacy and falling into emotional potholes of resistance. Ideas may inspire us, but without tangible and concrete coping, dreams make us guilty because they remind us of how far we have not come. Unfortunately, there are few skills lessons that come from our public discourse on race relations that can teach us to eradicate racial illiteracy in face-to-face schooling relationships, let alone between Democrats and Republicans. Racism or dreaming about a time when racism is gone may be too complex a concept or image for individuals to navigate on a daily basis. Individuals cannot learn from dreams or protests alone to problem-solve daily racial conflicts.

In addition to stimulating guilt based on our failure, dreaming about race relations leads us to judge progress in race relations based on the character of individuals to "do the right thing." Often, what poses as race relations is the process of trying to determine who is racist and who is not. That is, *racially stressful conflicts are moments more likely to reveal lapses of competence than lapses in character.* Moreover, acts of racial incompetence are not simply committed by White people, nor are these acts deterred by the moral character of the actors. It's not White people, but Whiteness ideology that matters in defining the elephant in the classroom, and as such, it would be better to follow the anxiety than to track for "the bad guy" or "the immoral dude." Too often, the avoidance and fear of engaging racial conflict is fueled by individuals' fear of being identified as racist or inferior in character and personality. But to modify a oft-quoted quip, "it's the Whiteness, stupid."

So, rather than consider eradicating racism, "Sharing the Dream," ushering in a "postracial America," or listing the measuring sticks for the demonstration of good character, I propose that we modify this public morality approach to the framing of race relations. That definition is a definition of personal goodness, will, and control where individuals are evaluated on the goodness or evilness of their hearts much more than on the good or evil in their daily actions. It presumes a common understanding of "good" or "evil." Just because individuals publicly state they hate racism doesn't mean they won't support and vote for policies that disproportionately disenfranchise persons of color.

Instead, racial politics frames racial fear as a reflection of stress that is ultimately fueled by the fear of appearing incompetent or inferior within social interaction and public discourse. Fearing racial conflict is human, but avoidance of racial interactions represents a coping behavior that can be seen and heard within the stress reactions of behavior, voice, and movement. Hostile reaction to this incompetence becoming public is as much a stress reaction as avoidance.

Racial stress is more tangible a construct than racism or character. Racial stress is not about character. Character implies personality, personality change, and morality coherence. Moral mandates do not always imply competence. Competence implies exposure, learning, practice, training, and skills. Large-scale systemic concepts or shallow moral mandates don't work well in teaching individuals what to do when faced with a moment of racial embarrassment. Racial stress management does. During stressful social interactions, it is human to diagnose the character of others, but it is misguided because there is little translation of these diagnoses into actions that resolve that stress. Being a good person isn't as relevant in these interactions. Good, caring people do not naturally know how to sail a boat or teach a classroom of middle schoolers without training. Becoming a teacher may reflect noble intentions but those intentions do not prepare you for teaching Black and Brown youth without training. The same is true about negotiating racial stress. Being a good person does not come with a racial stress negotiation instruction booklet.

I focus on competence rather than character because I want to isolate those pillars and consequences of racism that can be seen, touched, heard, and felt—not idealized. Racism as a concept can remain invisible if character is the criterion of progress. Incompetence or the inability or failure to resolve a racially conflictual interaction is more tangible and can be evaluated. Racism is amorphous. Incompetence resides at the level of individuals and interactions. Racism is systemic and multidimensional. Using the concept of systemic racism in schools may be useful for explaining the effects of oppressive policies on student achievement, but it is not the best way to understand and resolve racial stress or to change how teachers, students, and parents navigate racial dynamics and politics in relationships daily. These moment-by-moment interactions are visceral, emotional, exciting, and stressful. By focusing on the stress of these racial interactions, the rhetorical discussion shifts from a conversation full of rational intellectualization to one of feelings and negotiation, from rigidly thinking and saying the right thing to working through tense moments after saying "the wrong thing." I want to understand how systemic racism and racial incompetence clash in social interactions where people breathe, live, survive, and act—and in schools. Being "nice" or "good" schools relieves them of responsible leadership to resolve specific racial conflicts with specific racial knowledge.

Those accused of being "racist" should not receive more attention than the racism. One of the biggest stressors in racial interactions and dialogue is the unspoken fear that an accusation of being "racist" could be launched at any time. This fear can be so overwhelming that once launched, all manner of dialogue and diplomacy is lost because many lack the social skills to navigate the interaction to the next socially meaningful level. Sometimes defending oneself from being called a "racist" dominates the discourse such that it becomes the conversation instead of the original racial conflict. Resolution is next to impossible, given that the drive to avoid being called "racist" is a show-stopping "line-in-the-sand" moment, the quintessential first word among a group of fighting words, and a moment ripe for intense public shame.

A morality-focused, character-based framing of racism assumes that individuals can simply search their feelings and know "I'm not a racist." By doing so, individuals may expect immunity from making decisions that support racial hegemony. Social psychology research reveals that when individuals choose to reject racism as a matter of convenience rather than conscience, it masks the fear of an alternative they have not yet been willing to explore (Amodio, Harmon-Jones, & Devine, 2003).

Rejecting claims of racism may represent a cry for help. Stating the words "I am not a racist" may be more accurately translated as "Please don't hurt me" or "Please don't blame me for being White" or "Please don't remind me of my White guilt." Moreover, to become antiracist because one fears that the alternative is too costly or embarrassing is an avoidance coping strategy. It is not a choice of courage, but of convenience. But what drives decisions of racial convenience? Is it a fear of being judged, being labeled as inferior, or being discovered as incompetent in "all things racial?" Is it the fear of losing access to economic resources? Yes. It's the fear that others will question my character and consider me one of those "bad people," a "racist," which to many represents the lowest form of humanity.

What I find most troubling about the firestorm that occurs during a "racist" characterization is when the defensive retractions and rebuttals about the characterization take attention away from the actual egregious act of racial discrimination. Implicit in this distraction is the collusion between the accusers and the accused in not clarifying their definition of racism. Just once, when the issue of racism comes up, I would like the interrogator to simply ask, "What is your definition of racism or racist?" When George Bush stated that Kanye West's calling him out as a racist and one "who doesn't like Black people" was "disgusting" and the darkest day of his presidency, I was heartbroken and dumbfounded. I wasn't heartbroken because Kanye accused Bush or just that Bush was distraught. I was most disturbed that no one asked Kanye or the president to explain what they meant by "racism"—not the liberal media, not the Black media, no one. Given there was no clear definition, we were left to accept the most benign or frightening definition possible. We could just as easily have replaced the word *racist* with *terrorist* and gotten the same result.

Schools can teach that while President Bush through soul-searching decided that he wasn't racist, any definition of systemic racism would reject that individuals alone can decide this. The characterization of him as "racist" became the real problem, not racism or Bush's decisions during the Hurricane Katrina crisis. Whether George Bush committed acts of racism is not debated in his "disgusting" comment. Educators should be debating these events in classrooms. The very act of characterization is questioned, not its truthfulness. To be able to sidestep the larger issues of racism by bait-and-switching it with the smaller issue of one's personal insult is a clever but troublesome strategy, conscious or unconscious. Nevertheless, children in schools can learn to identify these clever strategies during racially charged situations, national and personal.

Conversely, the failure of politicians, educators, and journalists to turn these into teachable moments increases public ignorance of racial politics. In schools, racial equity is often about not saying the wrong thing, not appearing to do the wrong thing, and not being "racist" without a sense of accountability for the lesson implicit in any conflict that occurs. Instead of advancing information and knowledge about how racism is systemic and debilitating to academic performance and well-being, educators have also framed these dynamics as character education, thus making it a moral imperative—a miseducated framing, in my opinion.

Again, if racism is about character, not competence, we might feel sorry for George Bush, since Kanye tainted his character. Ironically, Kanye found sympathy for Mr. Bush's feelings some years later after he went through a scathing public critique of his character, following his intrusion in Taylor Swift's Grammy award–winning moment. To both of these men, I ask, Why should Americans care about the public embarrassment of celebrities more than the larger tragic outcomes of racism? Battling racism should be educational and schools should be at the center of the teaching and learning. It should not include defending our individual character and reputation. We should expect more knowledge and skills in the negotiation of racial politics from our leadership or role models. It is tragic that the public learned little to nothing about how racism works from these public "debates." Although racial humiliation for the few should not outweigh the effects of racism on the many, it does. Why should one individual's guilt or stress reaction become the center of the lesson about racism instead of the negative impact of the racist acts themselves? Why should the poor, the underachieving, and the not so famous bear the burden of protecting the shame of the rich and famous? Educators must take these popular events and teach daily.

What can schools learn from these public gaffs, games, and "scandals"? They can ask questions like "Was competence or character more important in this racial characterization?" Kanye or journalists could have understood that the fulcrum of his criticism of the president should not be balanced upon Bush's character or his public humiliation. The righteousness of his criticism should illuminate the president's lack of foresight. The intellectual disaster was the depth of racial incompetence revealed in this public encounter. Kanye could have described how Bush's hesitation, actions, and decisions led to racially disparate treatment for victims of Hurricane Katrina and tied it to a history of systemically racist decisionmaking that led to similar outcomes. He or informed journalists could have educated us all by not making it personal. A "morally good" President Bush is no less responsible for decisions or indecisions that lead to racially discriminatory acts that endanger American lives.

Unfortunately, the racial fears of the many outweigh the racialized life experiences of the few. In schools, we make judgments of quality of schooling by test score averages and gaps in those scores without focusing on the unique racialized academic challenges that Black youth experience. Healthy race relations should target the effects racism has on individual and collective well-being. Attitudes and percentages don't cause racism. Systems do. Our emotional ignorance and denial yet persistent allegiance to a racist past contribute to racism. Our blindness to racial difference and disproportionality in schooling contributes to racism. Our refusal or failure to act specifically on behalf of oppressed communities of color in schooling contributes to racism.

So what if many feel guilty for racial feelings they have? These feelings are natural, as are feelings of anger and fear. But they are insufficient for changing how children and schools learn to face racial disparities and overcome them. In summary, when the fears of the majority who endorse a Whiteness ideology outweigh the discrimination experiences of the minority, they become a distraction from the disparity problems and the educational imperative to solve those problems.

Schools can be reformed to teach racial literacy and stress management skills, not simply deliver information about race status disparity. Racial disparities that result from decisions that are not racist in their intention are racist nonetheless, irrespective of the emotional shame of the "deciders." The comments of these popular icons reflect many in our society whose knowledge and discernment of racial injustice or stress is limited or distorted. This colorblindness and racial blindness may rest at the kindergarten level of understanding racism because the definitions of the colorblind are often egocentrically focused on how one feels at a particular moment, not on how others are affected by the systemic racialized actions, statements, and decisions of powerful people. Schools can play a major role in illuminating the avoidance of racial matters by all Americans, and showing that these are coping strategies that are both intentional and unintentional.

Schools can teach children to observe instead of run from racial discourse. If actions speak louder than thoughts or feelings, then what actions can we see during racially stressful moments or interactions that reveal an acquiescence or resistance to the elephant of racial hierarchy? Children can learn to see stress. We can see fear through the stuttering of words, the blinking eyes, the hesitance in thoughts, through the censoring of one's agency, through the movement away from a topic or a space, and through the excessive boasting or defensiveness of a political position when confronted. Without casting negative aspersions upon them, these reactions reveal the underlying tensions that individuals undergo when confronted with questions about their racial credibility.

So what represents racism at the level of social interactions? Racism can be found in social interactions that hover around racial tension like a kind of dance. It is in the interactional moments of our lives and our existence that we determine who is kind and who is not, who is open and who is closed, who is courageous and who is cowardly. Social interactions are stressful, but students in school can learn that stress is manageable if we study its nature, its habits, its effects, and its modifiability. How anxiety-producing is this racial encounter for me? Does my level of anxiety, if any, reveal something about myself, my upbringing or my decisionmaking? Does my anxiety reveal that I don't know what to say or do when these arise? Does this anxiety reveal that my efforts at avoidance have failed me and I notice that I frequently fear a racial tribunal or firing squad awaits me? Can anyone or everyone see that I don't know what to do or say when I'm questioned about my credibility to negotiate racial conflicts?

Managing anxiety is a matter of competence, not character. The fear of being found out as inferior, as incompetent, as stupid, as being a "bad person" might be very intense. I say "might" because not everyone who is clueless about negotiating racial encounters wants to resolve them. Still, racial hostility toward others may simply be a mask or excuse to avoid self-reflection or deflect self-blame. It's running from the shame of incompetence that drives American race relations. Now, character can be revealed by how we face our incompetence. But it's the shame of incompetence that keeps us from facing what we don't know, from asking for help, and from taking the risk of becoming a student of racial politics. Schools can reform how we learn to manage our racial anxieties.

When Racial Hierarchy Is Challenged, Black and Brown People Become Expendable

In their work "The Avant-Garde of White Supremacy," Martinot and Sexton (2003) remind us that the "ignorability" of violence toward Black people in racial profiling, namely police brutality, is a consequence of our collective refusal to challenge racial hierarchy as the best way to judge quality. Similarly, in education, the acquiescence to the primacy of Whiteness ideas, thoughts, and behaviors in schools relies heavily upon and perhaps dictates the expendability and marginalization of Black and Brown humanity. To reiterate further, I believe that, under public, personal, and institutional duress, the humanity of Black and Latino intelligence, creativity, sacrifice, history, and humanity will be sacrificed for the greater societal "good." Martinot and Sexton remark about acquiescence by stating:

> Most theories of white supremacy seek to plumb the depths of its excessiveness, beyond the ordinary; they miss the fact that racism is a mundane affair. The fundamental excess of the paradigm of policing which infuses this culture is wholly banal. Those theories overlook that fact in favour of extant extravagance, spectacle, or the "deep psychology" of rogue elements and become complicit in perpetuating white supremacy. The reality is an invidious ethos of excess that, instead, constitutes the surface of everything in this society. For some time now, the intellectual quest for racism's supposedly hidden meaning has afforded a refuge from confrontations with this banality, even its possible acknowledgement. The most egregious aspect of this banality is our tacit acquiescence to the rules of race and power, to the legitimacy white supremacy says it has, regardless of

their total violation of reason and comprehensibility. Our "tacit acquiescence" is the real silent source of white supremacist tenacity and power. (p. 173)

Implicit within the concept of colorblindness—or better yet, racial blindness—is an inability to see racial hierarchy and the variety of behavioral and psychological strategies that accompany it. Racial hierarchy or supremacy is the notion that some racial groups are more evolved than others on multiple dimensions—relevance, smartness, potential, and humanity (Martinot & Sexton, 2003). Critical race theory assumes racial discrimination is unavoidable because those who benefit from White supremacy have little interest in giving up those financial, status, social, and psychological benefits for the sake of racial equality (Harris & Wallace, 2008; Lopez, 2000). This conflict of interest has highlighted that the creation of a racial hierarchy is purposeful, not simply random or accidental (Bell, 1992). The intransigence of racism as a phenomenon that maintains privilege for the powerful majority in our society fundamentally supports narratives of exclusion because it keeps those privileged from giving up "just desserts." Consequently, some argue for the necessity of racial literacy and training on behalf of White parents of Black children in multiracial families to challenge any racial hierarchy that demonizes the potential of Black culture, intelligence, and civic contribution (Twine, 2004).

The element of Black inferiority within a narrative of racial hierarchy is purposeful because it allows for a host of conscious and unconscious racial microaggressive insults against Black students and families to occur with little accountability (Sue et al., 2007). Ironically, many people regardless of their racial background believe in this narrative. Given the mass socialization of racial hierarchy in American society, no one is immune to the notion that "Blackness is inferior." This narrative can wreak havoc in classrooms from elementary through college education, but it is invisible—what Bourdieu calls "habitus," or that which "goes without saying" (Bourdieu, 1990). The Black and Brown inferiority and expendability narrative is invisible in crime reports on television and in school reform efforts around the achievement gap. Whether through the paternalizing efforts to "save" Black people or "incarcerate" them as miscreants, this narrative influences Black folks across the spectrum of employment success or educational attainment. Schools, however, can illuminate and teach students and parents to see and debate this narrative.

To be sure, the "Expendable Black and Brown Humanity" narrative is a game. But most players don't know it as a contest or that it represents a script that individuals, groups, and systems follow when threatened. Anyone can play this game. Despite how Black life, ideas, and creativity have been foundational to this country's economic, artistic, humanity, and intellectual growth over centuries, the worth of Black life remains paltry, particularly when White racial supremacy is challenged. One psychological rationale for such a strong position on the preeminence of racial hierarchy in American race relations is research on social comparison and how in- and out-group politics predicts the tokenized status and expendable outcomes of the out-group.

Some years back, my wife and I were visiting independent schools for our son to attend kindergarten and in the visits we heard lots of stories about the quality of each school's academic standing and rigor. During a tour of one school, a representative, teacher, and former parent of the school shared her excitement about the school, its positive effect on her child, and the longevity of the teaching corps. Given my own concern about faculty diversity and the important role it plays in student learning, I asked her, "How important is diversity of the faculty to this school's administration and mission?" The guide was stunned by the question, as evidenced by her pause, hesitation, and very slight and subtle stutter. Perhaps being asked a "diversity" question from a Black parent was new to her. I remember these "fear of racial incompetence" moments because of the work I do, but it was hard to miss even if you weren't looking for it. Following a very polite gathering of herself, she smoothly uttered the following argument: "We are very serious about the diversity at this school, but our focus is on getting the best-qualified teachers for each area of study given our history and tradition of academic excellence."

Now, in my consultations to PWS across the country, parents, teachers, and students have told me of their reactions to, experiences with, and oppression from this same argument. But for me to hear it so explicitly as a prospective parent looking to enroll my child, it was jarring. It wasn't simply about the work I do. Had I projected a view in that moment to her regarding how at risk my child would be in an environment that equated diversity with some notion of compromised or inferior academics? Now, as parents, we have license to fear the worst and best of our children's potential and demise within schools. So I realize that no school is perfect and all schools may hold to these ideas that "diversity undermines academic excellence" without stating them. Still, it was the invisibility and lack of question regarding the statement that was most disturbing. When parents, teachers, and students describe similar moments in schools, they are mostly disturbed by the ease with which others don't even see their biases with respect to difference. This is what Sue et al. (2007) calls *a microinsult* or a *negative hidden snub* in a message to a person of color that might be unknown by the perpetrator.

I never assumed that this school would give up on academic excellence in a search for diverse faculty, but she did and perhaps the school did. In schools where this perception or stereotype exists, perhaps someone holding the opposing view could just as easily wonder why such a connection would ever be made. When my wife and I asked further about the faculty of color present, the guide named a few people, but it was clear the number was small. We said nothing more at the time, but on a feedback questionnaire about the visit and the tour, I suggested the school not equate diversity with a lack of academic excellence for future visitors, as it may send the "wrong" message.

Another disturbing aspect of this interaction that stood out to me was the way in which our guide, after being thrown off course initially, so easily drifted into that explanation. While she clearly showed signs of stress from the question, there was an element of security that came with her answer that reduced her anxiety so she could return to a steady, polite, and welcoming demeanor. It appeared to me that she had practiced this response. In effect, she had demonstrated a skill, a practiced act to reduce her stress during a racial encounter. I began to wonder then, "For whom would this response not be offensive? For whom would it reduce anxiety or fear about enrolling their child in the school?"

After getting over my own anger at the false association between diversity and deficiency, I slowly realized that perhaps some parents would appreciate this response and see it as a positive reason to choose this school. As a cultural statement, it communicated a strong commitment of the school to a racial hierarchy that needs no explanation and deserves no questioning. The guide's statement was a political position for which there was or is no meaningful evidence, but if it sells the school, it is meaningful in a cultural customer service sense. So *I* was missing the cultural relevance of that statement to others. Perhaps it was I, not the guide, who was blind about how this "game" is played. The stress-reduction benefit of her argument was not meant for us or others like us who see diversity as an inherent advancement of academic excellence. Again, it was her stress reaction and my distress that were the clues to a larger set of questions I needed to ask. I wonder if school leaders, parents, and students can ask these questions for themselves when they are distressed.

My experience with the school tour forced me to question, "While blindness is a crucial element to maintenance of racial hierarchy and privilege, what evidence might we see of the hierarchy if we were looking?" The "Expendable Humanity" view, for example, has a history in the great American enslavement experience as well as in recent disasters like Hurricane Katrina. The historical and lived experiences of Black and Brown people are fraught with systemic acquiescence to the tragic but inevitable disrespect of their worldviews and their behaviors. When Black people survive a hurricane by looking for food to feed their families, they are thieves and criminals, but when White citizens do so, they are resourceful survivors.

Diversity initiatives in school are often viewed as not central to the curriculum or mission of the school, while diversity coordinators are often younger, less powerful in implementing policy changes and become tokenized by the school's lack of commitment to integrating diversity matters within strategic plans and pedagogy (Hall & Stevenson, 2007). Diversity activities of curriculum planning and personnel are often the most vulnerable for elimination should budgetary or political constraints increase. In exploring the psychological challenges, stress reactions, and coping responses of students, teachers, parents, and administrators in PWS and predominantly Black schools, I have learned that racial stress, hierarchy, and coping are no less important in these contexts, although they are manifested differently.

Racial hierarchy defines diversity in predominantly White settings in a particular way. While I believe the physical (demographics of PWS) and psychological presence of Whiteness defines the quality of schooling, it is better to study this hierarchy without ascribing blame to any particular group. Whiteness and the differential emotional, intellectual, and social meanings attributed to Whiteness rather than the percentage of White people is a better way to explain how cultural values and their clashing may define the politics of race relations in schools. By Whiteness, I mean how individuals and groups construct meaning in a world in which racial hierarchy is a standard against which coping models are developed and evaluated. So, it's possible to find in predominantly diverse or Black schools the same adherence to a superior racial hierarchy. In a 1990 edition and reprinting of Carter G. Woodson's classic work, *The Mis-education of the Negro,* Woodson commented in the early 20th century on how racial hierarchy taught in schools affects the self-esteem of Black people:

> If you teach the Negro that he has accomplished as much good as any other race he will aspire to equality and justice without regard to race. Such an effort would upset the program of the oppressor in Africa and America. Play up before the Negro, then, his crimes and shortcomings. Let him learn to admire the Hebrew, the Greek, the Latin and the Teuton. Lead the Negro to detest the man of African blood—to hate himself. (p. 130)

Belief in the supremacy of Whiteness is one way to frame this hierarchy, while colorblindness is another (Lewis, 2004). Often, the fear of offending friends and colleagues is why many students, teachers, and parents refuse to discuss racial hierarchy in schools or society. To do so is perhaps to violate an unspoken rule—never question that when we say "better" or "best" in our culture, we mean "most things White." It's the standard by which we judge most of our successes and failures, our heroes, villains, and antivillains, our best and brightest, our leaders and followers. It's not about White people, or it's not about White people being better as much as about people regardless of racial background who believe in an ideology of Whiteness is better and look for its brand in the seemingly normal politics of everyday life. It's about the "acquiescence."

In contrast, many Americans have been viewing Blackness (in whatever definition we ascribe to Blackness) as a stable and negative caricature for centuries. Elijah Anderson (2011) discusses this dichotomy in his ethnography of downtown cosmopolitan interactions in urban environments in which Black people are rarely present in these upscale public spaces. Their lack of presence gives way to a false sense of calm in these public spaces such that numerical scarcity of Black people is equated with peaceful civilization. Like jets flying across the sky, they maintain a slight, almost invisible presence. But Anderson suggests that this calm setting can explode in these public spaces once Black individuals cross into these spaces in greater numbers or visibility, because in the minds of many Whites, the Black stereotype of the "iconic ghetto" is triggered by that shifting presence of Black people.

As an ideology, the inferiority of Blackness is the perfect foil to the paternalistic hero Whiteness narrative of American racial politics. Guess (2006) suggests that the Black/White binary in race relations has forgotten to mention the role of Whiteness and, consequently, racial inequality cannot be resolved. Challenging the "heroism" of Whiteness is key to developing racial literacy or a racial lens that can see the forest and trees of race relations. To save or to incarcerate Black people are two tenets of the hero narrative that "goes without saying" and represents two sides of the same coin of racial hierarchy. Why? Simply put, it's because to save or incarcerate Black people is to assume the inferiority of potential and the need for remediability of humanity. So-called reform solutions perpetuate the justification of inhumane perceptions and treatment as much as negative criminality caricatures because the relationship to the savior or the jailor never changes. The plot and the punch line are still focused on the importance of the "Whiteness" or the hero as well as its invisibility (Lewis, 2004; Schomberg, 2013). To espouse Whiteness or colorblindness is to describe all things Black or non-White as despising entities. It means to control non-White phenomena or Blackness through ownership, distortion, subtexting, salvation, incarceration, and destruction of Black ideas, symbols, attitudes, styles, movements, firsts, exceptions, and presidents. The "invisibility" of these psychological machinations defines the culture or stage of race relations, especially in schools.

Not everyone sees it this way. In fact, some find it preposterous and conspiratorial to assume this racial hierarchy exists in everyday life. I want to illuminate the emotional, intellectual, and social challenges for those who not only see but experience this racial hierarchy as traumatizing, a phenomenon not endemic to one racial group. This hierarchy of Whiteness or colorblindness is not without its cracks, and there are some who find it not so invisible and are shocked that others cannot or will not entertain its presence (Bonilla-Silva, 2001; King & Smith, 2005). Not knowing how to respond to these poisoning and promising politics is a tragedy about a train wreck waiting to happen. But not seeing the hierarchy is far worse.

But what if this type of hierarchical reasoning and expendable humanity happens in schools and classrooms, not just public spaces? The sad and meaningful lesson we can learn from racial hierarchy reasoning is that the same political, poisonous, and promising processes that occur in relation to the largest racial elephant in the room (a Black president) apply to smaller racial elephants as well. These racial conflicts exist in classrooms, on street corners, on school boards, on city councils, in voting laws, in local elections, and in homes across America. Unfortunately, in schools and deeply embedded within the rhetoric of school reform, this racial hierarchy has become a trademark of success or failure, intelligence or incompetence. "Race to the top" is a battle cry for competition, as if the best and brightest only need the call for a race to awaken them from the slumber of laziness or incentive deprivation. It's the context, silly, and rarely do politicians argue for financial resources to take a holistic ecological, health, and racialized disparities approach to the achievement gap dilemma.

The models of education over the past decade have asserted that inferior education comes from the lack of competition (Bulkley, 2005; Scott, 2011). The academic hierarchy of best and brightest provides individuals with a rating system that prospective participants use to judge the quality of the "the thing." The educational hierarchy becomes a thing to be conquered, a mountain to be climbed, but in many ways perpetuates the same White supremacy politics (Ladson-Billings & Tate, 1995). Those who cannot speak this language, compete, or internalize this rating system will not make able mountain climbers. The "educationally disabled" schools, teachers, students, and parents are at risk of being scapegoated, a predictable result that has become systematized and turned into a technology or derivative. The problem remains in the people, not the process or the program's underlying colorblindness.

So, if the scapegoating of despised out-groups is an accepted process in climbing the hierarchy or mountain of race relations and avoidance is a natural coping strategy, several questions arise for schools to consider. How do schools perpetuate the reasoning of racial hierarchy through teaching, character-building, and discipline? How do individuals emotionally and behaviorally respond when the politics of racial hierarchy become more visible? Schools represent ladders of social mobility, but how does one climb the ladder of success if it involves navigating racial conflict through avoidance? What is the cost, if any, of racial stress to self-esteem, achievement, and self-sufficiency that results from climbing the ladder? Is it better for students, teachers, and parents to ignore or engage these stressful moments in which the demands of racial hierarchy become visible in order to remain on that ladder? How do these questions highlight the futility or possibility of a credible postracial America? How do we have or continue to fail to have racial conversations that challenge hierarchies of Whiteness, Blackness, or blindness so that we can reach the postracial promise land that political pundits keep claiming? Or finally, how might the underachievement of Black and Latino children be understood more accurately as an expectation and reasonable expenditure of our miseducated reforms rather than an unfortunate consequence? These questions and interactions of cultural mismatch around values, attitudes, styles, and meaning-making arise as elephants but stay hidden within a sophisticated etiquette of conflict avoidance.

Schools Are Places of Avoidant Racial Socialization and Politics

Schools are centers of racial socialization and represent the one place where social ethics, economic warfare, national politics, and racial conflict emerge, collide, erupt, or lay hidden daily. What if the fabrication and socialization of the importance of racial hierarchy, racial card gaming, and detecting "racists" character begin in school? What if the platform of one's political party clashes with economic, cultural, gender, and racial warfare at school? What if school is the place where students go to learn about stereotypes and how to use them? It is, after all, an institution of learning and where youth spend most of their waking day. School is a microcosm of American societal success and failure, and is a racially socializing institution (Arrington et al., 2003). Not only do schools teach about citizenship, they teach youth how to avoid racial matters while simultaneously desiring racial supremacy or internalizing racial inferiority as foundational principles of that civility. Carter G. Woodson (1990) captures this sentiment powerfully by targeting school classrooms as the place where racial violence begins:

> To handicap a student by teaching him that his black face is a curse and that his struggle to change his condition is hopeless is the worst sort of lynching. It kills one's aspirations and dooms him to vagabondage and crime. It is strange, then that the friends of truth and the promoters of freedom have not risen up against the present propaganda in the schools and crushed it. This crusade is much more important than the anti-lynching movement, because there would be no lynching if it did not start in the schoolroom. (p. 8)

How, if at all, do we see and challenge this hidden curriculum, this elephant of racial socialization? Stress. Stress and our reactions to it are our best warning symptoms for identifying where elephants of racial hierarchy exist in the school setting.

The ways we use stereotypes before, during, and after racially stressful interactions can reveal more about how educators perpetuate racial hierarchy than the games of ferreting out "racists" or "don't get caught saying the wrong racial thing." Playing these games distracts from questioning the hegemony of racial superiority. Educators must respond to a higher level of complexity by teaching youth how not just to see these elephants of racial hierarchy, but to ride them into a different sunset in a multicultural world that is changing by the minute. As we become more diverse as a society, our educational response to the intolerance of difference must be to teach skills that promote the recognition and identification of racial hierarchy politics and their dehumanization of Black and Brown talent—especially in school.

In a school, achievement gap challenges reveal more about the lack of instruction or learning, what Pedro Noguera and others call "Ain't Been Taught That" (ABTT), than the potential of the youth (Hileman & Clark, 2012). The more obvious concern about racial conflict is in how well teachers can teach and students can learn during racially stressful moments. To focus on the problem of name-calling ("racist") and its cessation, rather than on the development of a skill set that challenges the psychological infrastructure that promotes racial labeling as a coping strategy, is to put the cart before the horse. Racial labeling and the fear of being labeled represent symptoms of a larger problem of incompetence in negotiating a racial conflict. This fear undermines teaching and learning because it diverts attention toward self-preservation of reputation and away from illuminating the insidious nature of racial politics. In a colorblind context, the racialized experiences of students of color are uniquely invisible to educational leaders, teachers, parents, and students themselves. Racial avoidance coping only systematizes this invisibility. Schools are systems that both systematize and civilize racial avoidance.

So, the fear of being labeled as an immoral person is intense in the fight for racial absolution and innocence, but that intensity is fueled by an unwieldy sense of helplessness in navigating racial encounters. To be afraid of racial encounters is not the problem. Not addressing the fear of racial encounters is. As individuals become more competent at a task, the less they fear being held out as incapable of performing that task and the more they will receive feedback from sundry quarters of their capable talents. The best way to address racial encounter incompetence is through guided feedback while practicing successful coping behaviors in situations that approximate the originally stressful context. Practice, practice, practice will be a familiar response to queries about resolving the intransigence of racial conflicts. That some teachers embody this racial competence in their teaching and others do not is what makes racial dilemmas in classrooms most interesting. That schools are jungles of racial socialization is not the problem. That these jungles are mostly socializing individuals how to avoid racial tensions in our society at the relationship level is the problem of racial illiteracy.

The Role of Schools to Teach and Practice Racial Literacy

We must expect schools to do better at educating children about the nuances, complexities, and consequences of stereotyping and racism than American journalism or parenting has been able to do. Successfully negotiating racial politics should be a core curriculum issue in American schooling. Racial progress or piety cannot be defined simply by having a Black friend, a diverse student body, having never said negative things against Black or Brown people, or having a relative who once marched with King (which in some circles is greater than having one Black friend). In school, quality race relations must become more sophisticated than pointing out with whom and where one is playing the "race card." Conversely, students and parents of color need healthier "comeback lines" to these claims of racial game-playing.

If racial politics don't represent a card game or a dream, then what is required to navigate them successfully? Literacy. To reiterate, *learning to see and resolve racial stress and conflict in relationships involves explicit racial literacy skills teaching and practice on how not to get "played" by the politics of racial inferiority. Racial literacy* is the ability to read, recast, and resolve racially stressful encounters. Illiteracy on racial politics would be an inability to read, recast, or resolve these moments and interactions.

As observers of the dance of the racial elephants in the classroom, boardroom, emergency room, courtroom, early childhood education, special education, principal's office, and oval office, it is imperative that we not just alert educators to the injustices of these interactions. We must examine the dance deeply and study its insidious nature. It's not just one event, one policy, one person, one mistake, one racist to conquer. We explore to illuminate but also to teach. So, how do we help educational leaders see the drama so they can choose to dance differently to their fears of racial matters in the classroom and the curriculum?

That question consumes the work of racial literacy. Not simply to "tattletale," "expose wounds and weak spots," or humiliate educators, politicians, celebrities, or entrepreneurs. Racial literacy requires that educational leaders study, illuminate, and teach about the multitude of investigations and findings into the nature of the elephant, and not out of fear of being found fraudulent. It is because excellence in children's learning, achievement, and full participation in American society is at stake.

Racial colorblindness and amnesia happen not because children aren't capable of managing the elephants of racial stress, but because educators, parents, and adult leadership have forgotten that facing, not avoiding, one's fears is the key to resolving all conflicts, especially racial ones. Whether it is immature, unconscious, or routine, racial avoidance reflects a dance around social injustice incompetence. Still, although we desperately need illumination of the jungle of racial politics and teaching of racial literacy skills, illumination is not enough and teaching is not enough. We need practice.

Using examples from predominantly White independent and public schools as the contexts for understanding and improving stressful race relations, I will advocate for program and curriculum development that promotes successful relationships between educators and Black and Brown youth. I hope to bring clarity to the achievement gap challenge by focusing on teacher-student relationships and the classroom process as the most proximal and powerful contexts for improving or undermining academic skills.

I'll propose arguments in favor of facing racial conflicts as an important way to increase academic engagement and achievement. Before laying out the challenges to facing racial conflicts in predominantly White settings, let's discuss in the next chapter how racial avoidance in American national politics seeps into American schooling. Racial amnesia is socialized and reinforced within the national reactions to a Black presidency, so much so that it explains why most of us so skillfully run from local racial politics as if we were running from dragons, lions, tigers, zombies, and yes, oh my—rampaging elephants.

CHAPTER 2

Recasting the History of Racial "Firsts"

Dancing Around Stereotypes in American Schools

I'm not trying to build fences or get too intense.
But my sense is that it's senseless
that we can't even make reference
to **that** boil waitin' to bloom
and to **that** cloud of "racist" that looms large
over the elephant standing like a dusty heirloom in the corner of the dusty room.
Were we crazy thinking that we could polish away the rusty with a broom, or sweep up this mess,
when it was the wind or tsunami or monsoon that blew in this unrest of the racial?

—Howard C. Stevenson, *Elephant Attention* (2012)

The ground which a colored man occupies in this country is, every inch of it, sternly disputed.

—Frederick Douglass, Speech at the American and Foreign Anti-Slavery Society annual meeting, New York City, May, 1853 (2000)

In this chapter, I will discuss the power of stereotyping to inhibit positive race relations and social interactions. I will try to link the power of racial imaging in societal political discourse, the racial stress experienced by protaganists from selected examples of the history of desegregation, and the emotionally reactive Black presidential backlash to the politics of racial coping in schools. The use of the dance metaphor in this chapter is instructive for describing the unconscious nature of stereotyping to prescribe roles that predict how race relations become conflictual and remain so in mutual reciprocation. The implications of scripted roles and stereotyping for the schooling of Black underachieving students is how racial inferiority pervades their academic and behavioral identity performances and failures. But inferiority and portents of failure are not socialized in isolation. They occur and play out within relationships with school leaders and systems, as McDermott (1987) makes clear:

> While failure is a well-established institutional fact, the ascription of failure to one person or group rather than another says nothing about the learning potentials of the persons or groups involved. Failure is waiting every morning in every classroom in America; before children or their teachers arrive, failure is there. As citizens, as teachers, even as reformers, our questions have been focused on who is going to be acquired by failure and who by success; there is only so much of each to go around. If we take seriously that failure is an institutional fabrication, a mock-up for scapegoating, a mystification, a culturally mandated foolishness that keeps us all in our respective places, what would an explanation of failure be, and why would we expect failure to have any relation to the traits of the children who come to our schools? (p. 363)

As Ray McDermott describes failure as "staged," so too are race relations.

RACIAL ROLE STRAIN: HOW STEREOTYPES BECOME STRAITJACKETS AND DANCE ROUTINES

Imagine American race relations as a dance between partners wearing straitjackets. Awkward, right? American racial interactions are often clumsy and reflect a dance between stereotypes of heroes, distressed victims, and villainous men and women who play their roles with righteous intensity. Even though we think we know how the story goes, we rarely want any other ending than what these roles can bring. If the good hero doesn't get his or her love interest, we are disturbed. If the bad villain wins the battles or the victim is not rescued, we become helpless and hopeless. Unfortunately, racial interactions in America still rely on offensive, rigid, and caricatured heterosexist archetypes of men, women, and children, the removal of which brings enormous stress. In the last chapter, I proposed that racial illiteracy and silence in schooling relationships is like an "elephant in the classroom." To extend the explanation of racial politics in schooling, I would call this dance around the elephant between stereotypical roles and expectations a form of racial straitjacketing.

Blackness in our society has been labeled as evil and Whiteness as good, strong, and smart despite nuanced takes on the slave and slavemaster dynamics in such movie scripts like *Django Unchained* (Schomberg, 2013). This racial script is not outdated, unfamiliar, even as it remains invisible.

The strain of continuing to respond to stereotypes and low expectations for Black students and families becomes heavy and stressful and leads to several questions like "Is Black underachievement a given or do I somehow play a role in its proliferation?" "What if *I* am keeping this dance routine by the way I commit to my racial role?" "What if my enslavement to this role is evident in my refusing to resist it, resisting in the wrong direction, or simply pretending there is no dance?" Sadly, Americans from diverse racial backgrounds may have chosen one of the many racial straitjackets to maintain the dance, because it is safe.

One racial straitjacket includes remaining congenial and not being disagreeable in cross- or same-race relationships. This straitjacket is often resident in the belief that a good education or a good school covers a multitude of past racial sins, such that navigating racial politics is unnecessary. Fitting comfortably into this racial straitjacket includes resisting the urge to raise racially contentious topics whether you are student, parent, teacher, principal, or president. Some people of color dance while wearing the straitjacket by avoiding any level of familial, collegial, and societal accusations of "racism" to reduce the anxiety that White friends, colleagues, classmates, and neighbors may experience and to not lose good schooling options. But if squelching racial discomfort is a role that influences one's well-being and achievement, is it worth it? What if I decide to choose a different racial role because maintaining the current role is becoming more stressful? In the face of racial rejection it takes a lot of courage to question the racial role one plays, but it takes strategy to remove the straitjacket.

As a metaphor for race relations, a family systems approach views the love-hate relationship between racial heroes and villains like a familiar dance that generates its own self-sustaining force. As time passes, this racial dance becomes routine and change of any kind imbalances the harmony between good and evil, and in the case of schools, smart and below average. Gallant heroes need maniacal villains as much as villains need heroes. This codependency is fraught with distancing and the burden of maintaining distance or scripted closeness through pejorative characterizations of the other. Despite their unique missions, the roles of heroes and villains are symbiotic.

In schools, the achievement expectations and accomplishments for Black youth are often laced with doubt and surprise. Acquiescence to low expectations of Black youth or surprise that some perform beyond the stereotype are two sides of the same coin of Black inferiority. Racial inferiority and supremacy expectations of Black and White students are as codependent a relationship as are villains to heroes. Either muffles the background music of racial hierarchy where Black accomplishment is perceived to be an aberration, not the norm.

The racial gamesmanship identified in Chapter 1 becomes more relational within the metaphor of dancing. The racial dance routine of "Don't

Upset White People by Discussing Racial Matters Jeopardy" fuels other spin-off choreographies ("Let's Make a Deal to Find the Racist So We Can All Go Back to Sleep," "Name that Stereotype," and "How Not to Be the Angry Black Man or Woman for a Day"). Although infantile, these and other routines serve a relational purpose. They bring rehearsed roles with clear instructions on the verbal and behavioral dos and don'ts when people are stressed about racial matters. Just like families. A family that dances together stays stuck together. Families need scapegoats, villains, priests, and heroes to keep harmony. As in families, any shift in one's racial role brings disharmony that family or school systems are often unwilling to tolerate without a fight. So the game of "Don't Expect Too Much from Black Students" is another confining racial dance routine worth challenging.

How the "First" Become the "Last" in American Schooling

Unfortunately, the postracial American rhetoric inadvertently portrays a view that wealthy and powerful members of society are clueless, forgetful, or in denial about the daily oppressions of the racially different. We all suffer from superiority envy. It's the "I may not be rich, but I'm so glad I'm not as poor as you" wealthy. The racial equivalent to this rhetoric is "Thank God I'm not Black" and this cry is more palpable in the daily political blogs, reality television shows, and 24/7 infotainment world. Happiness for many Americans rests in watching someone else's tragedy, which is assumed when racial politics are discussed. As long as one can see someone else's life ruined, lies uncovered, mistakes revealed, and shame displayed, happiness is just a channel click away.

Superiority envy reflects less about what we think of others and more about ourselves as well as an acquiescence to our station in the racial hierarchy. But still, the rhetoric of democracy covers these underlying racial and wealth politics like the American flag covers a casket. What lies in the casket are our values to fight for the poorest and different among us. It makes you wonder if the phrase "I'm rich, bitch," is written in small font on the American flag.

What does this have to do with firsts and racial stress and schooling, you may ask? Well, by not talking about or analyzing the history of White supremacy and contemporary racial disparity in the United States, Black students and families are left unprepared to reject the internalization of the stereotyping inherent to that history. Without instructions or knowledge of how to connect the stereotyping of the past to daily social or racial interaction, the silent or blatant hostility within the climate of racial conversations in homes, neighborhoods, and schools intensifies. Black people who have been the first in their profession or talent stream carry the burden of history and future as the world projects upon them dreams and nightmares. For

Barack Obama, American's first Black president, much of this repressed and vitriolic hostility is foisted upon his symbolic representation. Obama has been attacked for simply breathing the wrong way, as if breathing has variation across skin color. Symbolically, it has become a death sentence to any conservative politician's career to support anything that President Obama proposes despite the brilliance, utility, or conservatism of those ideas. Schools can learn a lot about racial literacy and incompetence through the retrenchment and angst expressed in these national racial politics.

Several tenets of critical race theory (CRT) explain this process of racial scapegoating and projection—a ritualized element of American democracy. Bell (1992) points out that within a White power structure, the American legal system, through the three principles of constitutional contradiction, interest convergence, and the high cost of racial remedies, is able to propose egalitarian principles without giving up financial, political, or cultural power. Groups and individuals who support this racial hierarchy will not support civil rights initiatives against their own self-interests in the present or future (Crenshaw, Gotanda, Peller, & Thomas, 1995). For many Americans, the Obama presidency is one such perceived threat to their racial self-interests.

Historically, White supremacy politics can be seen in the subtle and blatant ways racial hostility, denial, and lashing out was cloaked in political piety and courtesy in the racial rhetoric of Orval Faubus, George Wallace, Bull Connor, and other southern power brokers. I'll call these men the *Preracialists*. But in the racial politics toward President Obama, similar supremacy rhetoric has become coded.

Symbolically, the "first Black president" has become a rallying cry for many who hide their racial fear of his status as a racialized president behind rhetorical claims of him as "Hitler," "Muslim," or "un-American" to now reassert this fear in political opinion. Clearly, Obama's presidency has illuminated racial elephants, not resolved them. These false claims that he is an American monster increase an atmosphere of racial threat and decrease racial conversations. No wonder folks are eager to deny the presence of racial conflict, even if it is clearly present. As individuals fail to face tensions exacerbated by racial paranoia, so do our abilities to talk through and resolve racially stressful encounters.

Such racial avoidance is brainwashing at best, and leaves educators, parents, and students racially illiterate and mute. The good news is that racial avoidance requires choice and thus is modifiable. Racial avoidance represents any attempt by an individual or group to ignore, deny, sidestep, or dismiss a racially stressful encounter, whether in one's mind or in one's social engagements. Despite the fact that "Racial Firsts," "Racial Lasts," and "Racial Backlash" are ritualized, we can predict how individuals will behave in the stressful company of racially different colleagues and classmates. If we can predict racial stress reactions, then we can prepare students and teachers to react in ways that won't compromise their intellectual and economic potential. Perhaps becoming racially literate means learning to refuse acting out racial roles that demand giving up some humanity for the sake of an equal and just education.

Stereotypes affect how individuals see themselves and their potential, but many scholars have argued that stereotypes are unique in their negative effects on Black student academic performance. Claude Steele's (2010) "stereotype threat" concept is the fear of behaving, thinking, or speaking in ways that confirm a stereotype about one's group. It is often a deficit-based stereotype associated with one's race, gender, or background. In this book, I will refer to racial stereotyping primarily.

The psychological challenge of stereotype threat isn't simply that people are exposed to negative caricatures of their racial potential and being, but that they might internalize those negative images. Torres and Charles (2004) have coined the term *metastereotypes* to mean symbols through which Black young adults internalize negative perceptions that Whites have of them. Torres and Charles assert that Black college students are amazingly accurate about what Whites think of them. Other negative consequences of stereotyping include within-race or reference-group disgust, the dynamics of which are implicit within Cohen and Garcia's (2005) notion of "collective threat." Collective threat is defined as situations in which

> although running no risk of personally lending support to a stereotype about their group, individuals are concerned about the potentially stereotype-confirming acts of other members of their group. We call this concern *collective threat,* as it issues from the collectively shared nature of social identities. We further suggest that in situations where one's group is negatively stereotyped, an "I am us" mindset may arise out of the awareness that the way one is viewed and defined depends, in part, on the way that other group members are viewed and defined. (p. 566)

Black "Firsts" often receive the most intense attack on their abilities and potential through racial stereotyping. Perhaps stereotypes are often about "words" and words that the "Firsts" have overcome, but they can damage the self-esteem of those who internalize these images as if they are true. Being last on the social and financial accomplishment ladder doesn't help and can confirm one's inferiority. Over time, this inferiority becomes a way of thinking, of living, of behaving, and of dancing. Without rewriting the traditional American racial script of White supremacy and recasting the traditional roles of slave and slave master, I doubt any reasonable understanding of the pressures on Black firsts can be had.

The Psychological Threats and Costs of the Racial "Firsts," the Few, and the Lonely

As far as race relations go, being a "First" is far scarier than we know. Most people want social progress as long as they can keep the racial hierarchy intact; hence, Frederick Douglass's words represent a brilliant critique of liberalism and conservatism—"they want crops without plowing up the ground" (Douglass, 1857). By recasting, I mean "plowing up the ground" in our personal racial identity struggles and in our relationships. I'm advocating more than just change, standing out in a crowd, or being unique. I'm advocating for in-the-moment (ITM) adaptability to see racial dancing. I'm advocating for what systems theorists, cultural critics, and school reformers are salivating for, second-order change. I'm advocating that folks take notes on how self and others respond to the process of change (or refuse to), signs that individuals and groups begin to dance differently (or refuse to). It's not just about change, but understanding how systems and individuals feel threatened by and resist change and invest enormous time and emotional resources in keeping change in racial politics from happening.

So the best recasting questions are not "Is racism over?" or "Have the achievement scores in the school changed?" or "Doesn't my one Black friend exempt me with a lifetime guarantee from being called a racist?" The best recasting questions ask, "Are the roles, scripts, straitjackets, and dance routines of racial inequality that stand as the substance of racism and underachievement in education, health, and justice modifiable?" and "What role do I play in maintaining those dance routines?"

Being the first carries advantages and disadvantages. To schoolchildren, being first in line means being the best, most liked, most accepted—the winner. Being the first to go to college in one's family or from one's neighborhood still remains for many an accomplishment too impossible to imagine. The first school to integrate in a town is no small deal. To use this event as a powerful statement of a school's legacy or mission statement is smart marketing. "Firsts" often portend future success for others. Unfortunately, the rarity of "Firsts" among Black professionals, artists, performers, and scientists in the 21st century can also remind us of retrenchment. This is especially true when one's singularity in difference leads to isolation and failure. Failure emboldens opponents to racial progress to claim that Black culture is stereotypically self-destructive.

Being first garners the attention and respect of others. But what if that attention is stressful and the respect is temporary? What if the influence from being the "First" does not bring the change imagined? What if the potential for change increases resistance to change? For every social equality change action, there is an equal and opposite social change reaction. This is how family systems theory helps us understand that change is a threat, no matter how beneficial that change may become.

The stress on many racial "Firsts" is not simply about being the first, but about being so while wearing a straitjacket, battling the pressure of being the one and only success story. Failure can come from not maintaining the success or from not pulling one's constituency in to benefit. Yet this exceptionality brings isolation and alienation. For students of color in school, alienation is often accompanied by pressures to not be the villain. Or in the racial dance of "don't be the angry Black man or woman," participation demands alienating oneself from any style, language, or behavior that could be labeled as stereotypically "Black." In other words, becoming the antivillain. An example of an antivillain includes students or educators of color who distance themselves from any racial labels in order to prevent marginalization. These stances maintain the dance of racial hierarchy by indirectly accepting the problem of "Blackness" as villainous while invisibly uplifting the role of Whiteness as hero. By dancing as the antivillains in juxtaposed rhythm to the stereotype of villain, students of color as minority protagonists solidify the tragic perception that more ordinary members of color are not as capable. This dance is very stressful.

Antivillain. The stress on Jackie Robinson was so enormous that some tout it as a contribution to his untimely death at the early age of 53 (Maisonet, 2012). Is the stress of being the racial "First" too costly? The stress on Jackie Robinson was not so much about being the first Black baseball player, but the first Black person to demonstrate the defectiveness of racial segregation. So, although playing baseball well was a requirement, he also had to prove that he wasn't a stereotype. The role of hero was off limits. The role of villain represented failure. Being the antivillain was his only choice. If he resisted and fought back too hard against the racial rejection and violence thrown at him, he would have become the villain in the eyes of Whiteness. If he tried to lead the entire nation through assertive but positive antiracist statements of American unity and pride, he would have had no followers and would have been attacked for speaking for everyone, a position that only a hero could occupy. One premise of the debilitating effects of racial stress is that the sacrificial role of antivillain remains an essential part of an unhealthy dance as people of color today try to prove they are not the stereotypes projected upon them. Sadly, many administrators, teachers, and students of color in PWS are the Jackie Robinsons of their time for those schools. They are the "Firsts" and the pressures on their academic, physical, and emotional health in being the antivillain is painful to watch. I can't tell you how many persons of color working and learning in PWS have told me how their physical health has been compromised by being the "First," the few, the only, or the lonely.

One way racial stress can manifest itself is when individuals are working so hard to be nice, remain racially neutral, avoid the role of villain, and play the role of antivillain simultaneously. Although "Firsts" relish or bask in the sunshine of pioneerism, they pay for it in the wasting of essential energy, emotion, and intellect on disproving the racial stereotype. Consequentially, the choosing of one's identity becomes difficult. One cost of being the "First" or the only is isolation. When students fear speaking up in class because their ideas may be considered inferior, playing the role of antivillain becomes a salient choice. When teachers withhold their viewpoints out of fear of being called "racist" or "playing the race card" by raising issues of race, playing the role of antivillain is a perfectly logical decision to make. A common challenge is when students and teachers of color doubt whether the majority culture in their school understands, appreciates, and know how to actively engage their racial experience. It influences how much they speak up or raise issues of racial difference or conflict, how they debate these issues with colleagues, and how they advocate for these issues on behalf of others struggling with racial stress.

THE HISTORY OF DANCING AROUND RACIAL STEREOTYPES IN SCHOOLING

Remember the Little Rock Nine? Remember the Black children in Alabama who tried to attend an all-White school for the sake of racial progress? Remember George Wallace, who made his famous "Stand in the Schoolhouse Door"? The threat levels for these actors must have been sky-high. I wonder what the Black students perceived of the behaviors of the National Guard troops, the Alabama and Arkansas governors, and their White classmates. How much anticipatory fear would they have had about their teachers prior to that eventful day? How stressful was their first day of school, first class, or first graded assignment? What of the first to be the best at academics or sports or to fail at either? In Melba Patillo Beals's (2011) autobiographical account of her experience as one of the Little Rock Nine in 1957, she recounts that first day walking into Central High School:

> Hundreds of Central High students milled about. I could see their astonishment. Some were peering out of windows high above us, some were watching from the yard, others were on the landing. Some were tearful, others angry.
>   I felt proud and sad at the same time. Proud that I lived in a country that would go this far to bring justice to a Little Rock girl like me, but sad that they had to go to such great lengths. Yes, this is the United States, I thought to myself. There is a reason, that I salute the flag. If these guys just go with us this first time, everything's going to be okay. (p. 132)

Over the next few pages of her account, Beals describes vividly the looks of the angry and tearful White students, the racial epithets from the students and the teachers toward the Little Rock Nine, and the stoic attitudes of the National Guardsmen who shuffled the Little Rock Nine to and from designated classrooms. What was most astonishing to me is Beals's focus on description and how little she details her emotional response to the events. It was almost as if she had no time or facility to feel during this monumental "First." There was a moment when she considered addressing an impropriety in one of her early classes of the day when a White boy was racially taunting her throughout the English lesson:

> I tried hard to ignore the boy, who had now begun a scathing dialogue with one of his companions. He carried on in a low tone, just above a whisper, which everyone could hear, but the teacher could legitimately ignore. "You ugly niggers think just because you got those army boys following you around you gonna stay here." I swallowed a sadness lump in the back of my throat. I wondered whether or not I should press the teacher to stop him from treating me that way. I decided against it because I thought she must be well aware of what he was doing. (p. 135)

Ms. Beals's experience of a "sadness lump in the back of my throat" is both a bodily stress reaction and a coping strategy. As the "First," she had no model for dealing with this kind of stress, and suppression of her trauma was the sole course of action. Trauma suppression is a common coping strategy of being the "First" and "the only." But it was a coping strategy nonetheless and is tied directly to the title of the book, *Warriors Don't Cry.* Not until she landed on the "peaceful island" of Mrs. Pickwick, the shorthand class teacher who had a no-nonsense approach to her classroom management, did she find relief. She didn't allow for any disruptive chatter or behavior of any kind, including racial epithets. Beals describes her stress relief, particularly her body reactions and coping strategies:

> I had been there about thirty minutes when I realized I was feeling kind of normal, enjoying the classwork and learning the shorthand characters. My stomach muscles let go a little, and I drew a long, deep breath. I didn't know Mrs. Pickwick, but I liked her and felt safe in her presence. I knew I would always be grateful to her for the moments of peace her class provided. (p. 136)

I think both now and in the 1950s, an individual can clearly see how one "First" could lead to the next and the next. Without all those difficult and painful "Firsts" in schooling, it is hard to imagine how race relations in America could have developed. But downplaying the intense backlash and political retreat from racial progress and rights for people of color would not be prudent. What if the backlash from those "Firsts" grew instead of disappeared and their effects and intensity remained just as powerful today as they did in 1957? Although it makes sense that the need for "Racial Firsts" would dissipate over time, it is eerily painful that while they continue for many African Americans and people of color, they may have less influence on social progress than we expect. One need only revisit the hateful and racist actions of Orval Faubus, the mayor of Little Rock who closed down all Little Rock schools for the 1958–1959 year. His actions reflected a "scorched earth" strategy ("The Lost Year") that blocked schooling for everyone, including White students, just to prove a point that these "Firsts" won't last. Some would argue that he was wrong and the "Firsts" did last. But when we examine the prevalence of and resistance to desegregation and the double resegregation of race and class in schools across the nation today, can we truly say that?

Contemporary Racial Dancing:
Postracialists and the Pitfalls of Racial "Firsts"

Although many social theories of varying racial backgrounds tout the postracial rhetoric, they rely heavily on the importance of symbolic images to argue that social change movements are no longer necessary. Given these historical changes in racial progress, proclamations of racism are viewed by some liberals and conservatives as outdated and archaic (Rodgers, 2010). The postracialists argue that racism was present when there was blatant violence and deprivation of access and mobility to, through, and beyond the American dream. To many, these conditions no longer exist and a Black president confirms that. These theorists call for a newer model for race relationship-building that excludes rehashing of historical tragedy, shuns accusations of racism, and shudders at the critique of the status quo as a racialized status quo.

What the postracialists forget is that although the politics of race has changed since the 1960s, the socialization of racial hierarchies remains and thrives. As a result, the racial oppression and civil rights prophets from the mid-20th century look foolish when they speak of a visible, violent, and hate-mongering racism. No palpable evidence of this "monster" exists—no dogs barking at the knees of innocent Black youth. So while the visceral violence of racial hatred disappeared from eyesight and television, the politics of racism went underground. For example, it became more legal within the last 20 years to incarcerate Black men and poor men and women with laws that were harsher for those who were poorer and Blacker, a point brilliantly argued by Michele Alexander (2010) in her book *The New Jim Crow*.

What the postracialists misunderstand is that symbols of racial progress no longer mean what they used to mean. Americans unfortunately remain as hopeful today as we were in 1943 about what the first Black president means for Black and American social progress. This hope persists despite witnessing poverty and poor-quality education to Black and Brown children increase over the past 7 decades (Wilson, 1996). "Firsts" no longer carry the same weight of social progression because the burden of progression is greater and requires a different psychology. The psychology of "Firsts" is the wrong educational reform strategy to change the racial illiteracy of American schooling and politics or the way Americans approach race relations. So the strategies of dismantling systemic racism are not in need of a major overhaul; it's our unexamined belief in the power of racial symbols that must shift. Sure, perhaps our language and knowledge need adjustment to meet current demographic changes across ethnic minority groups or racial disparities in the health, justice, and education systems. But what should really get our anger up and garner our full attention is that the school segregation and life outcomes for poor and Black children remain eerily similar to and worse than the conditions of the mid-20th century (Orfield, 2009; Orfield et al., 2012). Where's the "angry Black man" or "angry Black woman" when you need them now?

If the racial "First" is more about the interaction or dance between the players than the role any individual plays, what purpose does being the first serve? What if being the racial "First" means playing a role that maintains the dance of racial hierarchy? What if the "First" is an exception to and not a rejection of the rule of racial inferiority? What if this same dance can be observed through the dynamics of racial threat, stress appraisal, stress management, and coping that occurs in PWS when Black and Latino students are present? For example, White flight from neighborhoods and Black middle-class flight from predominantly Black and Latino urban schools reflects a fear of racial progress, social mobility, and achievement decline. I don't believe American schooling has counted the emotional costs to be the "First" or one of a few students or faculty of color in these settings. How costly is playing the role of antivillain or of being the racial "First" in the daily life of PWS? Would the "First" and the few cope differently if they knew that one cost of attempting to disprove racial stereotypes is that it preserves racial inequality?

Unfortunately, being the "First" may mean being the "Last" if it threatened the racial status quo. Racial hostility makes more sense if it is understood as a threat to undermine established racial hierarchy. Predicting backlash, would you change how you exercised your power as leader, educator, or parent? Would you change how you prepared for the emotional cost of being first?

In the Obama presidential campaign, there were multiple reports of the campaign experiencing death threats and violence toward the workers and offices (Wingfield & Feagin, 2009). But the campaign's insistence on playing down these displays of fear revealed a particular strategy toward racial interactions, racial rhetoric, and racial symbolism. It revealed a brilliant "temporary colorblindness" ideology crafted mostly for winning the election. But if it wasn't temporary, what purpose to racial equality does it serve not to make these threat reactions public and speak against them? Not remarking on these threats would be an acknowledgment that Americans are not ready for anything postracial. Not postracial schooling, not postracial journalism, postracial politics and certainly not postracial policing. If the Obama administration played down acts of racial violence during the campaign in order to secure a presidency that would one day directly address racial violence in a more powerful position, then that would have been astute.

But if the "racial blindness" is neither a strategy nor temporary, then what benefit for Black and poor people can be gained from the symbolic power of the first Black president? Unfortunately, this postracial blindness strategy has become a movement, a misguided "postracial" movement that not only won't see color, but is amnesic of the history of American racial violence. Martin Luther King Jr. (1963) once stated that "shallow understanding from people of good will is more frustrating than absolute misunderstanding from people of ill will." When Joe Wilson screamed out at a State of the Union address, "You lie," Jimmy Carter remarked that this event was "based on racism." He went further to say "there is an inherent feeling among many in this country that an African-American should not be president. Those kind of things are not just casual outcomes of a sincere debate on whether we should have a national program on health care. It's deeper than that" (Spillius, 2009). Black and poor people need the kind of aggressive advocacy that calls out injustice daily, not a vaguely hopeful revolution that selectively forgets the history of racism in America.

Dance of American Democracy and Racial Equity: In Love with the Idea of Love

Many postracial Americans are too willing to romanticize racial "Firsts" as powerful, but unwilling to identify the threats and backlash that follow even small changes in racial and wealth equity that come from symbolic progress. As Americans, we fall in love with the idea of "Firsts" so much that we fail to consider their relevance to social change. I'm not suggesting contemporary "Firsts" are not influential, just not powerful enough to influence face-to-face racial interactions. We embraced the idea that the first Black president would automatically bring equity to other societal institutions. We hailed victory before the war on racial inequity was completed. We are so in love with the idea of racial equality that we become more blind and apathetic about any evidence of change in the lives of Black, Brown, and White people who occupy the lowest economic places in our society. We forget about the day-to-day struggles of hunger and the difficulty of finding food, of poverty and generations of poverty, of unemployment, racial discrimination, and the difficulties of getting hired. Because Black presence—first or not—frightens us.

As Americans, we are so in love with the idea of democracy that actual democracy pales by comparison and in some cases creates disgust in us. Daily face-to-face race relations don't encourage idealism. Relationships are messy, time-consuming, and unpredictable. We are in love with the idea of loving racial equity so much that actual racial equity is too arduous. We believe our symbol of racial equity will carry us into the sunset of shoulder-to-shoulder blissful hand-holding. This symbol of the 1960s dream will carry us all into the sunset singing, "We shall overcome." Ironically, American education is the most visible stage upon which our romanticization of racial equity, uplift, and transcendence and our historical amnesia of racial backlash are most witnessed as contradictory and hypocritical. For me, it's this dream that must change, not the strategy to dismantle racial equity through protest and preparation. We need new dreams of how to remain contentious when our voice is silenced. Education needs a resocialization and redefinition of the meaning of racial conflict that can be debated in classrooms, a definition of racial conflict that is resolvable between teachers and parents or schools and impoverished neighborhoods. We need no more sunsets without rain or crops without plowing up the ground.

Still, despite all this proclamation of change, there is a psychological cost to forgetting our racial history. Americans don't want to hear about the schoolhouse-to-jailhouse pipeline or that "protect and serve" does not mean the same thing in many Black and Brown neighborhoods as it does in many White neighborhoods (Sentencing Project, 2012). We don't want to hear about the limitations of civil rights symbolic progress. Steady and slow advancement may be true for many Black Americans but not for all. Some were able to climb the mountain to the top but that doesn't mean those at the bottom weren't smart or able enough to learn how to read, or do science, or excel at math. We still maintained stereotypes of racial inferiority even as we became too weary of instituting racial desegregation as a solution to Black achievement problems. In some cases, Black and Latino students receive a better education in integrated schools, but it's not the sitting next to White students that makes the difference. It's the added resources that come from these environments. Integration has not remedied the resource gap that Black and Latino students continually face in schools, and suspension and expulsion rates have skyrocketed since the 1970s, an arguably tragic statement of resistance to integration (Lewin, 2012). Nor has integration diminished the belief in and internalization of racial inferiority or the trauma that accompanies it. It has become politically correct, albeit economically costly, to forget those who can't race to the top of the educational ladder. We minimize the power of African history to persons of African descent at our collective peril.

So this false adoration of democracy is what critical race theorists point to as the fulcrum that undermines racial equality and partially explains why practical social activism in the lives of poor Black, Brown, and White people rarely gets actualized. It is self-interest and the threat of loss of that self-interest that explains why powerful White institutions in American society use racial rhetoric to prevent the shift in the dance of racial equity. It's a psychological war. Several icons of American history have resisted wearing a racial straitjacket while dancing with racial stereotypes. I would like to highlight the unearthed lessons of healing implicit within the stories and writings of four heroes of racial civil progress. They are Kenneth Clark, Sarah Collins Rudolph, Mamie Till, and W.E.B. DuBois, and their stories exemplify the need for and emotional benefits of racial literacy and the direct confrontation of racial stereotypes.

Racial Stress of Battling Stereotypes Within Science: The Case of Kenneth Clark

Kenneth Clark was a "First." In the 1950s, 1960s, and 1970s, no Black psychologist had reached the level of notoriety and acclaim for scientific research on Black children than Kenneth Clark. Kenneth Clark is arguably one of the most prominent psychologists of the 20th century based on his research in the 1940s with his wife, Mamie Clark, that influenced the *Brown v. Board of Education* decision in 1954. This research was the first psychological research of any kind to be used and found integral in the decision of a Supreme Court case. Arguably, the research findings of the Clarks were based on a stereotype internalization thesis; that is, Black children were vulnerable to believing their emotional, psychological, and intellectual potential was inferior simply because they were not allowed to learn with White children. The psychological argument that inferior schooling and potential was race-related was stunning, particularly since the premise this research proposed was that it was the learning with Black children that harmed one's academic future.

Kenneth Clark went on to become the first Black president of the American Psychological Association. His research and work became well known internationally and he and Mamie Clarke pursued civil rights and social change on behalf of Black students through their research. Yet Kenneth Clark's life experience reveals more comprehensively how coping with expendable Black humanity politics is stressful, tragic, and complicated. Despite his best intellectual and advocacy efforts, Dr. Clark did not feel that his knowledge and research made a dent in the larger politics of racial antagonism, hierarchy, and discrimination. By 1965, Clark was disgusted with America's failure to embrace the humanity of Black children and stated so:

I am tired of civil rights. Maybe I should develop some ideas concerning the enormous waste of human intelligence sacrificed to the struggle for racial justice in America at this period of the 20th century. How long can our nation continue the tremendous wastage of human intellectual resources demanded by racism? (p. 1)

His view that America had sold its democratic soul for the sake of maintaining racial denigration of Black children and education was strong and did not dissipate years later (Benjamin, 2006):

Thirty years after *Brown*, I must accept the fact that my wife left this earth despondent at seeing that damage to children is being knowingly and silently accepted by a nation that claims to be democratic. Thirty years after *Brown*, I feel a sense of hopelessness, rather than optimism, because the underlying theme of *Plessy* and the explicit statements of *Dred Scott* persist. The majority of Americans still believe in and vote on the assumption that Blacks are not worthy of the respect, and the acceptance of their humanity, which our democracy provides to others. (p. 229)

Dr. Clark's comments are reminders of the traumatic effects of racism and racial politics on the well-being of individuals, even psychological researchers who have devoted their lives to eradicating racial injustice. These comments reflect a deep distrust of the ways democratic systems and institutions fail to embrace a racial egalitarianism that could lead to a reversal in power shifts in majority-minority group relations. Kenneth Clark understood what it meant to believe in American egalitarianism rhetoric only to be disappointed by the painful reality that racial supremacy outweighs research evidence, the universality of human potential, and basic common sense. Educational institutions cannot afford to remain blind to racial or ethnic identity politics that encourages the homogenization of racial/ethnic differences for the purpose of minimizing the anxiety of those who consciously or unconsciously endorse Whiteness.

Critical race theory reminds us of the dangers of accepting the habitus of racial hegemony in which we reject any subgroup as acceptable members of society unless they agree to reject any images or actions of angry revolution. But what else explains the persistence of a narrative of Black human expendability and the stress that Black people suffer because of it?

Sacrificing Racial Healing for Racial Survival: Bombing Trauma of the Fifth Little Girl

Not everyone can understand the costs of avoiding racially stressful moments. It has taken an emotional toll across generations of Black protest, progress, and regression (DeGruy-Leary, 2005; Shelton, Richeson, Salvatore, & Hill, 2006; Shelton & Stewart, 2004). But a closer look at history allows us to reframe past racial tragedy and discover new insights. These insights become useful lessons to combat contemporary racism.

The tragedy of the four little girls killed in the Birmingham bombing by White supremacists in 1963 hid more trauma than it illuminated racism. There was another girl (also known as the fifth little girl) in the church when it was bombed, but she survived. Sarah Collins Rudolph, sister to Addie Mae Collins (who was one of the four girls killed, along with Carole Robertson, Cynthia Wesley, and Denise McNair), is a survivor. Her story is powerfully traumatic and inspirational, mostly by its invisibility (Ott, 2013). Sarah Collins Rudolph lost her left eye in the bombing and the prosthetic eye that was given to her was so flimsy and ill-fitting that she was constantly terrified it might fall out. As a child, she endured unspeakable humiliation about her looks as she was constantly ridiculed. She experienced nightmares and other posttraumatic stress symptoms such as jumping whenever she heard loud noises.

What I found most troublesome about her story was not just that her trauma led to a life of pain, alcoholism, and eventual recovery. It was not the horror of living daily with pieces of glass permanently embedded in her eyes, chest, and abdomen too life-threatening to remove. It was not the scars on her face and body that reminded her daily of the bombing. The most painful aspect of her story for me was how the church responded to the bombing. According to Ms. Rudolph, the church never spoke about it.

Even after the church had been rebuilt, the fear of more bombing and terrorism from the KKK left the people of the church silent, as if talking about it would bring more horror. It is amazing to me that so often, the trauma of an oppressed people is so great that our own cultural, spiritual, and community resources are not seen as powerful or relevant enough to address that trauma directly. Where else but the center of spiritual and civil rights renewal would it be best to share trauma and receive healing? Was this "dirty laundry" of the bombing so tragic that they couldn't provide feedback to the "fifth little girl" about her nightmares, humiliation, and self-doubt? This has led me to posit that Black communities and people who don't directly battle oppression emotionally or psychologically are most likely to manage stress in ways that exacerbate our trauma. Unfortunately, oppressed people are often too willing, adept, and quick to sacrifice our emotional healing for the sake of our physical survival. I think this same dynamic or dance takes place in education.

Healing from trauma requires sharing the trauma. Storytelling. Protest cannot heal emotional trauma. Silence about tragedy worsens the effects of trauma on physical and emotional well-being. Sometimes we are too eager to focus on making sure students are force-fed knowledge for the sake of proving "equity" or "out of fear of not making annual yearly progress" or "to pass the tests," that educators sacrifice learning. Educators forget in their policymaking that emotional well-being, feeling safe about your existence and ideas, not experiencing daily rejection in school, and receiving support for your difference are essential ingredients before deep learning can occur. Educational policies and practices from the No Child Left Behind legislation have led to destructive "survival" strategies such that cheating on tests by school system leaders made sense. Cheating has become a reasonable coping strategy to deal with the trauma of not making annual yearly progress standards. What's up with that? It's the practice of sacrificing learning for the sake of survival.

Our search for the "good school" is no less a survival issue. Even wealthy Black and Brown parents look to PWS as the best schools because PWS have more resources and more opportunities. But are they capable of addressing the emotional, psychological, and intellectual challenges of racial stress for students of color? I don't think so.

After understanding Kenneth Clark's dilemmas and demons and re-examining Sarah Collins Rudolph's ongoing trauma from the 16th Street bombing, I would like to make the case that in these stories there exist gems of lessons on racial healing, not simply survival. From Kenneth Clark's life, we learn the lesson that research evidence is not enough to turn the tide of racism, but it does give some tools for people to consider changing their racial positions. From the story of Sarah Collins Rudolph, we learn that addressing our emotional responses to racial discrimination, stereotyping, and violence may be more important than legal remedies. These lessons of healing allow us to consider the question, "How can Americans reexamine history and mine lessons that contribute to a psychological wholeness or healthy approach to racial stereotyping?"

Recasting the Stereotypes and Scripts of Racial Dancing: Mamie Till's Ultimate Comeback Line

The Emmett Till story is a classic challenge to the script of American race relations and to the ritualized racial dance in which White men are the heroes, Black and Brown men and women are the criminals, and White women are the innocent victims. One element of disturbance about this tragic American story is that it undermines the expected narrative of how powerful people are good people and "weak" people are bad. We are confused about who the bad guys are in Emmett Till's murder, and the heroes are the most unlikely of characters. We have many Emmett Till stories going on across America, and not simply with Black boys as the targets of the dance of racial blindness and violence. Despite the many powerful examples of sacrifice in the civil rights movement, no single act of change could be as powerful in the 20th century as Mamie Till's decision to keep her tortured son's casket open at the funeral.

Mamie Till, an African American woman from Chicago, sent her son, Emmett, to live with family in Money, Mississippi. While there, he and his cousins walked into a small country grocery store to buy candy. As Emmett Till and his cousins were leaving the store, he whistled at a White woman, Carolyn Bryant, the wife of the owner of the store, Roy Bryant. She went to get a gun. The boys ran but 3 days later, Roy Bryant and J. W. Milam (Bryant's half-brother) kidnapped Emmett Till from his uncle's home. They took him to a barn where, with the assistance of other men, they tortured and shot Emmett, and afterward used barbed wire to wrap a 75-pound fan from a cotton gin around his murdered body before dropping him in the Tallahassee River in the hope that evidence of their crime would never be found.

Within 3 days of his kidnapping on August 31, 1955, Emmett's body surfaced and was found by a boy fishing. Despite the local authorities' attempts to cremate Emmett's body to hide the murder, Mamie fought to prevent this and won. She acted quickly and decisively. When it was time for the funeral of her 14-year-old son, she did something even more remarkable. She left the casket of her son's body open so the world could see what Roy Bryant, J. W. Milam, and southern racism had done to him. This psychological judo move changed the dance of racism in 1950s where, as long as the world could see no evil, the evil of racism in the South did not exist. The dance between southern hospitality and Whiteness and the power to hide the evil of racism was disrupted, thanks to the heroism of Mamie Till. Instead, southern hospitality and Whiteness became partners, synonymous with racial terrorism against Black children. Moreover, the typical dance move response of Black people to White racism did not have to be to simply grin and bear it. Because of Mamie Till, and at the expense of her own son, America learned to fight back.

"How Does It Feel to Be a Problem?"
DuBois Recasts and Stares Down the Face of Racial Stereotyping

Acknowledging that individuals can respond to racial stereotyping in assertive rather than passive ways begs the need for an underlying psychological strategy to do so. Besides Woodson, Douglass, and countless others, no one else in history has written as eloquently about psychological strategies to recast the script of racial hierarchy and take on different roles in this dance around racial stereotyping as W.E.B. DuBois. As one of the most ardent architects of an efficient psychological defense against racial inferiority and stereotypes, W.E.B. DuBois suggests we look directly at the stereotype in order to render it meaningless.

Questioning the inferiority stereotype of one's humanity is the beginning of racial literacy. In order to address the implicit bias of science and public opinion about Black people, W.E.B. DuBois (1903) asked a rhetorical question—"How does it feel to be a problem?"—that remains today as a powerful clue toward an antidote against racial subordination and a doorway for healing racial stress.

The psychological process of repeatedly asking the wrong racial questions have been artfully discussed by W.E.B. DuBois. In his essay "Of Our Spiritual Strivings," DuBois raises a rhetorical question of enormous magnitude. It illuminates an essential dilemma in the development of racial literacy for individuals across the developmental life-span spectrum. He poses the tragedy of how, regardless of a Black person's station or success in life, his or her life experience remains couched within the question of "How does it feel to be a problem?"

> Between me and the other world there is ever an unasked question; unasked by some through feelings of delicacy; by others through the difficulty of rightly framing it. All, nevertheless, flutter round it. They approach me in a half-hesitant way, eye me curiously or compassionately, and then, instead of saying directly, How does it feel to be a problem? They say, I know an excellent colored man in my town; or, I fought at Mechanicsville; or, Do not these Southern outrages make your blood boil? At these I smile, or am interested, or reduce the boiling to a simmer, as the occasion may require. To the real question, How does it feel to be a problem? I answer seldom a word. (DuBois, 1903, p. 1)

What I find remarkable about DuBois's comment is his stress management approach to these racial queries or interactions. He is obviously stressed ("reduce the boiling to a simmer"), but not simply from the comments. Although their queries reveal their own anxiety of approaching a "colored man" (in "half-hesitant," "flutter" fashion), they too are trying to manage their racial discomfort. What these random men and women say is intended to prove to the "colored man" that they are not racist or unfriendly, like so many "other" bigoted White people in the world.

No, there is another level of microaggressions that strains DuBois. It's the implied question, "How does it feel to be a problem?" This metalevel racial microaggression is a fundamental statement and rejection of the humanity of the "colored man" or even DuBois in this situation. It means that whether Black individuals are perceived as unsuccessful or successful, they are still thought of as inferior. If you are successful, the question is still about "How does it feel to be a success among a people of inferior ability and potential?" Dubois seems to be sarcastic in his recounting of the comments, but he also provides a variety of metalevel coping strategies ("smile," "am interested," "reduce").

This question can just as easily be found in compliments as in insults, particularly in public discourse. For example, Black folks hear often from colleagues and friends who say, "When I think of you I don't see color," or "You don't seem Black to me." These are comments that reflect one end of the continuum of perceived Black inferiority. Allow me to translate. "How does it feel to be someone who means something to me as long as you are not Black or behave in ways that would lead me to think of you as Black?"

What disturbed DuBois the most was not the spastic, threat reactions of the "other" but the acquiescence to the "atmospheric racial inferiority" that pollutes the ignorance or innocence of these interactions. It was the unquestioned breathing in of a racial hierarchy upon which Blackness is at the bottom. Consequently, all the coping strategies in the world are insufficient to address this carbon monoxide of Black racial inferiority, what Claude Steele and Joshua Aronson (1995) refer to as "threat in the air." But DuBois's most profound coping strategy to address the metaracial microaggression was quite simple—choice. DuBois (1903) stated that "at these I smile, or am interested, or reduce the boiling to a simmer, as the occasion may require." To the real question of atmospheric inferiority, "I answer seldom a word." Having a choice is part of healing from the trauma of being perceived as a "problem." We can choose to reject racial inferiority in any form from anyone, including ourselves.

Staring down or directly challenging racial stereotypes starts with a psychological rejection of one's inferiority but it will also take action that individuals muster against actual discrimination. Consider Mamie Till, one of the mothers of the civil rights movement, and how she decided to act when confronted with not only the terroristic killing of her only son because he was Black, but the justice system's cover-up of his murder. This act represented a public "racial comeback line" in opposition to systemic racial discrimination and it was witnessed from around the world.

What if a different beginning, middle, and ending could be written for race relations by examining and rewriting the expected roles in daily racial interactions? What if, as the most absurd foil to this often-used script, each character decided to become a role different from one dictated by his or her stereotype? In this rewrite, what if each character realized how much his or her acquiescence to the role has been a choice—a choice that is the key to unlocking role imprisonment—or, as we say in the "biz," typecasting, product satiation, overindulgent dysfunctional codependency, or another new school reform idea? Imagine how ironic it is that proposing another same ole new school reform idea would be maintaining the status quo of class and racial inequality in public schooling. What if parents in schools demanded racial stress and literacy training for their children and teachers instead of just getting them enrolled into a good school? What if we are asking the wrong questions?

After identifying why racial conversations are important but so paralyzing and witnessing so many educators respond in panic and avoidance of these conversations, how do we overcome this challenge? In the cartoons of the elephant and the scientists in Chapter 1, we learned that perspective matters and that blindness can be both a skill and a bad habit. Two reasons clarify why each investigator insists that his or her "discovery" solves the mystery of the elephant and why people remain comfortable in their blindness to reject alternative explanatory theories.

One reason for scientist gridlock with respect to racial elephants is the lack of a holistic theory or perspective. The other reason is the repeated asking of the wrong questions about group comparisons regarding race status and hierarchy instead of the racialized experiences of people who are different and how stressful those racialized experiences are. This is especially true in the achievement gap discussion.

The achievement gap is the great mystery that every educational researcher is trying to solve in schooling. But the gap is only one symptom of a larger problem that threatens Black students. John Fantuzzo and colleagues found that the academic gap literature does not adequately account for the greater academic risks that Black students or students from low-income neighborhoods experience in schooling compared with White students (Fantuzzo, LeBoeuf, & Rouse, 2012). Additionally, researchers fail to measure the racialized life risk experiences of Black students, and yet they continue to speak on the academic gap through a racially avoidant lens. Why not investigate how Black students succeed despite their having to match White students' academic output with fewer social resources, more school-based discrimination and bias, and fewer intimate teacher-student relationships? Does not the focus of these questions or the absence of other questions reveal the investigators' biases?

This failure to consider multiple and alternate explanations for our findings is clearly a vantage point problem, but also a racial one. The angle at which we capture an image is key to the interpretation of that image, and so is the case for how we problem-solve the social and schooling challenges of Black students. If we take as premise or fail to question the premise that Black life, relating, and being are lesser or inferior examples of humanity, then most of our questions will be tainted with this inferiority lens. So too could the research outcomes represent flawed and fear-driven thinking that assumes the lesser potential of Black people.

DANCE ROUTINES FOR HEALING, NOT SURVIVAL: COUNTERING STEREOTYPES BY RECASTING THEIR STRESSFULNESS

A healthy coping response to the straitjacket experience of being racially stereotyped and the behavioral and psychological confrontation of that stereotyping is what I call *recasting*. Recasting is an assertive presence of mind or coping by individuals or groups to psychologically reframe the stereotypical expectations and rejections from self, others, and society for the purpose of modifying roles, reactions, and behaviors to become less dehumanizing and more emotionally, spiritually, culturally, and socially healthy. Recasting is the socialization, creation, and communication of healthy and competent racial comeback emotions, thoughts, and behaviors that buffer and counter the stress from threats that others undergo of Black presence, voice, and existence. In essence, recasting is choosing to change one's role in the racial dance of White supremacy and Black inferiority and reducing the stressfulness that occurs from the change.

The distress from recasting in families can disrupt the homeostasis to which each of us has been accustomed. Questions arise when recasting occurs: "Will I be blamed for the imbalance of power and peace within our system if I stop playing my role?" "Will I lose my family or will they reject me?" "Who must I become if I no longer play my role?" We all become increasingly aware of the stress we've endured for playing family roles or dancing to music that we didn't choose—once we stop playing. We often feel dehumanized at having been given these roles. We may feel ashamed that while these roles bring clarity and peace, they may also bring more alienation than meaning.

Racial roles are no less dehumanizing or powerful. Despite their straitjacketed nature, our racialized roles are not invisible. They stand out in a crowd, like the feathers of a peacock, like a herd of elephants in the savannah. They are the only ones of their kind in a sea of ordinary, like the only Black student in a classroom of Whites. By their unique difference against the landscape, both superhuman and vulnerable, they stand out as the "First" or the "few" who appear to some, simply by their uniqueness, to be threatening; simply by their presence, to be plotting; simply by their voice, to be screaming.

Recasting causes stress by not only disturbing the status quo of race relations, but by raising the nagging realization that a role is not fixed. Recasting encourages the assertion, "I can choose my role!" There is stress from being the only Black student, of meeting same-race and cross-race expectations of Black people, or of dancing to different music. To be different is to be both courageous and to risk ridicule and hostility. If we can reduce the stress that comes from taking on a different role, we can choose a different role. Recasting can happen by plan or serendipitously, but its primary purpose is in identifying and altering the stress and dehumanization of stereotyped roles and behaviors, affording an opportunity to resist and reject that dehumanization and reshape one's behaviors, thoughts, and emotions to more assertively choose different roles, one's participation in the dance, and ultimately one's psychological freedom. Racial straitjacketing is a psychological reality. Woodson's (1990) brilliant rhetorical framing of this straitjacketed psychological allegiance to "Whiteness," its influence on Black behavior and role, and the use of education to train Black people for this straitjacketed role is a poignant cry for Black self-determination:

> When you control a man's thinking you do not have to worry about his actions. You do not have to tell him not to stand here or go yonder. He will find his "proper place" and will stay in it. You do not need to send him to the back door. He will go without being told. In fact, if there is no back door, he will cut one for his special benefit. His education makes it necessary. (p. 5)

Recasting involves a change of heart and voice within one's role and "choosing not" as much as "choosing to." Recasting is an emotional boldness, a psychological struggle with a series of painful decisions to reconstruct life's relationships through careful note-taking. Given that race relations is a game of chess, not checkers, in its political complexity, note-taking on the emotional and behavioral reactions of self and others (when one recasts) is essential for understanding how to reduce the stress of being different. Recasting involves examining yet refusing to play a stereotyped racial role that is psychologically unhealthy, dangerous, or incomplete. It is assertively refusing to accept one's stereotypical station in life. Recasting involves being courageous enough to rewrite and tell one's story and not follow a stereotypical script. Recasting means being one of the "First" or the "few" to see and disturb racial dancing.

The writings and musings of W.E.B. DuBois and other scholars who left America to live in Africa and other places around the world reflect a similar disgust with American idealism and its lack of concrete advocacy for change in the fundamental rules, institutions, and practices of White supremacy (Martinot & Sexton, 2003). This disgust comes before, during, after, and despite major social shifts of educational integration and civil rights legislation. Haven't we made the progress that makes racial discrimination a thing of the past? What are Black scholars, leaders, and families left to do if Black humanity, scholarship, and potential continue to be compromised, rejected, and rendered expendable? What are scholars, leaders, and families from any racial origin left to do if there is no inferior Blackness in the world? At the core of this disgust lingers the haunting notion that addressing the racial scripts of expendable Black humanity begins within us. What if I contribute to these scripts by failing to tell my stories of angst about or triumph over racial disparity? What if I contribute to racial disparity by not challenging the internalization of racial stereotyping in the smallest of venues or moments? What if by not speaking up I am playing the caretaker role of the racial elephant in the classroom that encourages racial straitjacketing and stereotyping for my peers, my students, and me?

Recasting School "Firsts" and Rewriting the Script of Expendable Black Humanity

Rather than re-create the wheel, blame the victim, or humiliate the racist, I recommend that racial equality advocates (preracial, postracial, and in hibernation) learn how to rewrite the script of Black expendability and demise. We must start with acknowledging that the script of Black inferiority is present in most facets of social life, and then we must agree to systematically reject its presence and influence.

If Black inferiority assumptions are lurking in our educational systems, curricula, and relationships, then we must assertively teach Black youth and families how to combat this inferiority and reject this form of miseducation (Twine, 2003, 2004). We do this not for the sake of propriety, piety, or political correctness. We most certainly shouldn't advocate for racial literacy in order to prove Black humanity is not inferior or to argue our right to exist. We do this so that it doesn't lead these beautiful minds and hearts toward deep-rooted anger and hostility toward in- and out-groups, or toward racial matters of any sort, whether blatant or triggered by the subtlest of images. Educators must disturb and recast dynamics of racial rejection in predominantly Black and Brown schools as well as PWS. Both contexts suffer from what Loury (2005) describes as

> "vicious circles" of cumulative causation: self-sustaining processes in which the failure of Blacks to make progress justifies for Whites the very prejudicial attitudes, that, when reflected upon in political and social action, ensure that Blacks will not advance. (p. 2)

Examples of these vicious circles of racial disparity can be found in poor health-care access health outcomes, unemployment, blocked access to schools of higher learning, poor schooling, increased and disproportionate incarceration, marginalized professional advancement, and a host of social mobility factors and situations.

To summarize, four key points reinforce the lessons of this chapter on the power of racial images and stereotypes:

1. Symbolic power from racial "Firsts" is less influential in reducing racial disparities in social, health, justice, and educational outcomes today than historically, when racial segregation was legal.
2. Racial stereotyping persists in the public dialogue and politics of race relations despite legal examples of racial progress in society.
3. Racial inferiority may represent a default coping strategy in a mutually reciprocal relationship with racial supremacy and may best be described as a dance of mutual dependence.

4. Many lessons of racial healing, not just racial survival, remain undiscovered in American history and an emotional reconnection to that history (rather than an informational regurgitation of that history) will only contribute to the development of healthy psychological strategies to recast racial stereotyping and reduce its negative effects.

First, the symbolic power of being the first to climb a racial mountain was very relevant in the latter half of the 20th century for social progress, but not as much now. Today, being the first to climb a mountain is woefully unrelated to teaching masses of folks at the bottom of the mountain how to competently climb that mountain. One explanation for the weak trickle-down power of Black symbolic "Firsts" is that societal changes and technological advancements minimize, resist, or make less relevant the power of this vehicle for social progress. New coping strategies are necessary to combat the mutation of racial hostility. Resolving the stress reactions toward irrational racial threat represents a novel way to address this relational gap.

Another reason for the limited power of Black "Firsts" symbolism is the distance. The symbols and people of accomplishment are so much further away from people of color without power. We need proximal influences of human behavior, not abstract distal ones. To be the first Black anything is not as significant for the larger Black community as it was before precisely because no one has figured out how to take this unique individual experience and translate or teach those skills of achievement and expectations to conquer stereotypes that influence the common person, the neighborhood, and the child. But this lack of connection from the top achievers to the bottom climbers can be strengthened if we consider practical, grassroots, direct face-to-face teaching of racial competencies and skills rather than "Since I made it, and I'm Black, you can too." The new political slogan to rebut the next claim of a postracial society should be, "It's the Love and the Economy, Stupid" or "Remember the History, Stupid" or "It's the Relationship, Stupid" or "It's the Skills, Stupid." Or maybe we should just stop calling people stupid.

Second, racial stereotypes persist in the mind of the American public despite our racial progress as a country. Because stereotypes are deeply ingrained in how many Americans make sense of racial politics, no one is immune from labeling. Several Black celebrities, such as Oprah Winfrey, LeBron James, and others, have found that their star status does not protect them from racial typecasting. Tiger Woods may be the most famous of "Firsts" to receive consistent stereotypical references. The racial innuendos and slights had occurred early in Tiger's career, beginning with Fuzzy Zoeller's racially stereotypical remarks (about serving fried chicken and collard greens) in 1997 and did not stop. Another example includes Kelly Tilghman's comments in 2008. As a golf reporter and play-by-play announcer for the Golf Channel, she suggested that the only way for golfers to beat Tiger Woods on the tour was that they might have to "lynch him in a back alley" (www.liveleak.com/view?i=902_1199898219). Her remarks are particularly interesting, given that she admitted to being surprised at her own comments, explaining that she and Woods were friends and that Woods didn't take offense at her remark. This led to a national controversy on racial stereotyping or political correctness in speech. In May 2013, when asked at a European Cup dinner whether he would invite Tiger for dinner, the Spanish golfer Sergio Garcia suggested Tiger "could come over every night, we will serve fried chicken." While Mr. Garcia tried to apologize about his statement he claimed, "In no way was the comment meant in a racist manner" (www.deadspin.com/sergio-garcia-makes-tiger-woods-fried-chicken-joke-a-509214406). I find it amazing how friends or enemies can make racially stereotypical statements that they may think and not mean to say, but then are shocked that they had little control over their own thinking and speaking. The persistence of racial stereotypes checkmates relationships.

The third summary statement is that ultimately, racial stereotypes serve the purpose of reducing threat—in particular, the fear of being inferior. But as these politics are mutually reciprocal, all players (winners and losers) in the White supremacy hunger games are victims of the same disease. Understanding this mutual dependence will be more constructive in eradicating racial illiteracy than calling someone a supremacist. Rather than accuse individuals who use racial stereotypes of being racist, it is smarter to hold them accountable for being incompetent at not screening what they are thinking or, more important, not credibly doing their professional roles. It goes without saying, however, that those who know so little about racial politics or the psychology of stereotyping are the last persons to know whether they've engaged in a racist incident. Stereotyping dumbs down our ability to make sense of complexity, especially racial complexity. But it may be that stereotyping is purposeful because it reduces collective and individual insecurity about not being as superior as expected. Perhaps the use of negative racial stereotypes (dumber, weaker, uglier, more aggressive) maintains the prevalence of positive racial stereotypes (smarter, stronger, prettier, more reasonable). Addressing that problem requires more than name-calling. This mutual reciprocity represents a form of give-and-take where two parties work in discordant unison, like the image of the awkward movement between two persons dancing to music while wearing straitjackets.

Fourth, racial stress, stereotyping, and discrimination require a healthy coping response, and examples of these healthy responses are hidden within Black history, waiting to be unearthed. But this requires reexperiencing the past from an emotional rather than informational position and then looking for these wonderful lessons. This reexcavation of the history of racial violence and triumph is not only possible but necessary before we can address racial disparities in education, health, work, or justice. The healing of that trauma has yet to be accomplished for a nation whose identity is rooted in history (DeGruy-Leary, 2005). Racial conflict avoidance, stereotyping, and emotional distancing represent common coping responses to racial inferiority in American culture and schooling, particularly in PWS. For the "First" and "few" in these schools, the usage of these coping responses can represent survival. To be sure, there are healthier responses to racial encounters. To be self-aware when asked a question about one's inferiority is one coping response and to not respond to wrong questions is another.

A contemporary civil rights protest on behalf of Black children may need to teach them to resolve racial politics directly in relationships, not circumspectly or generally in society through more Martin Luther King Jr. holiday celebrations. Civil disobedience may need to include mentoring them as they develop the emotional and racial coping skills to successfully assert themselves in conversations across the life span from the cradle to the grave and in classrooms from pre-K to graduate school. Children will need explicit preparation to identify and manage the stressful elephants that are identity-driven by racial, class, sexual orientation, and gender politics. They will need repeated practice and historical knowledge to anticipate how they could inadvertently become the elephant in the classroom if they play the role of antivillain. They will need to learn how to challenge postracial rhetoric with a reminder of a tragic preracial history. But who teaches them? Parents and educators will have to prepare themselves emotionally before youth can learn to resist racial rejection wherever it should arise. Still, both parents and children will require healing from the trauma of this racial rejection, healing that is not found in protest or education.

But for a greater understanding of why racial avoidance, stereotyping, and distancing are commonly used and socially reinforced, we have to look at more primal reasons. In the next chapter, I will examine how our primal fear of being stereotyped promotes racial avoidance but also interferes with openness to learning. Racial avoidance coupled with racial incompetence is a formula for racially stressful social interactions—and looks like a dance in real time. I will argue that the dance around stereotypes and racial stressors in schooling and society can be shifted ever so slightly toward emotionally healthy outcomes—but only if as educators, parents, and students, we agree to face our racial fears.

CHAPTER 3

Fearing Racial Discourse

The Socialization of Racial Threat in Schools

No. It was our musty elephant that exhumed up and
dragged in the fume.
No broom can clean this spew up,
that we all threw up.
We need a bigger tomb to bury the sorrow
and the worry that years of fears have brewed up,
pretending that the skin color didn't father me or bother you;
didn't other me or mother you.
We both know that the dark will make you holler
and bring out that other you.
We both know that you're afraid that the darker brother
is gonna smother you 'til you're blue.
No need to sweat it, I get it.
Everybody in the lighter hue *and* the darker hue has
got the same fear of the darker smother brother too.

—Howard C. Stevenson, *Elephant Attention* (2012)

Racism is more than just a word, a card game, or a dream. Racial discrimination steals years of living from individuals. It leads to health outcomes that change the futures of families and leave youth in self-doubt about how the world supports their humanity. In this chapter, I seek to connect the fear of racial conflict to the distrust of relationships with school authority figures. It is my contention that reduction in the quality of these key adult–Black youth and peer–Black youth relationships undermines learning in schools. Thus, unresolved racial fear is harmful to the quality of teaching relationships, which in turn influences the achievement outcomes of Black youth.

To many students, teachers, and parents, anticipating a racial conversation feels like facing a bully—emotionally stressful, threatening to reputation, and unpredictably dangerous to life and limb. It is a common theme of school and playground politics that the only way to defeat a bully is stand up to that bully. But often our fear of the bully is scarier because of reputation and rumor than face-to-face contact. Most of us ignore the bully, hoping that he or she won't exist or see us to harm us. Still, the bully remains dangerous by his or her potential for conflict. So it is with race, which has often been described as a social construction that has no real basis in factual reality (Frankenberg, 1993; Lopez, 2000). Ignoring racial interactions or politics is meant to minimize conflict and avoid face-to-face conflict. Nevertheless, the danger of avoiding racial politics in schools is in the consequences of psychological harm to those students and teachers who cannot avoid being seen as the bully because of the tension their difference raises.

So having a conversation about race is not easy. Racial tension that comes from debating racial matters, using the right language to describe racial matters, and resolving racial conflicts without ridicule overwhelms the relationships of most Americans.

In this chapter, I argue that individuals' avoidance of racial conflicts in thoughts and behaviors prior to and during conversation, social interaction, or other face-to-face encounters can be so intense that it undermines the quality and depth of those relationships. This intensity of racial stress is increased the more avoidance coping is used, particularly in schools where social courtesies and cultures of niceness rarely address racial conflicts as resolvable (Arrington et al., 2003). Planning how to cope with the fear of racial politics from others is necessary and healthy when one is surviving within stressful contexts. Facing and combating the stress of racial encounters represents what I call racial assertiveness. Without it, students and educators will be emotionally vulnerable to racial illiteracy and stereotyping.

FEAR OF WHITE GAZE: IF RACE IS A SOCIAL CONSTRUCTION, WHY IS IT SO SCARY?

The ephemeral social construction of race has led some anthropologists and authors to claim racial politics to be unreal, irrelevant, nonexistent (Hilton & MacDonald, 2008; Howard, 2010; Omi & Winant, 1994), except for the common agreement between societal members that race matters. Conversely, American science continues to debate the social construction of racial superiority and inferiority (Searle, 1995). The centuries-old debate of who is smarter, faster, tougher, sexier, stronger, more feminine, more masculine, more attractive, wealthier, and poorer rages on. Old stereotypes still influence how people cope. What's scary about that, you ask? Nothing, unless the socially constructed racial stereotype attributed to you contributes to how negatively people treat you.

Current research knowledge about racial interactions makes clear that anticipating that one will be called "racist" is so humiliating that it increases involuntary verbal and bodily reactions (Eberhardt, 2005). Racial tension that comes from the fear of public racial ridicule has increased dramatically. Individuals will avoid or defend their racial innocence with such ferocity that actual face-to-face contact with the racial matter/insult is not necessary to cause such anxiety (Gudykunst, 1995; Gudykunst & Shapiro, 1996). The notion that race is socially constructed often ignores the very real social ecology of racial stress that surrounds Black youth striving in schools and society (Johnson, Slaughter-Defoe, & Bannerjee, 2012).

Fear drives the debates on whether America has become a postracial society, whether the achievement gap is resolvable, whether charter schools and entrepreneurial schooling are effective, and whether sending Black youth to "good" predominantly White schools will eradicate racism. Because many perceive racial tension as overwhelming in a racially divided public discourse (Cafferty, 2012), reducing the tension can resolve the thorny racial conflicts inherent in postracial, achievement gap, and "good schooling" politics.

There is a similar fear of racial politics in the privatizing of public schooling and public access to private schooling (Orfield & Frankenberg, 2013; Slaughter-Defoe et al., 2011). Although we have almost agreed on the weak academic and career preparation performance of many urban public schools for poor students, some educational reformers are blindly and blissfully promoting charter schooling and turning over public systems to entrepreneurs as the solutions. Independent or private schooling has the opposite challenge. Black parents are increasingly looking to private schools to ensure their children receive a good education to reduce the achievement gap, yet these schools often feel helpless in addressing diversity directly and often socialize students to fit into prep school culture (Kuriloff, Soto, & Garver, 2012). Still, no serious racial conversation or racial literacy teaching is occurring that addresses the fears of educators, families, and students to prepare students to negotiate and resolve personal, familial, or societal conflicts related to racial disparities. In discussing how racial fear influences Black students' well-being in predominantly White primary and secondary schools, I share two examples from my experience as an Ivy-League professor of Black students overthinking racial stereotypes and falling prey to the danger of appearing smart.

Overthinking Racial Stereotypes

I served as the faculty master of the W.E.B. DuBois College House at the University of Pennsylvania for 8 years, planning the academic agenda of a living learning center of activity around the theme of "What does it take to create a village?" I had the honor as a live-in faculty member to hear the musings, genius, and fearful whispers of creative students, mostly African American, as they struggled to survive the academic and social pressures of an Ivy-League university. One day, I overheard four Black male freshmen whispering about their angst about whether to go to play basketball in the gym. The argument centered on their worry that people at Penn would think they were only at Penn because of their basketball abilities. I couldn't help myself, so I interrupted.

> *HS:* Guys, why would you be worried that someone here is going to think that you are only here because of basketball?
>
> *Students:* Because in just 2 or 3 weeks, people have been asking us are we on the team or not.
>
> *HS:* Yes, but you all are not on the team and once basketball season starts, they won't see you on the court.
>
> *Students:* But it just gets to be a pain, the way people look at you, like you don't belong here and the only way you could get here is if you are on an athletic scholarship.
>
> *HS:* First, Penn doesn't give scholarships. Two, you passed all the tests, jumped all the hurdles to get in. Oh, and three, you are here, just like everybody else. Do you think they will stop believing that you all are basketball players just because you stop playing basketball?
>
> [Students are dumbfounded and all out of comeback lines.]
>
> *HS:* They won't. Even after you graduate, they'll think that. Do you like basketball?
>
> *Students:* Yes!
>
> *HS:* Does it help you feel better about yourself, relieve some stress?
>
> *Students:* Yes!
>
> *HS:* Then you better play because of that so you can get through school and make it to graduation. These classes are hard but you need ways to feel good about yourself. If basketball is the way you take care of your health and have fun and relax, you better use it or lose it. Besides, have any of you got any game to speak of?
>
> [Students laugh. There are plenty of comeback lines, bravado, and trash-talking as they walk out on their way to the gym.]

The conversation continued throughout the year as we discussed the pressures of racial stereotyping on their performance. What is remarkable to me about this exchange is the pressure that many Black students feel regarding their right to exist and their need to defend that existence in educational spaces. It's as if they must justify to themselves and others that they belong in school and deserve to learn from the best educators. The politics of racial literacy in this story is how much the fear of being perceived as inferior preoccupies one's social as well as academic life. These boys needed healthy comeback arguments to challenge their own racial self-disgust, which they projected onto others on campus.

The Pressure to Appear Smart

I stumbled into another conversation, with a Black senior who was cry-ing in the gallery hall as I walked by through the College House. When I asked her if she was all right, she told me that she was worried she wouldn't be able to get access to a class in her major, chemistry, for her final semester, which she needed to graduate. I told her that given that she was a senior, I was pretty sure she would get permission and then she admitted that she wasn't really crying about that. She was mostly sad by the fact that she hated chemistry and her 4 years had been difficult. So I asked her why she chose chemistry and she stated at first it was because of wanting to go to med school but that later she no longer wanted to become a medical doctor. But she stayed in chemistry because whenever people queried her about her major, she would tell them chemistry and she liked the responses she would get. They would say how smart she was and she would be so proud. Despite my suggestion that she change her major (even though it was kind of late in the game), she wanted to remain in chemistry. She got into the required class, graduated, and decided to pursue an entirely different career, happily.

These incidents make concrete for me what is meant by stereotype threat (Steele, 2010; Steele & Aronson, 1995). Racial stereotype threat is the fear of confirming a racial stereotype about one's group. In education, the racial stereotype about African Americans not being smart enough is quite salient in an Ivy-League school and it invoked a level of vulnerability for the college students in the last two examples. Playing basketball invoked the risk of confirming a stereotype about Black males being more athleti-cally than intellectually talented.

The freshmen probably would have gone to play basketball without my "intervention." But I wanted to challenge their assumptions about playing, highlight the bizarre racial hierarchy to which they were psychologically enslaving themselves, and encourage them to alter the level of stress they attributed to playing. It's the stress of considering how others might think of them racially that educators, counselors, parents, and students misunder-stand. Unresolved grief or anxiety about the meaning that others make of behavior, status, and potential can be burdensome on an individual's effort, agency, and academic identity when poor performance is the racially stereo-typical expectation.

For many but not all Black students, predominantly White K–12 schools also embody this perfect storm of racial stereotyping stress where intellec-tual inferiority, athletic superiority, and smartness image politics collide daily. I assert that this storm persists mostly by schools failing to face and reprocess how these stereotypes exist in the world, and how they can exist unchallenged in the learning practices, academic expectations, and intellec-tual pecking orders that occur in K–12 classroom interactions. It is the most salient assertion of this book that this stress or microaggressive onslaught of racial inferiority stays with us until we challenge it, psychologically and emotionally—with our words in voice, writing, and dancing.

Collective Threat in a Predominantly White School

I gave a keynote talk once at a predominantly White school having a diversity day in which the high schoolers were taking the responsibility of organizing and leading the events. I spent more time than usual meeting with the planning committee of students and their faculty advisors, including a school visit and tour although usually a phone conference is all that is necessary for a 10-minute keynote. The students were eager and stressed about diversity day, as this was their first time hosting a full day instead of random events. I observed the anxiety of the students and their faculty advisors as the students whispered and showed trepidation on their faces as they escorted me into a waiting area. These looks and whispers did not abate over the course of the next hour when the day's events would begin.

I encouraged the upper school students and faculty of about 150 participants to consider facing, not fearing, racial conversations as a statement of diversity in action rather than diversity in name only. I shared a story about my mother's experience with racial problem solving (see the story in the Introduction) and sat down. The story involved humor about what it's like to be a child looking at racial hostility when you don't have the authority or power to speak up against it. It was a story about how you vicariously experience trauma from watching a loved one endure racial rejection and how you try to prevent a racial conflict by distracting that loved one from the impending clash. It was a story of how children learn to racially cope vicariously while watching family cope with racial encounters. It was a story about how to directly confront racial disrespect in public places and how those skills are just as relevant for resolving racial disrespect that students experience in schools. Finally, it was a story about the insidious and demeaning power of silence and how not talking about the racial elephant in the room is a danger to critical thinking in education.

The audience was conservative in their response but receptive and pleasant. As soon as I finished and as the applause subsided, on my way to sit down, one of the very few Black administrators at the school took the podium unannounced and, against the protocol of the schedule, began to discount my entire speech. He chided my assertion on the importance of facing racial challenges and stressors in one's learning. He was not in any of the earlier planning meetings, nor did I ever hear of his input to the day's agenda. He suggested that the students didn't have to speak up or share their feelings about race if they didn't want to. He continued to speak in a hostile tone to the audience without interruption about the importance of individual responsibility, some of which I blanked on, as I was quite disturbed by the intrusion. When he finished, there was an eerie pall over the audience and the stage guests, not knowing what to do or say. If only the microphone had fallen with a reverb bounce to break the silence. It would have been better had someone pulled the fire alarm. But there was just awkward silence. The student representative who was scheduled to speak next then spoke in halting fashion about how the day's schedule would go and thanked the audience, and then students confusingly dispersed from the auditorium to their morning diversity workshops.

I was shocked and hurt. I told the only other Black educator about my shock but I never fully addressed the situation. Although I felt hurt, I also felt like I should have done something more direct in that moment. I wanted to retaliate and by not doing so, I felt weak for not defending myself. I could have dismissed his dismissal, but that would have not only been disruptive to the goal of the "diversity day," it would have undermined the students' courageous efforts to push their school's growth. I thought hard and long about it. I hated that feeling of helplessness and humiliation, but I felt better when I shared my helplessness with the other colleague who validated the experience. The more I tell it, the more I feel better. The ability to review perceived victimization can be helpful, but the emotional healing from racial microaggressions begins with validation.

Taking life's experiences as instructive is not about retaliation but resolution of one's angst—and in this case, angst about not acting. This is the beginning of developing a racially assertive coping response to these moments of racial rejection. Storytelling allows us to reflect on what could have been done differently, what feeling I want to have when I leave, and what message I want to leave—not only what should have been done to make me feel less weak or embarrassed. Could I have spoken up or did I do right by remaining quiet? Would I have made everyone so uncomfortable that they would have blanked out and not heard a word I said? What I should have done was to take back the mic and debate my hostile colleague by asking a simple question, "What's wrong with talking directly about racial matters?" I should have stated that I didn't appreciate his dismissal of my comments and that if he had a problem with my message, or me, the appropriate step was to talk to me. To use the podium to express his personal political position on race was rude to the audience, to the student leaders who planned the event, and to me as the guest scholar.

In schools, teachers and students of color face similar moments of dismissal, and I recommend gentle confrontation in the moment of the conflict for the best emotionally healthy result. My racial rejection moment is not dissimilar from the many moments students and teachers of color face daily in predominantly White schools where the choice to assert their voice in opposition to racial microaggressions seems unavailable.

I should have known that the whispering of the student leaders was not a good sign. It was a signal that it wasn't safe to bring up or challenge diversity conflicts or simply talk about diversity. Whispering reflects an apprehension of panic within racially tense contexts. In the many research interviews and studies on racial socialization with respondents of color, the interviewees whisper as if White people are listening into our interview. It's a funny moment when it happens because I often wonder exactly who my respondents feel is listening in. Often, that whispering is a way to stay true to the tenor and verity of the truth spoken, if not staying true to the tone. This hiding and truth-telling must be acknowledged as a coping strategy that is both useful and alienating. I found it alienating both because I felt I had to go searching for what else the whisperer was "not saying" and because it forced me to consider how I myself whisper to hide the shame of raising racial discord in predominantly White social settings. Over time, my failure in trying not to scare White people has taught me not only have I little to no control over reducing others' fears of my style, voice, passiveness, or assertiveness, I am ignorant of how my best invisibility moves are in and of themselves creepier. The failure of "whispering" in both body and voice has led me to develop a more useful coping strategy of "calling out the fear" (albeit sometimes sarcastically) in the moment of others' fearful reactions or what will be discussed later as a "Healthy Racial Comeback Line."

THE NEUROSCIENCE OF RACIAL FEAR IN PREDOMINANTLY WHITE CONTEXTS

The anxieties of negotiating race relations wreak havoc for anyone who fears being attacked for their views about race. What should concern educators is a more complex reality. A greater concern than potential attack is the fact that racial supremacy underlies much of our educational endeavors, even as it remains unspoken. White supremacy in education exists like violence toward Black people in spoken and unspoken law enforcement policies on racial profiling. It's subtle and commonplace, and hides as violence in what Martinot and Sexton (2003) call "nonchalance in contemporary racial talk" (p. 173). This supremacy masks a fear of and retaliation toward Black presence, whether it is on a street corner or in the halls of academia in the form of students or faculty (Essed, 1999). It is not always easy to identify this fear and its structural embedment in mainstream institutions like schools and police. But fear is observable.

In fact, thanks to neuroscience laboratory research and the use of physiological and neuroimaging measurement, we have learned a lot about how racially stigmatized and nonstigmatized individuals fear and awkwardly respond to racial conflict (Hebl, Tickle, & Heatherton, 2000). Whites who work hard to hide their racial fears will often exhibit halting emotional expressions, involuntary spastic movements, and awkward verbal eruptions when in the presence of Black people (Eberhardt, 2005). Recent research has uncovered startling findings of unconscious bias in Whites that brings more credibility to Blacks' concerns about how they may be perceived negatively. It confirms for many folks of color that those verbal and nonverbal "spastic reactions" from Whites in particular, but from racially stressed individuals in general, often reflect racially negative sentiments (Apfelbaum, Pauker, Ambady, Sommers, & Norton, 2008; Apfelbaum, Sommers, & Norton, 2008; Eberhardt, Goff, Purdie, & Davies, 2004; Mays, Cochran, & Barnes, 2007; Torres & Charles, 2004). Eberhardt (2005) describes the benefits of physiological measures as "considerable":

> Because many of these measures are more continuous than traditional behavioral measures, they offer a wealth of information on the time course of responses. Some measures allow researchers to physically locate the phenomena of interest, such that precise predictions can be made regarding when and where race effects will emerge. Moreover, physiological tools often allow measurement of mental states without eliciting overt behavioral responses or decisions from participants. (p. 182)

Anxiety Uncertainty Management Theory explains the physiological strain of racial encounters and the role that racial/ethnic socialization may play as a mediator of stress and coping (Crocker, Major, & Steele, 1998; Gudykunst, 1995, 2005; Gudykunst & Shapiro, 1996; Trawalter, Todd, Baird, & Richeson, 2008). During racial interactions, the pressure for individuals to self-regulate their thinking and behaviors so as not to attract derision is so intense that it can be fatiguing. The uncertainty of what to say and do during these encounters is the essential element of this pressure. The depletion of emotional resources compromises executive functioning and can lead to cognitive dissonance, or tension about two or more conflicting beliefs (Stephan & Stephan, 1985, 2001). An individual's belief in the immorality of racism or racist thoughts and behavior conflicts with his or her negative attitudes toward Black people. This cycle of ignorance, fear, dissonance, excessive self-regulation, and resource depletion is illuminating. Racial stress and strain reveals individuals' fear about mishandling racial/ethnic encounters and may lead to saying or doing something inappropriate and involuntary (Hebl et al., 2000). Even children can be stressed by racial/ethnic encounters in diverse contexts (Killen, Lee-Kim, McGlothlin, & Stangor, 2002). Gudykunst's (2005) antidote to anxiety uncertainty is mindfulness, or the focused consciousness of one's thoughts, like rehearsing what an individual can say during an expected interaction with a coworker, student, or parent.

When Relationships with Black People Become Racially Stressful

My examples of racial anxiety have focused on Black individuals coping within predominantly White educational contexts. Most of the social psychology laboratory research on racial anxiety over the past 2 decades has focused on the anxiety of Whites in interracial interactions, particularly with Black people. Although many White Americans become very anxious *during* encounters with Black Americans, it is also true that this anxiety *precedes* face-to-face cross-race encounters with Black Americans (Blascovich, Mendes, Hunter, & Lickel, 2000; Crocker et al., 1998; Devine & Vasquez, 1998; Hyers & Swim, 1998; Shelton, 2003; Stephan & Stephan, 1985). This research identifies that Black–White interracial interactions can ignite physiological reactions in some Whites that represent fight, flight, and fright responses such as heart palpitations, avoidance of eye contact, and emotional and physical distancing, even in Whites who report being low in prejudice toward Black people (Blascovich, Mendes, Hunter, Lickel, & Kowai-Bell, 2001; Blascovich & Tomaka, 1996; Devine, Evett, & Vasquez-Suson, 1996).

The fear of appearing racist can reveal honest and uncensored responses to queries of racial impropriety, particularly for Whites, because one feels physiologically threatened by the cross-racial social interaction.

Physiological and neuroimaging measurement can accurately assess anxiety related to racial stimuli and sidestep the "politically correct" self-report responses that accompany national polls and questionnaires about race relations. Neuroscience research has helped reveal underlying levels of anxious autonomic responses that many individuals work hard to hide. As racial and ethnic diversity in the United States has increased over the last 50 years, the decrease in the percentage of the population of Whites has led to research that investigates how Whites react to racially overwhelming interactions in workplace, public, and school settings. In summarizing the literature on Black-White racial interactions in the workplace, Avery, Hebl, Richeson, and Ambady (2009) write:

> Some of the more pertinent findings show that (a) White Americans often find interracial interactions discomforting; (b) their discomfort, despite their best efforts to conceal it, is commonly apparent to their Black partners; (c) the cognitive resources expended in interracial interactions can impair various types of performance; (d) anxiety concerning these interactions tends to lead to avoidance of minorities; and (e) the most intense feelings about interracial interactions involve contact with Black individuals. (p. 1382)

They suggest that businesses won't maximize the productivity benefits of diverse workforces if they can't foster successful interracial interactions. Schools also benefit intellectually from racially diverse student bodies (Linn & Welner, 2007).

Who's watching also matters in an individual's anxiety level when responding to racial encounters without racial prejudice. Amodio, Harmon-Jones, and Devine (2003) found that White adults differed in their activation of affective race bias depending upon their internal or external motivations to respond without prejudice. Individuals who are highly internally motivated to respond without prejudice worry less about others' anger or disapproval of them when they act in nonprejudicial ways, in contrast to highly externally motivated individuals. An example of high internal motivation is one who would speak up in a classroom or faculty meeting challenging one's school's admissions racial bias practice in selecting mostly White students, which has continued for years, despite the school's robust diversity in admissions policy. Adults high in internal motivations (IMS) and low in external motivations (EMS) showed less affective race bias than any other group, while high or low IMS participants showed significantly less affective race bias than high EMS participants. This research suggests that individuals who can't develop personal rationales for controlling racial bias may not be equipped to self-critique their misperceptions and stereotypes. Based on the view that smiling Black faces would ignite less threatening responses than sad or neutral faces, Richeson and Trawalter (2005) found that Whites high in external motivations to avoid prejudice were more likely to respond anxiously when presented with Black neutral faces (as opposed to sad or happy) compared with highly internally motivated Whites. So these motivations affect the attentional cognitions of adults when in the presence of Black faces, such that for some Whites, interracial relations are very anxiety-producing. This research points to the stress that may come from anticipating others' views of their behaviors before, during, and after racial encounters.

Other studies found that participants are more likely to associate Black and not White faces with criminality and ape-like features, irrespective of other factors (Eberhardt et al., 2004; Rattan & Dweck, 2010). Trawalter, Todd, Baird, and Richeson (2008) state that the stereotype of the dangerous and threatening young Black male has become so ingrained in the "collective American unconscious that Black men now capture attention, much like evolved threats such as spiders and snakes" (p. 1322). These types of reactions are unfortunate, but whether they are primal, learned, or tragically archetypal, these reactions might be better defined as a racial anxiety disorder of sorts if they distort and hamper interactions with persons of color (Azibo, 2003; Soto, Dawson-Andoh, & BeLue, 2011; Whaley & Davis, 2007). The fear of Black boys in schools by White teachers is a concern for parents and education reform advocates, as it may explain disproportionately inappropriate and harsh discipline strategies such as suspension and expulsion for these boys (Stevenson, 2003). My basic point is that we can't ignore the influence of racial fear among adults and school authority figures in their relationships with Black students and in how Black youth and other youth of color experience schooling and struggle to achieve in the classroom.

While this research on adult reactions to appearing "racist" reveals how school authority figures influence school climate, research on how children behave in the context of racially different children is very relevant to a racial/ethnic socialization understanding of schooling (Killen et al., 2002). Recent evidence reveals that older children (10- or 11-year-olds) who have learned about racial stereotypes may perform more poorly than younger children (8- or 9-year-olds) on a social categorization task that requires participants to identify racial differences. The older children were afraid to appear prejudiced and thus did not complete the task as efficiently (Apfelbaum et al., 2008). The authors summarize their research:

> In short, though cross-sectional, our work is consistent with the presence of a developmental anomaly: that a consequence of increased understanding of norms pertaining to race is the tendency to avoid acknowledging race altogether. (p. 1516)

Research on the effects of television viewing and preschoolers' prejudicial views is most notably relevant in the show *Sesame Street* (Lovelace, Scheiner, Dollberg, Segui, & Black, 1994). When a racially diverse group of preschoolers was asked to construct a neighborhood of diverse families, most children integrated the families of different racial groups as if they were living together. A significant percentage of the European American children, particularly the 5-year-old White children, failed to integrate Black families with the White families. *Sesame Street* researchers modified the television programming to address the White preschoolers' concerns for why the parents of those families did not support the integration by showing parents endorsing the interracial relationships in sleepover and game-playing interactions (Lovelace et al., 1994). The results were positive in changing White preschoolers' prejudicial attitudes. The study suggested that preschoolers don't have adult conceptions of racial prejudice, but they observe how their parents make these judgments in everyday life.

In short, youth at a certain age learn to see and fear the social outcasting that comes from thinking and speaking wrongly about race and thus keep their true thoughts and feelings to themselves to avoid expressing any biases behaviorally where possible (Pollock, 2004; Schofield, 2007; Slaughter-Defoe, 2012).

Fearing, Facing, and Bearing Racial Stress in School

Most schools fail to teach about the societal and emotional injustices of how children are educated, how families receive health care, or how neighborhoods receive basic protection and emergency services (Orfield, 2008).

But hiring adequate numbers of teachers of color is also difficult for schools to accomplish. Many teachers of color are marginalized by being few in number on faculty rosters (McDonald, Harvey, & Brown, 2005). Even diversity-friendly school administrators struggle with how to diversify their teacher workforces (Tack & Patitu, 1992).

The history of race and racism in education is a recent phenomenon (Tatum, 2003) as the politics of race at societal, institutional, and relational levels has led to administrations failing to see racism as a core barrier within schooling, let alone core to their practices and policies (Orfield & Frankenberg, 2013; Slaughter-Defoe et al., 2011). Unfortunately, the hesitation of institutions to directly engage racial conflicts may reveal degrees of incompetence and apprehension among leaders, especially in the field of education. Educators are left with the responsibility of providing adequate and exceptional schooling that influences learning at the relationship level. Whatever the history of race and racism means, racially literate schooling examines how those dynamics influence the quality of and caring within the teacher-student relationships that support student achievement (Foster, 2008; Gibson, 2007; Noddings, 1988, 2007; Ozer, Wolf, & Kong, 2008). Students of color experience these relationships less positively than their peers (Thompson & Schultz, 2003).

Educators remain responsible for addressing racial politics that are unwieldy and include the identification and negotiation of spoken and unspoken racial dialogue. These racial identification and negotiation skills are necessary but not plentiful among many educators. They require complex knowledge, critical thinking, self-awareness, and relational skills. This lack of racial literacy is pronounced in Predominantly White Schools (Orfield, 2008). What could be the danger in trying to identify and resolve racial differences in the experiences, education, and well-being of children and youth? Except for the emotions that are raised among and between individuals regarding their competence in problem-solving racial conflicts in the school setting, there should be nothing "wrong" with raising and addressing racially tense matters, unless you don't know what you are doing.

Several reasons explain why school leaders, students, and parents abdicate responsibility for addressing racial conflicts. One reason is the appearance of incompetence in managing racial conflicts. Reasons for student reticence to identify and negotiate racial matters include the diminution of emotional, intellectual, and social safety. In schools where leaders are ignorant of how racial diversity influences social conversation and climate, students of color will risk enormous social rejection by speaking up about racial matters. Conversely, others are rewarded for avoiding racial matters in both knowledge and communication. The result is an unhealthy racial climate. The burden shows up in student and leader hesitation to assertively share and debate racial ideas in the classroom.

This burden becomes heavier whenever school staff and majority-culture students who feel incompetent rely solely on avoidance coping strategies to maintain their public dignity. It can be stressful for individuals who work hard to not be racist, who do not say negative things about people of color, or who do not align directly or indirectly with bigotry in thought, word, or deed. Consequently, those struggling with not appearing racist will seek to protect themselves (for example, from being accused of not teaching Black students as equitably as White students). Consequently, there is less intellectual and emotional energy available to make meaning of the racial conundrums for youth who are racially different (Thompson & Schultz, 2003). There are a host of rewards for avoiding racially stressful interactions in school climates that prize niceness as a fundamental cultural value. Racial avoidance of racial matters can become the most appropriate thing to do as an expression of a cultural value if it is philosophically linked to how schools see themselves. For many PWS and school leaders, to avoid appearing racist is a cultural identity struggle. To avoid appearing racist may be the most equitable thing a "good school" can do, become, and teach.

Even if racial avoidance is hidden in the cultural fabric of school etiquette, it can be observed. School personnel that dance around and run from racial tensions in school classrooms and playgrounds cannot hide these reactions. It takes courage to admit to these threat reactions. Courage here is defined not simply by having conversations about racial matters but by taking stock of the verbal and nonverbal social interactions that reveal racial tensions, their intensity, influence, and targets. Table 3.1 reveals how educators might behave and react when fearing or facing racial encounters, which are anticipated, perceived, and experienced as racially conflictual social interactions. It is my contention that these behaviors and reactions are not simply observable but malleable.

Racial stress in many school interactions is not lessened or made invisible by ignoring or silencing conversation about racism, or the "R" word. In particular, conflicts within the teacher–Black student relationship are often ripe with fears that these conflicts are racial, even if they are not. While the silencing of conversation about racial stress exacerbates myths of intellectual inferiority or supremacy and hides emotional wounds, it mostly compromises learning if left unaddressed ("Should we say or not say the 'N' word when reading *Huckleberry Finn*?).

While this avoidance of the "R" word inadvertently promotes the superiority of a colorblind philosophy, it is the way in which people avoid racial matters that reveals how safe a school can become. These "ways" or behaviors are observable. Safety can best be understood within the quality of teacher-student, family-school, police-youth, and parent-teacher relationships. The assumption is this: If authority figures in school and society are intensely worried that their incompetence (perceived or actual) in success-

TABLE 3.1. Interactions That Show Fear or Facing of Racial Encounters

Fearing Racial Encounters	Facing Racial Encounters
When feeling personally challenged during encounter, worries about appearing as racist, having character flaw; views racism as a moral and personal issue	While feeling personally challenged, can see racial encounter is more important than personal fears; views racism is systemic and political
More concerned with the negative consequences of racial conflict than resolution	More concerned about the emotional consequences of racial conflicts and the educational lessons to be learned
Views racial stress as a *threat* (tsunami that will overwhelm) or an interaction that reveals a problem that is unsolvable	Views racial stress and conflict as a challenge (mountain worth climbing) or an interaction that reveals a problem to be solved
Less competent at racial negotiation because avoidance is primary coping strategy	More competent at racial negotiation because curiosity is primary coping strategy
Avoidance of encounters increases fears and focus on political correctness	Engagement of racial encounters increases competence in racial literacy skills
Perceives diversity issues as too complicated or costly to navigate so embraces a vague universal notion of diversity	Understands each diversity issue is different based on language, history of oppression, and triumph
Less interested or skillful about racial conflict resolution and more interested in preventing a public humiliation or political disaster	More interested in resolving racial conflicts directly as a statement of school's ability to teach students about the world
Educational leaders delegate responsibility to others for the development and implementation of diversity in school mission, policies, and curriculum	Educational leaders take responsibility for the development and implementation of diversity in school mission, policies, curriculum, and practices

fully negotiating racially conflictual social interactions with youth of color will be exposed, the quality of those relationships will be compromised. The most common explanation is that no one can effectively provide his or her best efforts when highly stressed. The good news is that as behavioral scientists, we know how to reduce fear and stress. The bad news is that fear must be acknowledged and stress reduction has to be actively practiced, not avoided.

The hardest part is getting individuals to admit to difficulty in emotionally managing social interaction and teaching or learning at the same time.

Basic skills to navigate and negotiate the racial tension of educating Black students from K–12 education are not only missing in educator training and professional development, they are missing within the curriculum for students who are preparing to succeed in a racially diverse world. There appears to be little room for critical racial literacy development in the classroom. If educators cannot acknowledge or bring a halt to this avoidance or ignorance of racial tension negotiation, how will anyone learn to resolve these issues?

One argument for the teaching of racial literacy in schools is the need for a buffer from the negative effects of racial microaggressions on the physical and mental health of people of color. Let's examine briefly some research on racism effects before we propose a theory to resolve racial stress in social interaction.

Catch-33: The Effects of Racial Blindness and Discrimination on Black Life

In 2003, I advanced a concept called Catch-33, which describes the psychological trauma of being Black in America while trying to battle racial hegemony (Cassidy, Davis, & Stevenson, 2003; Stevenson, 2003). It is an essential element of the narrative of Black life expendability proposed in this book. The idea is that if Black people can be vilified as problematic regardless of their status, educational level, accomplishment, service to country, and history, they are in a perpetual Catch-22 reality ("Damned if you do, damned if you don't"). Catch-33 represents a "Just Damned" position as individuals realize that Catch-22 experiences are not temporary but systemic and are going to occur across the life span. Whether young or old, in health and educational institutions, from those who take oaths of "do no harm" and "protect and serve," we find disproportionate and discriminatory hostility and harm toward Black people. It's the psychological effect of this narrative and its reality on one's well-being that drives my interest in not simply naming racial elephants, but tracking and remediating the short- and long-term negative effects of their invisibility and influence, especially in school classrooms.

One Catch-33 scenario is evidenced in how the discriminatory punishment and arrest rate of Black and Latino male youth from within schools is disproportionate to their misbehaviors (Advancement Project, 2005; Skiba, Michael, Nardo, & Peterson, 2002; Skiba & Rausch, 2006). This disturbing collaboration of juvenile justice and educational systems is fueled by stereotypical judgments that affect even preschoolers. Gilliam (2005) studied 3,898 preschool classrooms (81% response rate) representing all 52 state-funded preschool systems operating across 40 states and found that African American preschoolers are twice as likely to be expelled as White or Latino children and five times as likely as Asian Americans (Dobbs, 2005; Gilliam, 2005). The authors conclude that although the pattern reveals disproportionate punishment based on biased overreactions, the disparate ratio disappears when a behavioral consultant is present to help schools understand the developmental meaning of preschoolers' "disruptive behaviors." Research has reaffirmed the tragedy of the Catch-33 racial disparity in unemployment and job seeking for African Americans as well (Bertrand & Mullainathan, 2003; Giuliano, Levine, & Leonard, 2006; McDonald, Lin, & Ao, 2009).

Whether young or old, African American adults (parents, teachers, and leaders) are also not immune to the negative effects of perceived and actual racism on physical health, mortality, and emotional well-being (Barnes et al., 2004, 2008; Cooper, Mills, Bardwell, Ziegler, & Dimsdale, 2009). After controlling for several factors, Black women who suffered both acute (followed around by guards in stores; perceived as less intelligent) and chronic (discriminated against at work and in housing) incidents of racial discrimination were more likely than their peers to develop breast cancer (Taylor et al., 2007). The increased risk of premature death for Black mothers (parents, teachers, leaders) who experience breast cancer affects the lives of countless youth and is reason enough to explore the stress-reduction benefits of racial socialization. The Catch-33 here for many Black adults is whether to reveal one's emotions regarding subtle or blatant discrimination and fall into the stereotype of the "Angry Black Man" (open heart), to suppress emotions that contribute to serious health risks such as cardiovascular heart disease (damaged heart), and to realize that racism continues despite one's actions (broken heart). The negative consequences for cardiovascular health appear to be more extensive when the discrimination is subtle than when it is blatant for Black men, probably because of the ambiguity of subtle racial microaggression.

Research has found that Black adolescents who experience racial discrimination in their preteen years are more likely to develop conduct problems and depression than peers who don't experience racial discrimination (Brody et al., 2006). The negative effects of racial discrimination on self-esteem and depression for adolescents of color has much research literature support (Greene, Way, & Pahl, 2006; Scott & House, 2005; Wong, Eccles, & Sameroff, 2003), but this work has shown that racial discrimination negatively influences youths' experience within schools (Nyborg & Curry, 2003; Seaton & Yip, 2009). A hostile racial climate in schools (one characterized by low academic expectations and harsh and racially disproportionate discipline practices) as perceived by Black and Latino students has been linked to lower student achievement and grades (Mattison & Aber, 2007). In school, the threat of stereotyping and stress from racial profiling and discrimination affects how well students invest and achieve in school. This was particularly true for college women's sense of belonging and agency toward math achievement (Good, Rattan, & Dweck, 2012). Racial profiling in urban America is a form of terrorism and represents a national threat to the lives of Black children and youth. Consequently, solutions to the Catch-33 dynamic of social interactions are essential if we expect to reform education. Those solutions are based on one notion: rejecting and responding to the inferiority assumptions implicit in Catch-33 situations.

Keenan Michael Key and Jordan Peele have a brilliant comedy skit on their show *Key and Peele*, called "Suburban Zombies," which takes this same Catch-33 dynamic to an absurdly hilarious level. The two of them start the skit as terrified survivors in an apocalyptic *Walking Dead*–like time period. They find themselves trapped in a White suburban neighborhood surrounded by White zombies. The funny part is that they begin to notice that the zombies are not trying to kill or eat them. In fact, it becomes eerily clear that the zombies are "racist" and are so afraid of them as Black men that the zombies "run" from Key and Peele to avoid being touched by them. One zombie couple lock their car door as they approach the vehicle while a two-parent, one-child family prevent their uneducated child from eating Key and Peele as they walk by. This is so funny to me that I dare not attempt to write while I'm laughing for risk of self-injury. The skit ends with them finding a group of Black families having a party in a backyard, unbitten and unharmed. One modification I might make to the skit is to have Black zombies at the party too, all realizing their common plight, and end the skit with Black humans and zombies living happily together—unassaulted forever. Another modification would be to have a few Black zombies in the neighborhood also avoiding Key and Peele. Although the larger message is essential for justifying racial literacy—Black people and their lives are scary, expendable, and interminably so—there exists a healthy coping response to that fear. It's okay and healthy to have a comeback line or a coping strategy that identifies the racial conflict (elephant) and speaks to its absurdity through humor or pushing that absurdity to its most illogical and ridiculous conclusion—thus rendering the racial microaggression or insult less harmful.

Catch-33 examples of racial oppression within the justice, educational, employment, and health systems explain why preparing young people for a racially hostile world may become as much a parenting given for African Americans as is teaching children manners or not to run in the street or play with matches (Stevenson, 2003; Sue, 2010). The variability in how much parents discuss racial barriers is significant and may depend on how much they perceive racial matters to be a threat to child development (Hughes et al., 2006). But if parents choose to, how do they teach children to see and deconstruct America's acceptance of an expendable Black humanity narrative without becoming jaded by it? How do parents prepare youth for a world (or classroom) where the reproduction of American racial stereotypes is evident everywhere, even in cartoons and advertisements? Some parents worry that enrolling children of color in PWS is subjecting them to a culture that unwittingly endorses the expendable Black humanity narrative as an inevitable and tragic consequence of better schooling (Slaughter-Defoe et al., 2011).

Facing and Recasting Racial Stress Through Racial Literacy

Exposing students to diverse ethnic foods or learning the meaning of the colors of the flags of different countries doesn't adequately prepare students for negotiating a diverse world. Still, how do students navigate the world of racial stereotyping? As institutions of higher learning, why can't classrooms represent the spaces where these and other social challenges are raised and debated? Instead of students, parents, and teachers reproducing these stereotypes through avoidance, how can these groups be taught to psychologically face and counter these stereotypes? Racial literacy, racial debate, and racial negotiation are cornerstone skills for students and educators alike, but they must be taught with a relevance to the current needs of education, with a focus on addressing the racial fears and specific task demands of educators and constituents, and for the problem solving of current societal challenges.

Rist (1970) identifies how the power of teacher interactions in blocking the social opportunities of students is not dissimilar from how societal barriers and hierarchies of privilege create social injustice and disparities. There are disparities in the ways teachers approach children of color, even in affluent White schools. Classroom interactions emulate societal discrimination and apprehension about racial risk taking. A major premise of this book is that teachers and students are stressed by unspoken challenges or adherences to a racial hierarchy that are observable through the social interactions in the classroom (Thompson & Schultz, 2003). Whether a student raises his hand to share his ideas while worrying that others may see his contribution as racially tainted or whether a teacher decides to continue a discussion that falls surreptitiously into the realm of "who has the right to use the 'N' word" are a few examples of stressful interactions that might tax teachers' and students' coping abilities. These "elephants" loom larger for students or teachers of color, who are often stereotypically framed as less able to learn or teach. The same could be true of teachers and students of any racial background who have to engage racially stressful interactions. Yet I would distinguish between the stress related to the challenges and practices of teaching students and the stress of teaching Black and Latino students. Student and teacher racial stress may best be subsumed in the following questions: "How well can I perform in my schoolwork as a Black student or in my teaching of Black students?" "Is the stress of performing competently in my teaching of Black students or of being one of the few Black students in my classroom overwhelming?"

Although I believe racial stress and incompetence hinders teaching and learning, I have been impressed with some teachers, students, parents, and educational leaders who are racially assertive regardless of the racial composition of the audience. My research over the last several years has begun to uncover behavioral expressions of racial suppression and assertiveness among students and faculty in schools. Coleman and Stevenson (2013) developed measures that specifically ask teachers in predominantly White independent schools about their racial socialization history, sense of racial self-efficacy, sense of school belonging, style of appraising classroom racial conflicts, perceptions of the school's openness to racial questioning, and use of racial assertiveness and coping during school conflicts. Teachers were also asked about their perceptions of their colleagues' and leaders' openness to support racial questioning, to face racial conflicts, and to commit to diversity mission and action in the school. They found that faculty of color from independent schools show different racial suppression and assertiveness responses than their White counterparts. Still, the biological race differences are less instructive or explanatory of teacher classroom behavior than the differences among teachers in racial stress and self-efficacy appraisals and levels. It so happens that clusters of faculty who view racial stress in the classroom as more of a challenge and less of a threat are significantly better at management of classroom structure and student defiance than clusters of teachers who view classroom racial stress as threatening (Stevenson, 2012).

My hesitance to react during the keynote incident in Chapter 3 is similar to the reticence of some teachers to engage obvious racial conflicts or misunderstandings in the classroom. It is basically a fright response. Our fright, flight, and fight reactions to racial or diversity conflicts are often reactive yet very telling of how self-efficacious and competent we are in navigating these types of stressors. These are quite natural reactions to traumatic experiences but if unresolved will lead to phobic under- and overreactions of hesitation and spastic malapropisms. Thankfully, there are ways to explain these fears and anxieties regarding racial encounters. With explanation comes the potential for resolution of racial fear.

It is my hope that educators can ask these questions openly so that any stress reaction (minimal or severe) can be reappraised and minimized. We start with the stress of teacher–Black student relationships because they have consistently been defined as less engaging with a greater degree of lower expectations for achievement than other teacher-student relationships (Adams, 1978; Bennett, 1976; Chang & Sue, 2003; Clark, 1965; Coates, 1972; Cooper, Baron, & Lowe, 1975; Dee, 2004; Murray, 1996; Oates, 2003; Richman, Bovelsky, Kroovand, Vacca, & West, 1997; Zirkel, 2005). But how do racial stereotypes, tensions, and worldviews influence these relationships and contribute to denial in social interactions?

Color and racial blindness are not the biggest barriers to improving American race relations. It's the combination of denial of racially stressful interactions and the incompetence of what to do when unable to avoid these racially stressful encounters that represents a tragedy in school-based race relations. Not to learn basic math in the early grades hampers the learning of algebra in middle school. The failure to acknowledge racial stress means our educational systems and leaders are not only less likely to see racially stressful moments, but they become less open to admitting that they see those moments. They become less knowledgeable or able to do so. How do we cure this unique form of racial blindness, denial, and incompetence? *Recasting*. Recast theory considers several factors that influence the successful maneuvering or coping with racial conflicts in school relationships, politics, teaching, and leadership.

In the next chapter, I will propose an intervention model based on recast theory to identify racial elephants, reduce racial stress, teach effective racial coping skills, and promote racial literacy of educators and within their institutions.

CHAPTER 4

Recasting Racial Threat:

A Model of Coping and Assertiveness During Conflicts

> The voice of the intelligence is drowned out by the roar of fear. It is ignored by the voice of desire. It is contradicted by the voice of shame. It is biased by hate and extinguished by anger. Most of all it is silenced by ignorance.
>
> —Karl A. Menninger

> I had a colleague once who got mad at me
> because I told him he was White.
> He got so mad that he wanted to fight me.
> But that wouldn't do so he walked away to spite me.
> So I followed him to enlighten him, ever so lightly.
>
> —Howard C. Stevenson, "The Politeness of Whiteness" (2011)

In this chapter, I illustrate a replicable theory and model that can be applied in different educational, health, and justice institutions for the purpose of reducing racial stress in relationships among students, parents, teachers, educational leaders, and health professionals. This chapter will explain recasting through a model of teaching or intervention that moves storytelling toward behavioral assertiveness. Recasting is an activity of repeated and guided self-reflection that increases awareness of "in-the-moment" (ITM) encounters. The following objectives of recasting toward racial literacy include target goals and strategies to accomplish those goals:

1. Observing the Stress and Scripts of Racial Politics Through Storytelling
2. Appraising the Stress of Face-to-Face Racial Encounters Through Journaling
3. Reappraising and Reducing the Stress of Racial Encounters Through Relaxation

4. Engaging Racial Conflicts Through Debating
5. Resolving Racial Conflicts Through Role-Playing

RECAST THEORY: RACIAL ENCOUNTER COPING APPRAISAL AND SOCIALIZATION THEORY

Other than families, schools represent the most efficient system of child and youth racial socialization and literacy in American society. Perhaps visual media will eclipse them both (Adams & Stevenson, 2012). Still, failing to challenge schools about the power they possess to proliferate racial illiteracy would be a childrearing abdication of the highest order. If schools avoid racial matters by acts of omission or commission, they can perpetuate a miseducation of sorts. Miseducation is what Carter G. Woodson warned about in regard to Blacks being improperly educated in schools and society to despise their historical, cultural, and intellectual contributions and potential to humanity. Conversely, to focus on school systems at the expense of losing attention on what individuals must cope with daily in micro-interactions is to perpetuate miseducation as well. Let's see if we might apply a both-and approach toward the development of racial literacy and not either overestimate the trickle-down power of symbolic influence or blame individuals. So a theory to address racial threat and stress must consider how it is manifested ITM of relationships and in the dance of political systems.

The theory I am proposing is called recast theory (Racial Encounter Coping Appraisal and Socialization Theory). This stress- and coping-based theory redefines subtle and blatant racial unrest and conflict as anxiety-ridden. Anxiety is not the only way to characterize racial conflict or racism, but it is more likely to explain the persistence of avoidance and denial behaviors when individuals undergo uncomfortable racial interactions. This theory in no way exonerates intentional racial hatred, bigotry, and violence. This racial coping appraisal and socialization theory borrows from the literatures on stress and coping, stereotype threat, physiological reactions to racial conflict, critical race theory, culturally relevant pedagogy, and the psychology of family systems. It promotes the reappraisal and stress reduction of racial interactions and portends hopeful outcomes for those who can reduce this stress.

Racial/ethnic socialization (R/ES) represents the sum total of verbal and nonverbal communication from families, society, and communities that define the rules for interpreting racial/ethnic conflict, progress, and resolution. Racial socialization includes the transmissions and acquisitions of racial coping messages and strategies from family, society, and community systems. As a mediator, R/ES supports the interpretations of racial interactions as irrelevant or relevant, positive or negative, and stressfully overwhelming or manageable. Furthermore, recast theory will examine different coping solutions for individuals who over- and underreact to racial stress.

Recast theory proposes that through practice and application in social interactions, racial socialization can minimize the negative influence of racial stress on racial coping by bolstering racial self-efficacy. Recasting is the process of reappraising racial stress as workable by virtue of racial socialization processes (affection, protection, correction), which are essential ingredients in developing racial literacy. Although we have explained racial stress and encounters in the first chapter, other concepts are foundational to recast theory, including racial self-efficacy, coping, socialization, and literacy.

Racial self-efficacy is the *belief* in one's capability to read, recast, and resolve racially stressful encounters. The protection, affection, and correction of this racial self-efficacy are essential ingredients in reducing racial stress and there are benefits related to the emotional and cognitive processing of one's thoughts and behaviors or related to taking personal action. Table 4.1 describes the processing and action benefits of racial self-efficacy in intra- and interpersonal perceptions and relations. As is true about racial stress being a function of racial matters, racial self-efficacy is not a generalized self-efficacy. Teachers who are high in racial self-efficacy score higher on statements like "I believe I can resolve a racial conflict in my classroom between students" or "between myself and a student's parent."

Racial coping includes "[racial] cognitive and behavioral efforts to manage [racial] demands that are appraised as taxing or exceeding the resources of the person" (Lazarus & Folkman, 1984, p. 141). Coping with racial encounters is another foundational concept and is defined according to Lazarus and Folkman's original definition of coping with slight modification. The practical implications of racial coping is that both cognitions and behaviors can be appraised and observed within racialized encounters and defined as successful or unsuccessful. The glue concept between stress, self-efficacy, and coping in recast theory is racial socialization. *Racial socialization* is the teaching of emotional, physiological, cognitive, and voice skill sets that aid in the recasting of racially stressful encounters and in the promotion of racial coping, and will be discussed later.

Racial literacy is the *ability* to read, recast, and resolve racially stressful encounters through the competent demonstration of intellectual, behavioral, and emotional skills of decoding and reducing racial stress during racial conflicts. Racial literacy is the culmination of a successful procurement of racial coping skill sets to navigate racially stressful encounters across various social contexts. As such, racial literacy is defined by the product of experiences of racial encounter stress, self-efficacy, socialization, and coping as the ability to read, recast, and resolve racially stressful encounters. Another

TABLE 4.1. Benefits of Racial Self-Efficacy

Processing Benefits	Action Benefits
Less likely to dissociate, withdraw or become paralyzed in racially stressful encounters	More likely to speak assertively about racial politics
Less likely to panic when losing peripheral vision and hearing	More likely to see that one has lost peripheral vision and hearing
Less likely to impulsively say something "politically incorrect"	More likely to use strategy to reduce one's stress in the moment
Less likely to allow personal, psychological, and physiological stress reactions to influence their perceptions of others	More likely to self-observe, self-correct, and use breathing to self-care and reduce panic when racially stressed
Less likely to view racially stressful encounters as maximally stressful or as a threat (tsunami)	More likely to listen and hear what others are saying in racial dialogue
	More likely to interpret body movements of others accurately
Less likely to give up when racial assertiveness is rejected by colleagues or context	More emotionally confident during racial interactions
Less likely to use silence as coping strategy for racial stress	More likely to view racially stressful encounters as challenges (mountain)
	More likely to ask for help during or after racial encounters

aspect in recast theory is the location or contexts within which racial literacy is necessary. Five locations or "jungles of racial/ethnic miseducation" are proposed later, as are the strategies to use in developing racial literacy (storytelling, journaling, relaxation, debating, and role-playing) in teacher and school leadership training, parent and youth school-based interventions, and in child social policy development.

As Iris Is to the Eye: Racial Socialization for Buffering and Reappraising Racial Stress

Racial and ethnic socialization (R/ES) has been studied quite extensively over the past 2 decades and its relationship to the healthy psychosocial and emotional functioning of youth and families of color is significant (American Psychological Association, 2008; Hughes et al., 2006; Lesane-Brown, 2006). It has been defined as "communications to children about ethnicity and race" (Hughes et al., 2006, p. 747) and as the reciprocal delivery and reception of messages and interactions between parents and children about managing racial/ethnic discrimination and promoting cultural affirmation across the developmental life span.

These series of reciprocal interactions and communications are not solely exercised between parents and children, but also between youth and societal authority figures such as police, teachers, and counselors, and between media and justice social systems, to name a few (Stevenson, 1998, 2003). I think racial/ethnic socialization plays a much broader and more complex role in helping individuals negotiate racial/ethnic interactions that are stressful. So this recast model broadens the definition of racial/ethnic socialization to include the *transmission and acquisition of intellectual, affective, and behavioral skills to protect and affirm racial self-efficacy, then to reappraise and negotiate racially stressful encounters within five psychosocial contexts: information and knowledge processing, relationship engagement, identity reconstruction, styles expression, and stereotype reproduction*. It is broader than previous definitions in that it focuses on three different stress management outcomes: (1) the purpose for explicit communication to youth about racial/ethnic negotiation; (2) the development of a variety of racial/ethnic negotiation skill sets; and (3) the illumination of varied learning contexts in which these skill sets need to be differentially applied.

What if the burden of preparing children to successfully cope within a racially ambivalent society requires skills-building practice more than lectures between parents and youth? What if racial coping competence involves not just the presence, prevalence, or content of racial messages, but detailed explanation of why Black youth need this kind of socialization? Parents warn and encourage their children often, but the reasons for the warnings and encouragements as well as what youth internalize matter as much as "what" they say.

As racial socialization is conceptualized in the research literature as a parental factor of influence on child development, it is not clear what specifically it is meant to influence. I am proposing that R/ES acts as an instigator of coping in the face of unpredictable social exclusion and that it functionally mediates the relationship between stress and coping, particularly its effect on racial self-efficacy. This is a theoretical shift away from a focus on the *content* of parental transmission and child or youth acquisition of racial/ethnic values (e.g., cultural pride) and toward the *purpose* of R/ES. Additionally, recast theory explains how those values relate to parent and youth behaviors and support their racial coping in stressful situations. Discrimination and the racial/ethnic stress that accompanies it is not enough to explain racial coping. Avoidance of stressful racial encounters is only one coping response. Without mediation or reduction of uncertainty, individuals will probably continue to exhibit avoidant behavioral coping skills during racially tense encounters (Gudykunst, 1995, 2005; Gudykunst & Shapiro, 1996). But there are other coping strategies that are less psychologically detrimental.

Racial socialization, whether benign or intentional, buttresses racial self-efficacy and identity in a way similar to how the iris supports the eye. The iris regulates the amount of light needed for the eye to gain perspective and clarity on an image. Racial socialization is an interpretive and information-processing mechanism that regulates the relevance of racial encounters. Racial socialization helps individuals judge whether racial encounters are tense moments that lead toward racial negotiation and competence or toward tidal waves of mass emotional destruction or both. Without the iris, the eye would go blind through the overexposure of light, or in this case, racial stress. Too much experience with racial stress without protection and affirmation may result in more withdrawal, low racial self-efficacy, and a sense of racial incompetence. This may explain why many individuals aspire to a color/racial blindness philosophy of race relations (Bonilla-Silva, 2001, 2003). It is simply easier than processing the complexity of resolving racial conflict. With a dysfunctional iris, too little light would be disastrous, as clarity on an image (racial/ethnic encounter) would wane. With too little light or racial competence, as in the case of "colorblindness," individuals and institutions can distort (under- or overestimate) the threat of racial encounters. This distortion undermines the effective management of racial stress and contributes to feeling overtaxed by the stereotyped impressions of stressful encounters. Figure 4.1 reveals that R/ES serves a mediating role between stress and coping with a particular influence on racial self-efficacy.

Racial Socialization as Legacy or Literacy? Reconceptualizing the role of racial socialization from that of an interesting "correlate" to an essential "mediator" has led to identifying two types of racial socialization research directions. *Legacy racial socialization* reflects the type of research that most of the literature is currently investigating—retrospective parental racial communication to children and youth while growing up. Its primary focus occurs through self-report from parents or youth about the frequency and agreement with past racial communication. Legacy racial socialization also includes past racial communication and learning from society, peers, community, media, and a host of socializing agents such as school. One assertion proposed by recast theory is that legacy racial socialization is much more reactive to negative events of discrimination in which parents and youth are forced to socialize in the face of stressful encounters.

Literacy racial socialization represents a more planned, proactive, preventive, and practiced socialization for protection from those negative events as well as for the affirmation of one's racial self-efficacy. Racial socialization as a form of literacy suggests that positive socialization can also be planned and practiced to counter the negative effects of discrimination. Racial socialization as legacy is less likely to teach specific racial coping skills for different contexts, catalyze competence in racial dialogue, replace avoidance

FIGURE 4.1. Recast Theory: The Mediating Role of Racial/Ethnic Socialization

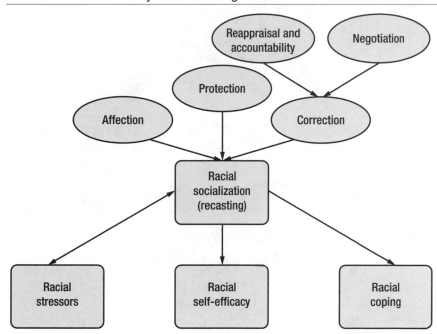

racial coping with racial conflict resolution, or teach a variety of examples of healthy situation-specific racial coping strategies. Literacy racial socialization is characterized by how well it leads individuals to skillfully and flexibly respond to insult and seek support within different contexts (school, home, neighborhood). Moreover, healthy R/ES should lead not only to effective and healthy survival of oppression but toward the self-actualization of creative talent. Talent and skills development can be self-reinforcing and with practice can lead individuals to counter societal stereotyping from micro- and macrosystems, from distal experiences of racial insult that occur societally or virtually, as well as from proximal experiences of face-to-face racial insult. R/ES can help individuals catalyze different definitions of self, other, and culture. Although it is true that youth can glean kernels of truth and skills from legacy racial socialization, its integration in the daily behaviors and social interactions is more implied and less practiced than with literacy racial socialization.

To call this a theory of recasting is to acknowledge the important role of racial socialization processes in not only buffering the negative effects of racial/ethnic stress and in bolstering racial self-efficacy, but also in the reappraisal and resolution of racially stressful encounters for encounters that take place across multiple contexts. How one can adjust coping within

FIGURE 4.2. Goals of Racial/Ethnic Socialization

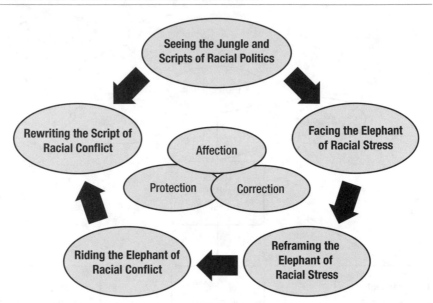

the moment of an encounter that becomes stressful is a highly desirable psychological outcome. In essence, the work of R/ES processes should move beyond the foundational role of buffering and affirming racial identity in order to ignite the psychological, emotional, and behavioral postures of stress reappraisal and conflict negotiation. As R/ES serves as an iris or buffer to racial conflict, increasing a healthy approach to racial stress increases the chances that this conflict can be recast as workable instead of as impossible.

So recast theory asks, "How can we identify the racial stressors in one's environment, bolster an individual's racial self-efficacy enough to recast those stressors as less threatening, and develop new racial coping skills to negotiate racially conflictual interactions that are intrapersonal and social?" In other words, recast theory seeks to help individuals, groups, and institutions meet five overarching objectives: (1) Become Aware of the Jungle and Scripts of Racial Politics, (2) Assess the Intensity of the Elephants of Racial Stress, (3) Touch or Reappraise the Elephants of Racial Stress, (4) Ride or Engage the Elephants of Racial Conflict, and (5) Rewrite or Resolve the Script of Racial Politics (Figure 4.2).

When I see racial mountain, you see racial tsunami. A major barrier to seeing the elephant of racial stress or the concomitant dance of denial in racial encounters is the negative meaning that individuals attribute to that racial conflict or to that racial dance. Some see racial conflicts as small and harmless as an anthill while others see them as a storm waiting to devastate.

Anthills are small and while teeming with activity; they ignite no particular fear, given their smallness and vulnerability. Moderate stress reactions might be described as "mountain-climbing" reactions. Mountains are considerably large and require some level of skill, determination, and summing up of courage to climb. Depending on their size, mountains can appear overwhelming but are nevertheless not impossible to scale. Extreme stress reactions are characterized as "tsunami" reactions. Tsunamis are devastating acts of nature that figuratively and literally engender fearful reactions of insurmountable despair.

In our research on classroom and school racial stress, my colleagues and I have developed measures of racial stress appraisal that ask teachers and educational leaders if they view racial stressors in the classroom as threats or challenges, and whether they have adequate resources and support to navigate and resolve these conflicts (Coleman & Stevenson, 2013).

If individuals can interpret a racially stressful encounter in multiple ways, what factors are likely to predict whether they have anthill, mountain climbing, or tsunami stress reactions? Well, one factor is the degree to which one has been exposed to racial socialization, received skills training, and internalized through repetition, practice, and feedback how to successfully negotiate racially stressful encounters (Stevenson & Arrington, 2009). But where is the application of these appraisal, self-efficacy, and stress management skills necessary? Or more specifically, where might racially stressful encounters occur?

Where Encounters Happen: Self-Efficacy and Coping in Diverse Socialization Contexts (Jungles)

While racial encounters are moments of dissonance inside of and between individuals, I am proposing that these encounters look and feel different within five socialization contexts or "jungles," including *information deconstruction, relationship bonding, identity reconstruction, style expression, and stereotype countering*. Although surviving and navigating each "jungle" requires the protection and affirmation of racial self-efficacy, reappraisal of racial stress, and negotiation and resolution of racial conflicts specific to these contexts, the racial and ethnic stressors and conflicts specific to each jungle are different, as is the utilization of racial/ethnic skills.

Information contexts require racial/ethnic skills of deconstruction and interpretation, while *relationship* contexts require building relationships skills; *identity* contexts require identity exploration and reconstruction skills; *style* contexts require style restraint and expression skills; and *stereotype* contexts require stereotype countering or endorsing skills (see Figure 4.3). Furthermore, not only might parents socialize to bolster racial and ethnic self-efficacy and stress management in youth, but so might other

FIGURE 4.3. Racial Socialization Contexts and Competing Tensions

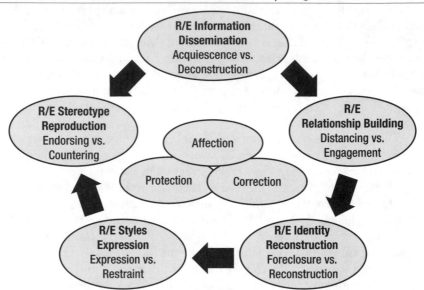

institutions. As a mediator of racial stress effects on racial coping, racial socialization has the potential of reducing or bolstering one's sense of racial competence by weakening or strengthening racial self-efficacy.

Information contexts communicate knowledge that is not benign. Canons about what constitutes knowledge within school curricula often raise many potential racial conflicts that require skills of translation and rebuttal. The dilemma of swallowing this information without critique versus deconstructing it to discover its support of racial hierarchical roles and expectations is not a small issue. Students, parents, and educational leaders might consider the consequences of students struggling with academic agency, identity, and achievement should they decide to challenge or accept the curricula as truth or knowledge. *Relationship-building* with teachers is perhaps the most important factor in student achievement as learning is increased because students gain not only more time but social capital and framing of the importance of the knowledge. It's one thing to deconstruct the racial meaning of a class lesson, book, or media event, but it is another to try to talk, listen, and negotiate a racial encounter with another person. The third social context of *identity construction* suggests that youth should have the freedom of securing a racial identity only after they've resisted or rejected the racial identity expected by others. Over time developmentally and after being resistant to outside influence, identity construction can be viewed as a choice after some resistance. Choosing one's racial identity has its own stressfulness that considers family and societal pressures on children to be a certain kind of person. The key tension is between foreclosing on an identity due to the stressfulness of the decision or the risk taking of reconstructing an identity based on deeper-level introspection.

The fourth social context of styles expressions suggests that racial literacy skills are necessary here to navigate successfully the public presentation of one's identity. Style is the "conscious or unconscious manipulation of language or mannerisms to influence favorably the hearers of a message" (Asante, 1987, p. 39). Black students will often be confronted about their grooming styles, shower habits, attitude habits, and walking and talking habits as to how much they mimic or stray away from common racial stereotypes and images.

The fifth and final social context that requires unique racial negotiation skills is that of stereotype reproduction. The skills to counter stereotypes daily are very necessary and unclear given the plethora of images and unchallenged assumptions that are attributed to Black life and culture. The most talented among us will see debate and artful argumentation as humorous but ninja-like in their subtle ways to protect and advance one's racial identity and well-being. Students need agency to counter stereotypes as much as they need it to learn math and science. Without active countering, recast theory suggests endorsing the stereotype is quite possible. This proposition supports and contradicts current research on this topic (Steele, 2010).

Recasting Racial Stress One Story at a Time: From Theory to Model

Because racial stress ignites our basest and most primitive fears, I want to spell out processes of resolution and agency in simpler ways than is possible using a theory. Our intentions within the madness of these fearful images and assumptions get lost as we become overwhelmed—too overwhelmed to listen to each other, let along appreciate the complexity of learning about racial dilemmas. Conversations get muddled, people get tongue-tied, feelings get hurt, and all without uttering what we really want to say about the racial world around us.

With the right degree of support and safety, the phobia of racial social interaction should dissipate over time, but not without exposure, experience, and practice. Based on years of working with students, parents, and teachers, I've constructed a model of racial literacy development. The recast model is designed to reduce and resolve racial stress in schools and everyday living by using racial socialization through recasting to bolster racial self-efficacy in individuals and groups. Through greater racial self-efficacy, individuals and groups are expected to identify and remediate the negative psychological effects of simplistic colorblindness, White supremacy, and ste-

FIGURE 4.4. Racial Literacy Components

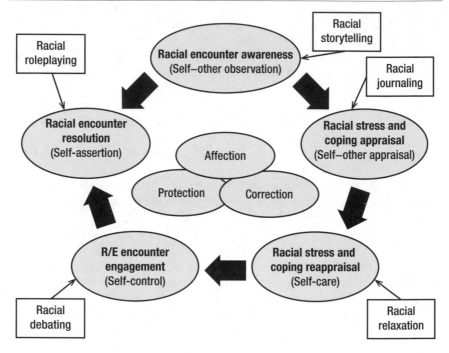

reotype threat. This remediation occurs through teaching and practice of racial coping skills that are specific to the situations students, parents, and teachers face in the classroom.

Upon completion of the training goals, strategies, and skills of the racial literacy model shown in Figure 4.4 individuals and groups should be able to (1) identify racial politics and encounters in their environment; (2) evaluate the stressfulness of racial encounters within themselves and others; (3) modify the stressfulness of racial encounters; (4) engage rather than avoid racial conflicts in the moment of the social interaction; and (5) resolve these racial conflicts satisfactorily. To reiterate, recasting overwhelming racial stress into workable racial stress involves the active use of skills necessary to see the dance of racial politics; choose dynamic roles beyond villain, hero, or victim; change one's movement or role in the dance; and respond competently within future racial encounters.

Figure 4.4 represents a more detailed and complex map of the relationship between racial literacy objectives, strategies, and basic skills. Each figure assumes that these objectives are influenced by the others but are best accomplished through the active presence of affection, protection, and correction processes. That is, without these three foundational aspects of human trust-building, none of these objectives or rest stops is possible. The call for a conversation around race will always be premature without the skills of negotiating the tensions that come with that conversation (Huber, 2013). Students, teachers, parents, and educators must expect, receive, and give affection (nurturance), protection (monitoring), and correction (accountability) while they take risks to become aware of and learn to resolve racial stress and conflict in daily social interactions. Without these ingredients, the risks of racial avoidance will be too great and the improvement of race relations and racial climates within schools too arduous to complete. Whites who begin conversations with others about race may give up during these "conversations" out of desperation and fear (Huber, 2013). If educators and parents give up due to fear, then students of color may be at risk for bearing the burden of this unresolved stress. A review of the research on schooling experiences suggests that Black and Latino children will carry most of that dehumanization burden as the lowest-status groups on the racial totem hierarchy. This invisible racial hierarchy of "who's smartest" or "who's more likely to succeed" is brutal, as it exacts emotional toll on students as they seek to be and survive in schools where racially disproportionate treatment is unacceptable (Martinot & Sexton, 2003).

In Figure 4.4, the objectives are framed as approaches to racial encounters; the strategies are thought of as socialization activities or practices for learning how to recast racially stressful interactions; and the skills are framed as intellectual, behavioral, and emotional outcomes that can be heard, felt, and seen. I propose that the training of educators, parents, and students should lead to greater racial/academic encounter objectives (encounter awareness, stress/coping appraisal, stress/coping reappraisal, encounter engagement, encounter resolution) that lead to ITM racial literacy skills (self-observation, self-correction, self-care, self-control, self-expression) by using specific socialization activities (storytelling, journaling, relaxation, debating, and role-playing).

"Self" here is defined in both individualistic and communal ways (Nobles, 2006). *Extended self* is an African psychological term that proposes a view of self as a collective reality (me, you, us), not simply an individual one (me, myself, and I). Both will be included in my framing of these core literacy skills. A more complex version of the recast model of racial literacy (and its elephant themes) is below and can be found in Table 4.2.

Questions that promote the development of the five racial literacy skills of racial encounter awareness, stress appraisal, stress reappraisal, conflict engagement, and conflict resolution are proposed. They are meant to stimulate suppressed memories, creative ideas, hidden blind spots, racial malapropisms, and stories about racial matters. For every exercise and strategy, I expect participants and facilitators to conduct ITM mindfulness that furthers the processing of thoughts, feelings, and behaviors of self and others using the following questions.

- Did you notice anything about yourself as you were sharing and listening?
- What feelings, thoughts, bodily reactions were you having?
- What feelings, thoughts, bodily reactions were you observing in others?

With these queries as the substance of ongoing ITM processing of racial stress and coping, the following racial literacy objectives of racial encounter awareness, stress appraisal, stress reappraisal, conflict engagement, and conflict resolution are proposed.

RACIAL ENCOUNTER AWARENESS: STORYTELLING TO SAFELY SEE STRESS IN SOCIAL INTERACTIONS

The initial challenge in developing racial literacy for individuals and institutions is to become aware of racial encounters happening in their environment between themselves and others. Each individual or institution can gain self-knowledge through observing oneself in the retelling of past experiences, memories, and in reflecting on current reactions to racially stressful interactions. Developing the ability to self-observe involves gaining knowledge about the history of racial/ethnic politics in society and in one's family of origin. It involves taking mental notes on your emotional reactions to that information. Learning more about historical events of racial conflicts can be very helpful in gaining a broader context of how racial encounters and their effects are not new, just avoided. This is awareness.

Racial Encounter Awareness (Self/Other Observation) as the first step toward racial literacy involves seeing the dance of racial politics and the many scripts and roles that encourage the maintenance of racial hierarchy in schools and society. Critical queries to stimulate self and other observations include

1. When did/will I experience a racial encounter (elephant in the room) and what did/will I do?
2. What were my past experiences with racial socialization? (What did my family tell me?)
3. What are my current experiences with racial socialization? (What do I tell my family?)
4. What stories of racial stress do I remember over the course of my lifetime?
5. What do I notice in others who get upset by racial matters, politics, and conflicts?

TABLE 4.2. Racial/Academic Encounter Objectives

R/A Encounter	Socialization activities to protect and affirm self-efficacy, reappraise stress, negotiate conflict (Affection, Protection, Correction)	R/A Basic Literacy Skills (Self-Affirmation)	R/A Socialization Contexts
Awareness	*Storytelling* Narration of past encounters and socialization; emotional reattachment to cultural history, psychology	Self/Other Observation	*Information* Proliferation Acquiescence versus Deconstruction
Stress/ Coping Appraisal	*Journaling* Chronicle and rate stressfulness of current racial microaggressions	Self/Other Appraisal	*Relationship-Building* Distancing versus Bonding
Stress/ Coping Reappraisal	*Relaxation* Relaxation and self-regulation during microaggressions and encounters	Self-Care/ Correction	*Identity Reconstruction* Foreclosure versus Exploration
Conflict/ Coping Engagement	*Debating* Rebutting stereotypes using research, conflict, healthy comeback lines, cultural style, and competition	Self-Control	*Styles Expression* Expression versus Restraint
Conflict/ Coping Resolution	*Role-Playing* Mainstream/bicultural coping Guided practice of negotiating racial/academic encounters with teachers, self, peers	Self-Assertiveness	*Stereotype Reproduction* Endorsement versus Countering

6. What are my assumptions about the importance, communication, and resolution of R/E politics?
7. What is my current knowledge of and emotional attachment to the history of my racial group?

The best strategy for seeing the denial of racial stress and conflicts in yourself and others is through *storytelling*. Through storytelling, individuals can learn how to observe emotional and physiological reactions to an event before or after the event occurs. In one's story there exists the freedom to explore challenges and successes without attack in ways that are not possible in social conversations around racial politics. Storytelling includes listening to the racial socialization stories of others, particularly family members.

Storytelling

The first challenge of developing racial literacy is recognition that racial stress and situations exist. Hence, the name of this first stop on the safari is "Seeing the Jungle of Racial Stress and Politics." Being able to reflect upon and process how people in a story are ignorant of, clueless about, avoidant toward, or engaged with racially tense matters in their speech, mannerisms, movements, and professional responsibilities is invaluable and therapeutic. Why? Because we are so often afraid to talk and feel about racial politics, the actual conversation around racial stress can be relieving and can undermine the burden of silence that fuels the power of racial denial. Listening to the stories of those who see the racial dynamic and talking about it is healing and represents a greater demonstration of ethical civility.

The utility of storytelling for developing racial literacy is that it places individuals in the center of the racial conflicts they face or fear daily. Storytelling, therefore, begs the question "What if I am the elephant?" It changes the use of "us versus them" framing to "us and them" where my story could be unique and part of others' stories. It could be both ethnocentric and relevant across other in-groups and out-groups without the choosing of sides. We will need to get back to the collective stories of "us" and the "them," but let's consider first how individuals manage racial stress before we discuss the implications for in- versus out-group psychology.

Storytelling can originate from spontaneous or planned interaction. It allows individuals to navigate racial politics by having a personal chip to throw into the debate. Telling stories of racial encounters past and present is the method designed to uncover and discover hidden emotions and racial socialization experiences. Storytellers are expected to answer questions that stimulate the detection of hidden dynamics, nonverbal communications, and interactions that may, in fact, be racial microaggressions. Sharing a story about a racial encounter raises emotions that can be examined. Identifying and managing these emotions are important in utilizing racial literacy skill sets.

Storytelling naturally teaches one to reflect on past experiences with racial tension and how they influence current coping approaches to racial stress and conflict without blame. Racial socialization and coping experiences are forgotten, recalled, and retold. Individuals are asked to reflect through stories of their early experiences, and communications from families, communities, and society, how they currently define and resolve racial conflict. A key question of interest here is "What was I told and what did I learn about racial politics while growing up?" A follow-up question is, "What am I being told now about racial politics from relationships at work, at home, in the media, and in my neighborhood?"

African American psychology research has grown over the past 3 decades and could be useful in school reform initiatives that emphasize racial literacy and self-awareness in professional development strategies. This field of study has strongly insisted that self-knowledge (both collective and individual; cultural, ethnic, and racial) is the highest form of knowledge (Neville, Tynes, & Utsey, 2010). This is not simply about the procurement of factual information. Knowing facts and figures about different cultural groups might help illuminate deeper elements of other cultural groups, but it is fairly useless in how one might become conversant in cross-racial relationships. The knowledge that is most useful in racial conversations is knowledge about our reactions when confronted by racial stress and conflict. So, to stimulate storytelling, I ask folks to engage in exercises that encourage them to discuss their exposure and experience of racial/ethnic socialization. Entitled "What I Was Told and Taught About Racial Politics," this set of activities is designed to stimulate memories of childhood experiences about racial communication that is both verbal and nonverbal. Verbal experiences could include proverbs, sayings, or quips that parents would say, for example. Nonverbal experiences could include memories of watching how adults or peers during one's childhood would respond to racial stress, conflict, and/or resolution. These storytelling activities are also meant to uncover assumptions that individuals have about the importance, competence, communication, and resolution of racial politics. But we begin with the "self."

Another self-knowledge goal of storytelling is to provide new exposure to information and knowledge about one's racial history, as discussed in Chapter 2. Teaching racial histories is not simply about sharing information. It should be about stimulating an emotional attachment to that racial history, no matter how tragic or triumphant. My hope is that participants become better storytellers over time, easily talking about personal and professional racial matters without censorship and shallow reflection. I expect them to demonstrate calm as they remember past racial experiences and find any relevance or connection to the racial lens-making of the present by themselves or others. I also expect them to develop a third ear or eye to see, hear, and reflect on the meaning in their stories that will be contradictory but mostly self-defined.

Creating Safe Spaces for Racial Risk Taking and Storytelling

To tell the story of one's experiences with racial stress and conflict is no easy feat. It is racial risk taking and without it, we can't make progress as a society. Racial risk taking is being vulnerable enough to share a story about a racial encounter (successful or not), knowing that others might perceive, diagnose, or treat you in a negative way for misinterpreting or mismanaging the encounter. It's the courage that Cornell West (1994) speaks of to face and directly talk about structural racial problems. Whenever I teach on these matters, I get excited when so many teachers, principals, parents, pastors, counselors, superintendents, and youth share an experience they've never shared before. It's like a vulnerable flower opening up to the world despite the potential threat of ridicule and attack from wind, rain, disease, and insect invasion. There is something healing about letting go of fear and regret about racial encounters we wish we could do over. But storytelling is not enough.

Although students in my courses may enjoy the "misery loves company" rule of classmate bonding, that bonding rarely includes divulging failure or trepidation about one's history of racial encounters. It's my job to create the atmosphere for that risk taking. It's what I would desire and demand from the teachers of my own children, from the counselors of my family members, from the community leaders and educational leaders of my neighborhood, and from the police and politicians in my city. I think the people I care for and love the most deserve safety—safety that the leaders in those environments from prekindergarten through graduate school would not only demand but be able to create. Any leader who could not create atmospheres where protection from physical attack, intellectual disregard, emotional muting, and behavioral misinterpretation is a given, should resign immediately.

So if and when I'm successful at creating this safety, I watch with anticipation and hope when my elementary, secondary, undergraduate, graduate, midcareer, postgraduate, and doctoral "students" struggle and take enormous risks to share their encounters. Because, by doing so, they reveal their bodily, cognitive, and emotional strengths and challenges. I take this seriously as a necessary step toward racial justice. While I am less hopeful that racial justice can happen through congressional action, I am hopeful that it can happen in a classroom—within a relationship between a teacher and a student.

Storytelling is only one stop on the safari. Hearing others' stories is just as important. So, watching yourself as you tell the stories of racial stress, conflict, and coping is essential. Ultimately, it involves perspective-taking of others' worldviews in addition to your own. An example of this "other perspective-taking" comes from Beverly Daniels Tatum's work on Black students who gather together in cafeterias in PWS.

Appraising Whiteness as Lens: Who Is Sitting Together at the Cafeteria?

When Beverly Daniels Tatum (2003) wrote her wonderful book, *Why Are All the Black Kids Sitting Together in the Cafeteria?* I was delighted that a different look at the perspective of White students was finally getting its due. It revealed the power of blindness for those who observe Black behaviors and consider them inherently problematic. In my many talks to PWS where students, parents, and faculty still wanted to understand "Black people and culture and style," frequently, these innocent questions were driven by an exaggerated belief and an irrational fear. The exaggerated belief was that if one could have the exact knowledge of how not to offend Black people in social encounters, then one could escape experiencing the irrational fear—being called "racist."

So, with these unspoken and barely spoken questions lingering in many audiences, I realize that most folks are too afraid to become introspective regarding resolving racial stress and conflict. The question they were asking without saying so was, "How does it feel for Black students sitting together to be a problem—that confuses me and causes me anxiety?"

Americans in general and in schools have been socialized to believe that when Black people congregate, it is dangerous activity that could be harmful. The only way to get out from under this ritual of problematizing Blackness is for students to generate new questions, become introspective, and ask, "Why would Black students sitting together bother me and my friends so much? Why I am also sitting together with people who look like me, talk like me, and act like me? Why do I hang out with people who understand most of my mannerisms, my colloquialisms, and style, too?"

The best comeback line for Tatum's questions should be, "So why do the White students sit together in the cafeteria to watch and talk about why the Black students are sitting together in the cafeteria?" The "observers" are gazing outward, not inward, but like the blind scientists discovering elephant body parts, they remain clueless. They are asking the same wrong questions without self-reflection. Meanwhile, as a researcher studying Black students in PWS for 2 decades, I often feel like Bill Murray in *Groundhog Day*. Still, developing racial self-reflection skills cannot be dependent on storytelling alone because memory is hampered by stressful experiences. Without a recording of the racially stressful experience, individuals are unable to fully self-reflect. This leads us to the second stop in the racial literacy process—racial encounter stress appraisal, or in practical language—writing down our stories.

RACIAL ENCOUNTER STRESS APPRAISAL: JOURNALING FOR DEEPER SELF-REFLECTION

A second objective of recasting is learning how to assess one's level of stress during racially conflictual situations. Racial Stress and Coping Appraisal (Self/Other Appraisal) is the beginning of assessing how well individuals understand their stress reactions as well as the reactions of others. Knowing the boundaries of the racial stress reactions from low to high is essential. In particular, individuals have to learn not only how they understand the extremes of their reactions to racial matters, but also how others (family, public, authority figures, colleagues) are likely to interpret those reactions. Critical queries to accomplish the objective of self and other appraisal of racial stress include the following: Is the past or future racial encounter a challenge or threat? How well can I take written, not just mental, notes on my reactions to the encounter through journaling? How well do I calculate, locate, and communicate my stress reactions (body, feelings, thoughts) to encounter and seek help?

Stress appraisal is important while conflict is happening. To be able to identify symptoms of stress in real time brings much more "control" to one's involuntary and undesired overreactions or clueless underreactions to racial conflicts. The best psychoeducational strategy to initiate this type of racial mindfulness is *journaling* about one's racialized life experiences. The strategy of journaling allows one to examine the threat level of current racial encounters with more detail than storytelling alone can afford. Writing down one's experiences can ignite other reflections, stories, and moments while building meta-analytic cognition or the ability to see oneself being oneself.

Journaling

Writing down one's stories and experiences and rating the stress about the incidents of microaggression is also essential for healing. The recasting of racial stress and self-efficacy happens here by virtue of our risk taking in admitting and listening to our emotional weaknesses during racial conflicts, whether imagined, perceived, or endured. Often, thoughts of brilliance come to our minds about our life experiences but we lose them because we don't write them down. Journaling becomes most powerful when we write down our observations of the nonverbal reactions we have had during racially stressful encounters. Writing down what others have said about us during these encounters is a gift and shows that we take our ideas and feelings seriously. If we have real friends, we can ask these friends to be witnesses as we journey through the safari of racial discourse and tell us how we look and sound. Writing and reflecting is key to developing racial self-efficacy and believing that we can see, face, and engage racial microaggression moments (when a student or peer unconsciously describes students of color using a stereotype of laziness or less intelligence, racial jokes that go too far, or speaking up against a racially discriminatory discipline policy as the only or one of a few faculty of color in PWS).

By self-appraisal, I do not mean self-blame. I mean the ability to see yourself closely and how you react to stressful situations within a safe context like a diary—a diary of racial coping. Journaling can deepen one's ability to self-observe yet reduce the stress and self-blame associated with racial conflict. As discussed in Chapter 2, participants are taught to rate the stressfulness of a racial conflict on a scale of 1 to 10 (where 1 is not stressful at all, like thinking about being one of the few faculty or students of color; and 6 or 7 is moderately stressful, like thinking about being a minority on the way to the school you work or attend; and 10 is extremely stressful, like during a faculty meeting or classroom session where the topic of racism in the school is brought up and everyone is looking at you, expecting you to either solve the problem, exonerate everyone in the room from ever being a racist, or channel Martin Luther King Jr. at that moment by reciting the "I Have a Dream" speech in "authentically Black" intonation and mannerisms).

The key questions individuals must ask themselves are "What do I fear about racial/ethnic politics or experiences and how threatening are they to me?" and "When I get stressed during racial encounters, what body movements, behaviors, thoughts, and emotions am I having and what do others see?" The more individuals can rate their racial stress, the more they can safely reappraise that stress to be less threatening.

Questioning racial stress during the journaling of one's story should raise awareness of several racial elephants. They include awareness of one's lack of knowledge about racial issues and which ones are most stressful and which are not. Another is the level of fear one has about what others think of his or her racial competence or level of commitment to diversity issues. Journaling reveals how easy or difficult it is to discern when racial dynamics, irrational thoughts, overreactions, and spastic anxious behaviors are present, and what to do about them. The work of "race-reflective journaling" (Howard, 2006; Milner, 2003) is the work of this step.

Writing your experiences about racial encounters is not the same as telling the story. In telling the story, one cannot always be sure to capture the most salient aspects of the encounter, particularly if you tell the story in front of strangers, or acquaintances like classmates. To be mindful of how you tell the story is important and what reactions you might not be aware of are also essential. Still, telling a story involves multiple cognitive, behavioral, and emotional reactions colliding and expanding simultaneously. So when my students are sharing, it is not uncommon for them to be halting, hesitant, apologetic, shamed, and angry that what they want to say is in their minds but not readily accessible. It's like an emotional aphasia. You vaguely and clearly know the feeling, and you may even see the words, but you can't transform those words into verbiage to save your life.

For many of my students, the sharing of an experience feels like their lives are dependent on saying it "just right." To add some anxiety to misery, I often accompany safety with stressful role-playing, in both-and fashion, by blocking attempts to "make nice-nice" or "say it perfectly" or "wait until I figure it out." I want them to say whatever comes to mind in that moment. Still, storytelling has these fits and starts that do not always lend to creating safety or depth of exploration, and that is where writing comes in.

Journaling allows for individuals to take a deeper look at their reactions to the story they tell or are telling in real time. To write one's story is to bring a self-critical eye to an event that clashes across emotional, behavioral, and intellectual expressions. By definition, writing is done alone. I have no one else to critique or support my risk taking but me as I write. People can take notes about themselves without the gaze of others. Memory is more accessible and less under attack when you are recounting experiences in writing, so details to these experiences can become more salient. In writing, while I can change the story in ways that privilege my actions in the experience, I can perhaps also be more revealing and honest about my failures.

Poetry, Letters, and Essays as Journaling

After years of conducting research in PWS, I came to the frustrating conclusion that I had become an enabler of racial elephantism or contracted a severe form of systemic racial avoidance. I had no one else to be angry at but me. I was in denial about how much racial politics was mucking up the data collection and blocking the research questions we were trying to answer. I was particularly angry at myself for acquiescing to the niceness in the schools and not asking tougher questions about some obvious racial conflicts. So I wrote an essay about my frustration.

So as I reread this essay while writing this book, I became reenergized and began to remember how stressed I was at the time and when rereading it. My stress score was a 10 at the time I wrote the essay. It was an 8 after I reread it in preparation for this book. The stress would affect me mostly in my stomach area as a nagging tension and tightness and would eventually move upward to get clogged somewhere around my throat. What I realized through writing this is that I felt powerless to do anything about my being an enabler when in fact most of my frustration could be explained at not speaking out either loudly or boldly enough to challenge the racial inertia and resistance I had experienced. This essay helped me stop acquiescing and led me to plan the kinds of confrontation I would use to alert schools to their racial blindness.

Educators cannot be afraid of others taking offense at our writing or our leadership and expect to develop self-appraisal skills. I wrote before speaking because I did not want to have to worry about what other people would think about being in the jungle of PWS. The choice of sharing can be a difficult one, but the process of journaling involves reliving experiences of shame and fear and feeling triumphant in giving up the enabling role and of choosing to not remain blind to racial tensions in schools and relationships. That acquiescence to the racial elephant in this case was to pretend that no racial stress existed for me in this work, when it obviously did. I notice that I'm shocked and invigorated by the boldness of assertion here. I'm stunned by how much over the last decade I've integrated this in my speech, teaching, and presentations more. I'm also convicted more when I catch myself being too polite at some emotional cost, simply for the sake of keeping others from being uncomfortable, which is really about *me* being less uncomfortable or racially stressed.

Writing Letters to Confront Racial Hierarchy in PWS

I've been discussing the importance of appraising the racial stress I experienced in doing research in PWSs, but what about appraising the racial stress in others? I once worked with a PWS by providing some daylong diversity training sessions around racial politics in schools, and after my first visit, the administrative team of mostly White faculty and educators was disappointed. They wanted more sophisticated diversity training that pushed the envelope and matched their own sense of maturity and growth on these matters. The trouble was that the school had so few students of color, even in the elementary school, that their racial diversity was nonexistent, with little chance for serious change over the next decade. I couldn't understand the disappointment except to say I didn't see how they would implement what I shared with them. The White alumni of the school were eagerly politicking to get their children into the few coveted openings in elementary school such that future numerical diversity would be next to impossible. If this wasn't Whiteness privilege in its most pristine state, then I didn't know what was.

I promised to return for a second visit, but in a lengthy letter before returning, I challenged them, suggesting that they wanted the appearance of diversity through their professional development but lacked the commitment to changing their school policies in direct actions that they claimed to want and would be supported by the training I had delivered. They wanted diversity in idea but not in action—"crops without plowing up the ground." They wanted a certificate of accomplishment without actually challenging their own school's decisions on admitting very few students of color. I returned to a much more attentive audience but my hope for serious change was diminished, given their reckoning of the costs of making stronger diversity actions in admissions, let alone curriculum. Nevertheless, I identified three barriers to these educational leaders in demonstrating a serious commitment to diversity in their school. In my experience of consulting with PWS, these barriers are fairly common challenges and include (1) leaving unresolved the conflict between the self-interest of the PWS and its goals for improving diversity; (2) proposing a vague and amorphous definition of diversity without actionable steps for diversity programming; and (3) creating little to no time to address the self-interest conflict or the amorphous diversity definition dilemmas. Below is an excerpt from the letter I wrote to them:

> One major barrier I see is the idea that you want diversity in your admissions, but to do so would mean the rejection of an alumnus's child or a friend of an alumnus's child (most likely to be wealthy and white) and also a rejection of potential monetary resources to the school in the now and the future. If this isn't the largest elephant in the room, please explain how and why it is not. It's a major pipeline concern. Lower school is one of the most powerful ways to project diversity in the future. If the majority of students are alumni students, what's the percentage? Who knows this info among the faculty, parents, administrators, and who doesn't? Pipeline through lower school by creating lifers is not foolproof by any means which is why retention dynamics require their own focus (again still requires a clear diversity agenda) and resources.
>
> This barrier hit me more after I left you than when I was there with you. You have the biggest reason in the world to not accept students who are poor or of a particular ethnic or racial background who also happen not to have resources. Start here. I may be underestimating or overestimating how much a barrier this is. Now you may say, "We have significant numbers of American racial minorities coming in 9th grade." To which I would say, "What do those numbers look like?" "What's the attrition rate like over the high school years for those ethnic/racial minorities?" "What are the income levels/issues of those students?" "Who is privileged by these dynamics and who is at risk?" "Who does not fit into our view of your school?" "Who do we make sure not to admit based on past experiences with ethnic/racial minorities?"
>
> A second major barrier is that your written definition of diversity (or the paragraphs to explain it in more detail) doesn't make clear the different political dynamics and priorities that you are facing at your school. You still haven't decided that you want to differentiate international from American-born students in your calculations. Despite what is required of you from other professional organizations, your schoolwide decisionmaking on this matter seems unresolved. Why is this important? It's only important if you believe that *matriculation*, *retention*, and *recruitment* issues with international students are different than American-born ethnic/racial groups. If you do not feel there are differences, then combining the numbers makes sense. But if you do feel there are differences, we should rethink how those differences require different strategies in each of those three areas.
>
> A third barrier is that you are too busy to have the dialogues necessary to address barriers 1 and 2. This is true for many of the schools

I have visited. One cultural value in most independent schools is that being busy is part of our identities BUT this busyness allows us to not reflect on what we do or deal with thorny issues like diversity or celebrate our development and growth. . . . To be busy means some issues will be foreground and others will become background and others still will be periphery or off the radar. This is human and natural. I think diversity is a peripheral topic within your school, not foreground. But if this is a choice rather than an "Oops," then that would make it more honest. To state that "we don't have the time to address this" is a slight copout. To say that "we have very little time and it is not a priority now because . . ." is more honest and allows the hearer (student, teachers, teachers of color, parents of students of color) to make an informed decision about your school. BUT, as a group you can't make these statements or decisions until you come to grips with what YOU all mean by diversity and abide by that definition.

The challenge for me when I look back at this letter is that while I was talking about the privilege of Whiteness, I never said this in the letter. I'm surer now that I would mention Whiteness if I had another chance, but I think they got the point then. But it does beg the question, "How direct should one be in teaching about or raising to attention the politics of Whiteness to PWS, knowing most leaders will resist and reject the idea altogether?" Facing that fear is a constant struggle in doing this research. I did feel as if I was rewriting the script of the dialogue that usually happens, and confronting the usual disconnect and discomfort between diversity trainer and school staff audience. Speaking directly to this discomfort was healing for me in that once finished, I felt I had assertively voiced my challenge of the Whiteness privilege.

When I was a junior, nontenured faculty member, I was stressed. The support I received from the two African American women faculty was immeasurable to my success. Still, there were unique racial experiences as the only Black male that left me isolated. Disagreeing with White male colleagues was a recurring type of encounter. If I challenge others, will that hurt my tenure chances, future, and emotional health? If I don't speak up, will I lose my dignity, my intellectual niche, or my emotional health? I remember the moment I refused to stress about the issue any more. I made a concerted decision to speak assertively despite the racial stress reactions I noticed in myself and my colleagues. I wrote and published a poem about one such encounter (Stevenson, 2011). An excerpt from the full poem is listed at the beginning of this chapter.

The incident involved a discussion with two White colleagues in public (street corner) in which I disagreed with one and raised my voice ever so slightly (my view, about a 4 on a scale of 1 to 10, with 10 being "shouting") to that one colleague, who immediately walked away from me. Upon asking the other colleague about what happened, he explained that the "walk-away" was out of fear that I might hurt him physically. I then decided to follow up further with the fearful colleague and ask why he had walked away in the middle of the street corner, my sentence, and my carefully articulated argument. So I followed him down the street, which frightened him more. I describe this event in ways to express my angst at being misinterpreted but also my wish for a "do-over." Mostly, I examine my emotional reappraisal of the stressful experience of facing and assertively challenging Whiteness. Another excerpt reflects the struggle to say exactly that inappropriate thing:

> I dreamt my whole life for this kind of rift.
> For when a colleague would lift up his hand
> to me in thought, word, or deed.
> To put me in my place, just so I could erase
> the years of politeness and slap the taste out
> of his proverbial eloquence.
> Enough of the words and the dance.
> Time for that fast talker to pray that I don't forget
> what time it is or remember where my secret anger is kept.
> (Stevenson, 2011, p. 182)

By emotionally processing this incident with others, I realized it was a seminal moment in my decision to be myself with and trust my White colleagues. I believed that few would be able to appreciate my racial difference in presence, my racial allegiance in identity, my racial knowledge in scholarship, and most of all, my racial assertiveness in voice. I was mostly right. Gaining tenure became less important than self-alienation as I concluded that there would have been greater detriment to my emotional well-being had I not begun to speak up. I struggled with staying quiet among colleagues who expressed their stereotypical views on racial inferiority. Having been a junior academic fly on the wall for 5 years, I collected many stories and statements made by colleagues. Central to my decision to speak up was the realization that although I was often angry about these racial politics, I could resolve my anger by conducting culturally relevant research that allowed me to measure and write about and on behalf of many others who struggle with racial microaggressions in relationships (Stevenson, 2002).

I remembered and cataloged both context and content and tried to process these experiences, feebly at times, into some cogent expression. This poem was part of it, but it started as a raw and angry essay—one I was too afraid to share publicly, and still am. But it led to the writing of many more essays related to my struggle in doing research and working in PWS. I have had my beliefs on mistrusting colleagues both confirmed and disconfirmed, but in journaling, I've learned to see now what I couldn't see then and how I've reappraised the moment. I also came to the conclusion that I don't want this racial distrust to ruin my mission or mojo. I came to a resolution in the end of the poem that embraced my need to confront the elephant of Whiteness with my colleagues while also collaborating with those who could handle this confrontation without running away.

Journaling, letter-writing, and poetry allow us to see and appraise our own elephants of racial stress by freeze-framing them and putting in slow motion our stories of racial encounters, the feelings we have about them, and, more important, what we want to say in response. These writing efforts allow us to visit these encounters from different angles, perhaps even in 360-degree fashion, rotating the experience ever so slightly to capture elements invisible before. My students will often complain that they are not good poets, as if their fear of my critique is enough to opt out of doing this exercise and write a bland paper on racism instead. But the writing is not as much about becoming a poet or author as it is about using poetry as a tool of excavation and discovery. What I hear in my students' requests for exemption is the angst at having to reexperience their feelings of incompetence in racially stressful moments. This doubt and incompetence is unearthed best through journal reflection and poetry writing because there is no crowd to humiliate the writer. There is no one else to blame (except me as the professor and grader) for exposing this shame of racial incompetence. There are fewer arguments for using avoidance of these racial moments and reflections when my students use journal writing and poetry to describe their racial feelings. And yes, while writing is done alone, and we often write as if someone is watching us or will read it and critique us, a professor is not a crowd.

So while storytelling lends itself to self-observation, I believe journal, letter, and poetry writing can increase one's ability to appraise stress levels in racial encounters. Although the first two stops on the safari are introspective in emphasis, the last three expect individuals to apply these learned self-awareness and stress appraisal skills *during* social interactions and conflicts, not before.

RACIAL ENCOUNTER REAPPRAISAL: RELAXATION IN-THE-MOMENT (ITM) OF RACIAL THREAT

Racial Stress and Coping Reappraisal (Self-Care/Correction) involves using relaxation during stressful encounters and may seem counterintuitive, particularly if one is learning how to take notes on one's emotional reactions. Recasting racial stress requires a deeper investigation of one's story. It involves self-appraisal, self-care and mindfulness of the racial stress that lies in one's positive and negative thoughts, behavioral missteps and triumphs, verbal assertions or gaffs, and bodily spastic involuntary or controlled movements. The queries of interest include, How well can I use relaxation to reduce my stress reactions to encounters "in the moment" of the encounter? How well do I recast a threatening encounter into a challenge? How well do I ask for help and access resources on racial literacy when I'm threatened?

Racial stress reappraisal or racial mindfulness is the goal of the third stop on the racial literacy safari. Racial stress reappraisal and relaxation take no more energy and work than racial mindlessness or colorblindness take in race relations etiquette. It's like the saying, "It takes fewer muscles to smile than to frown." Recasting racial stress involves applying this mindfulness in the moment of the encounter. An example is when a White student makes a racially awkward statement (for example, during a U.S. history class session on enslavement, a White student mentions, "I wouldn't mind having slaves around to help me get a lot of work done"). What could the teacher do? Instead of ignoring the comment, the teacher first breathes and exhales (BE), calculates his or her stress level, locates his or her bodily reaction to that comment, communicates the fear that he or she has about the costs and benefits of engaging in this classroom moment in self-talk, then speaks his or her thoughts. A racially competent response might be to open up to the class with "Class, what just happened here?" or "I'm a little uncomfortable at the last comment that was made but I see that you were just talking freely without thought as to how others might feel. So I'd like to get others' thoughts about the costs and benefits of enslavement."

Relaxation

Relaxation during racially stressful conflicts represents the essence of the "both-and" concept and being able to listen to one's inner peace and mission can be infectious. The benefits to hearing others' voices and meaning despite the distress or noise in the situation are immeasurable in building trust. If the first lie in racial conflict avoidance is to yourself, the first step in healing is listening to one's inner voice. Although I list this third among the strategies, it's actually the first skill to teach, so that folks use it during all the other steps in the journey. Relaxation during stress can increase one's courage to face racial threats.

Racial stress reappraisal is defined by reducing one's stress during the racial conflict, otherwise known as *self-care* or *self-correction*. The key question that individuals must ask themselves are "If I notice stress on my body, can I reduce the stress and adjust my reactions to the encounter instead of avoiding the encounter altogether?" The strategy to reach this goal is *relaxation skills building or mindfulness*. Although listening is an important theme throughout the model, self-care is essential. Listening is difficult if fight, flight, and fright reactions are occurring. The fear of public humiliation from mishandling a racial encounter or saying the wrong thing can block out one's ability to hear or see.

To address the fear of public humiliation during workshops, I will sometimes ask teachers, counselors, and students to role-play a racial encounter and say the most inappropriate thing that reflects their basest feelings or fears of the interaction. With teachers, the most challenging racial encounter is when an angry Black parent walks into the parent-teacher conference session to complain about how racist the teacher is in mistreating the student. (Now, I hope that's not because I've just told the story about my mother's forthrightness in the grocery store, but you never know.) Anyway, this scenario appears to engender a host of fears about not saying the wrong thing or feeling incompetent but not admitting to it. Still, the most inappropriate thought or statement could be "I better call the police before this parent hurts me." By expressing the honest but inappropriate statement, one can experience the worst level of stress. The strategy is to practice breathing and exhaling while under stress, thus rendering it less incapacitating.

Calm in the Racial Chaos

The lessons from neuroscience research on racial perceptions are helpful because they explain how listening is impossible if fright, fight, and flight reactions are ignited. Through relaxation, one's physiological stress reactions can be managed so that listening and seeing racial blind spots in storytelling and journaling and daily living become possible. Thus, individuals can begin to experience success in their reframing and reappraisal of racially stressful conflict. Primarily, I expect readers to try and reframe racially conflictual moments that are tsunami-like and deemed impossible to resolve into moments that are mountain climbing experiences (difficult, perhaps, but not insurmountable). Once reappraisal of the racial stress is shifted downward, individuals and institutions can develop self-efficacy beliefs such as "I believe I can be a teacher/student/parent/school that does not avoid racial conflicts" or, in the case of the angry Black parent, "I believe I can listen through a parent's anger at me about their child's mistreatment that the parent believes is due to racism."

So how does one relax in the middle of racial chaos? Breathing and exhaling. There are a host of mindfulness strategies that can be employed, some from yoga and physical exercise (which is my favorite form of mindfulness). But in the moment of perceived battle, individuals need simply to know how to breathe and exhale (BE). Sure, it would be great if we could prepare for all racial situations (something we will talk about later), but it's their predictability that raises the level of stress. Breathing and exhaling—and the competence to do so at any time, under any circumstance—is a gift. The youth and parents I have worked with over many years have learned to use this simple skill to open up their hearing, pause before reacting (underreacting or overreacting), and speak clearly or give a confident response during an encounter.

The activities of storytelling and journaling may raise stress levels and inhibit processing. So I advocate for using relaxation strategies during those activities. As soon as racial risk taking through storytelling and journaling occurs, I make it a point to ask, "Did you notice anything about yourself while you were telling or journaling your story about the racial jungle or the racial elephants in the classroom, conversation, backroom, faculty meeting, assembly, parent conference, discipline council, IEP planning, or hallway or while growing up?" If you are storytelling or journaling or writing poetry on your own, jot down notes about your emotional reactions (calculate, locate, and communicate the stress or the reactions experienced in the moment).

It is possible to relax while you are stressed from racial conflicts seen and unseen, that happened, that are happening or about to happen, and that may expose the weakest aspects of your character in front of lots of people. What I expect to happen when individuals begin to reappraise racial stress in schooling relationships is that they

1. Begin to see the racial glass as half-full, rather than half-empty.
2. Ask for help or resources to manage racial stress.
3. Look for trustworthy friends or colleagues to share their fears.
4. View racial conflicts as mountains worth climbing, not insurmountable obstacles.
5. Increase confidence or racial self-efficacy beliefs.
6. Can identify and detail skill challenges in classrooms, parent-teacher relationships, collegiality, with students.
7. Develop "allies" or a posse of racial/ethnic support systems.

As individuals become competent at relaxation and listening during racial conflicts, the fourth step of racial encounter engagement becomes more feasible.

RACIAL ENCOUNTER ENGAGEMENT: DEBATING RACIAL ILLITERACY IN SELF AND OTHERS

Racial Encounter Engagement (Self-Control) involves the initial engagement with racial conflicts in social spaces. Self-control comes from practicing healthy comeback lines and responses in debating competition. Relevant queries of interest include, "How well did I engage (appraise and reappraise) a racially stressful encounter? How often and how well did I practice debating opposing arguments to R/E inferiority and use healthy coping responses to racially stressful encounters I face in school?"

What if teachers allowed the tense classroom discussions about race to continue and guided them toward critical thinking moments rather than change the topic? Conflicts would arise naturally in the classroom and, with careful leadership and skills-building, students could assess their emotions and fears without putting them away. Teaching individuals to identify and then speak their voice in the middle of the racial conflict could become a practice, an expectation, a curricular goal. This skill is usable anywhere outside of the classroom. Debating about racial matters and stereotypes is the best strategy to prepare for taking the risk to engage racial encounters.

Debating builds character and self-control as individuals determine whether they can demonstrate courage under fire. Debating requires a regulation of emotions and a show of endurance under duress. This kind of courage cannot be grasped without struggle. On occasion, I demand that participants become as combative as possible. This test of courage is more powerful than teaching a lesson on racial self-control. Debating racial stereotypes allows one to have the argument that was never had and to practice rejecting stereotypes.

Once when visiting a gathering of several predominantly White public and private schools, I was giving a talk on racial literacy to African American parents. The mood of the room was electric. Through the storytelling process, many had examples of racial stress they wanted to resolve. One parent stood up and discussed the pain she experienced when her oldest daughter, now in college, and who was an alumna of the local school, chose to not go to her senior class prom because no one would ask her to go. Black girls were rarely asked and this humiliation was hard to bear. The pain was reignited as she expressed fears that her youngest daughter in middle school might confront the same challenge.

Other parents began to weigh in with similar stories and fears of what to do about several dilemmas. One, they felt that Black girls were lowest on the social popularity totem pole, with White males at the top. Black girls would rarely be asked to go to the prom by White males. The Black boys, next to the bottom of the pole, were still prized, particularly if they were athletes, but because there were so few, the choices were slim to none. Another factor complicating this fact was that many of these Black boys were known since kindergarten or 1st grade and thus were more like brothers than dates you would take to the prom.

Another dilemma was that the Black girls in these schools were reluctant to date outside of their race because they were more attracted to Black boys. Most of the Black boys had no such restriction when it came to dating cross-racially, and they would rarely be left without a date for the prom. Now, most people I've asked report that their prom was a horrible experience, but it's the freedom and choice to have that horrible experience that was eluding the Black girls. What makes the prom so special is the drama of preparation for the night, the anticipation. It's like opening a gift box. What is in the box is much less exciting than the emotion of the unwrapping—the shopping for the right dress, the photo-taking drama, and the hundreds of pictures at different houses and sites, the family members and neighbors who dote, the teenage boys or girls who ogle and lust, the limousine service (for some), and of course, the pampering. The prep is often more exciting than the prom itself.

As these dilemmas were laid out, it became clear that the Black girls were more vulnerable than any other group in PWS and this pain was palpable in the room. Short of taking one's relative, there appeared to be no options. Several mothers started crying about it as they recounted trying to calm down their daughters and make them feel better about missing out on the prom.

Now I thought the question they posed was important but essentially wrong. It was "How do we change the chances for Black girls in PWS to go to the prom, by improving their social position or by increasing diversity in the school so that there will be more Black male choices?" The unspoken question was, "How does it feel to be a problem as helpless parents—who can't make your beautiful daughters more beautiful to others in a PWS?" This question was wrong because it didn't address the fundamental challenge of the elephant of Whiteness staring them in the face. That is, they were not ready to acknowledge how the Whiteness hierarchy of beauty that existed in their schools influenced dating patterns. This elephant assumed that being White was more beautiful than being Black. and that acquiescing to that hierarchy in any way was an endorsement of the notion that "White is more beautiful and Black is not." Better questions included (1) "How much sooner before one's senior year at a PWS might we consider that Black girls have a different schooling experience?" And if (1) is true, then (2) "How might we prepare them to reject the absurdity of a racialized hierarchy of attractiveness and popularity, where they are helpless to change their position at the lowest rung?"

I suggested that until they came to grips (debate) with the more fundamental and painful reality that being a Black girl in a PWS includes facing these negative and ridiculous microaggressions that assert, "Black is not beautiful," the default coping strategy of inaction would always end with a visceral sense of helpless anger. I suggested that the numbers of schools represented at the talk could agree to plan for the senior prom at least 3 years earlier and invite a consortium of schools to develop a same-race network of students in order to broaden the pool of eligible dates. This would hold other schools accountable to the idea that Whiteness must be planned for—for any issue in which one's social status might be stigmatized, stressful, or exclusionary. Still, to do this kind of planning involves seeing the elephant of racial hierarchy and making hard choices about responding to that insult. Several questions can be used to trigger healthy engagement and debate of racial stereotyping, conflict, or Whiteness ideology in a school setting:

- How do I avoid running from stress before, during, and after the R/E conflicts?
- How do I not avoid R/E conflicts by admitting to my fears and ask for help?
- How do I survive R/E conflicts by affirming the worldviews of others?
- How do I put more energy into listening and not reacting to my fears?
- How do I create arguments to challenge stereotypes and inferiority?
- How do I publicly present my arguments to challenge stereotyping?
- How do I develop healthy, witty, protective comeback lines to racial insults?

To speak boldly during conflict is a risky endeavor, but it gets easier if educational leaders, teachers, and parents can help students prepare for predictable racial encounters and practice raising questions and opposing opinions to an issue, all the while using relaxation strategies and mindfulness to observe the sensitivities of others who may feel differently. This preparation, practice, and vigilance can trigger more meaningful moments of agreement or disagreement about racial dilemmas. Moreover, with less hostility or self-interest preservation in these dilemmas, individuals and groups may be better prepared for the final stage of racial literacy development: encounter resolution.

HEALTHY COMEBACK LINES: FACING RACIAL STEREOTYPES HEAD ON

Debating can also occur in a moment of social interaction rather than in a longer dialogue or forum of argumentation. In fact, having a quick retort or comeback line to a racial insult or microaggression in a social moment can be stress-relieving. Racial socialization research suggests that a healthy response to racial stress requires some form of buffering. Specifically, the four key functions of parental racial socialization—*affirmation, protection, reappraisal, and negotiation*—are important. The *affirmation* and *protection* of racial coping self-efficacy (the belief that one can successfully negotiate racially stressful encounters) can lead to the reappraisal of racial stress (reducing the stress in the moment of the encounter using breathing and relaxation exercises). In reaction to racial stress, individuals are under pressure to resolve these moments with skillful competence, a dignified response, or at least a witty comeback line.

If it is true that Black parents, like educational leaders, are struggling to see or disrupt the dance of racial encounter and avoidance in PWS, then leadership and parenting must change. Survival can no longer be the battle objective for racial justice. Schooling cannot prepare children for the world with education that prepares them simply to exist as "survivors." They must excel in learning, not just keep pace. Several recasting approaches to the politics of racial dancing include knowing how racial stress influences underachievement, expecting racial backlash in schools, being prepared for racial microaggressions, and using emotionally healthy comeback lines and thoughts when caught in a dehumanizing racial encounter.

What are emotionally healthy comeback lines? These are planned and practiced responses to the predictable racially avoidant, assaultive, or ignorant microaggressions that are likely to endanger individuals' emotional, psychological, or physical well-being. They are not simply statements but also actions and behaviors. If one is being stopped and harassed by a cop while walking or standing on a street corner, it is probably not a healthy thing to respond to that harassment with "F— you, officer" or running away, especially if you happen to be male and Black or Latino. That would be an unhealthy comeback line. However, respectful responses that can maintain one's dignity without humiliating oneself can be practiced. Healthy comeback lines are cathartic and reduce tension, especially if humor can be injected. These comeback lines are recasting strategies, since they have the potential to reduce the "sting" of the racial encounter.

This reduction is important because the enormous amount of racial stress experienced in keeping this dance going (police racial brutality is justified by my acquiescence or my rebellion where the former is pretending there is no harassment and the latter is overreacting without realizing it to be a potential "do or die" situation) is significantly more emotionally debilitating than shifting my role.

For 8 years, I have lived as faculty master at the W.E.B. DuBois College House at 3900 Walnut Street in West Philadelphia. My office at the Graduate School of Education is at 3700 Walnut Street. Often running to make appointments, I notice people's fear reactions. It so happens that a Black man running down the street scares people. In these moments of running (in slow motion), I see a host of emotional reactions as I run behind, beside, and eventually beyond them. These recurring and predictable set of facial, body, and emotional images flash before my eyes.

As a response to these images, I am of two minds. One mind invokes the coping strategies of my father, which is to pray for the fearful ones, hope

God heals their fear, and keep running. The other mind involves invoking the spirit of my mother and commenting on every look with "What you lookin' at?" or "What, you never seen a Black man running before?" I've never tried shouting this comeback line—"Black man running!" but I've been tempted to on many occasions.

Sometimes, I may be so moved to slow down to a fast-paced walk. But I found out that running fast and then slowing down quickly looks creepy to the fearful and makes them more scared, as if I'm about to pounce. Fast or slow doesn't stop the fear. Other times I say, "Excuse me" at least 10 feet behind as they hear me coming and watch as the adrenaline rush in their brains shoots skyward. Then I ponder sharing my business card or vitae as I run pass—or maybe I should just wear a sign listing my accomplishments. Because, of course, if they knew I was professor at Penn, with a PhD in clinical psychology and 25 years of working with abused and depressed children and broken and impoverished families, and that I owned a dog once, that would be more than enough to allay their worries.

Unfortunately, there is not enough time to explain what kind of Black man I am in the 1–2 minutes it takes me to run two blocks (okay, I am fast, but maybe it takes 4 minutes). And then there is the bigger problem—that talking to them and interrupting will increase their fear reactions. Still, I can't pretend that I don't see the clutching of the purse, the shifting of the gait, the surprise in the eyes, or the heavy gasps of breathing in the body, neck, and shoulders. Perhaps it has nothing to do with my Black man–ness. Perhaps I'm too paranoid? The question they ask without saying is, "How does it feel to be a problem—that might hurt me?"

So I have on occasion decided to "speak truth to stereotypes" without cursing people out. One day as I was running to get to my office, I did not slow down or walk slowly, but the fear reactions were especially pronounced as I walked into the elevator in my office building. Instead of pretending I didn't see anything, I decided to speak: "Hey folks, I'm not going to steal anything from you all today, okay? I'm just late." I thought this was funny and I still laugh when I think about it. Not so for my elevator mates. In fact, the slew of reactions to my comment ranged much more dramatically than when I didn't speak. In addition to the usual pupil dilation and involuntary body shaking, I saw bizarre "both-and" fear reactions. Some people were both relieved and guilty while others reacted with relief and denial or a nervous under-the-breath chuckle as if *I* was strange for suggesting they thought I was going to assault them. Then some showed an emotional and physiological incongruous reaction: being literally afraid, then relieved, and then pretending through feeble control of both facial and body movements to not appear fearful or relieved at what just happened. It's funny to me but as I tried to control my spontaneous guffaw at such plastic spasticity,

I just stood smiling, looked upward at the ceiling as the slowest elevator in the world took us all uncomfortably to the next floor, got off, and as I left, said, "Have a nice day."

The stereotype that the actors in this story are dancing around is that of the "potentially dangerous or criminal Black male." The therapeutic benefits of a comeback line includes making visible the hidden racial tension surrounding an unspoken stereotype, the practice of assertively calling out the stereotype and the tension it creates, the repositioning of the stereotype as residing in the minds of observers rather than the observed, the rejection of the internalization of the insult of the stereotype, and the increasing of empowerment for similar racial moments in the future.

RACIAL ENCOUNTER RESOLUTION: ROLE-PLAYING FOR DIMINISHING RACIAL THREAT

Racial Encounter Resolution (Self-Assertiveness) involves bringing to completion the psychological effects of racial stress and problem-solving the racial conflicts in schooling relationships. Role-play is the strategy to accomplish resolution. Queries designed to bring about racial assertiveness include, "How well did I practice and resolve this racial encounter through role-play? How well did I try and retry to use racial literacy skills in my school during stressful racial encounters? How well did I continue to calculate, locate, and communicate my stress levels while role-playing an encounter? How well did I practice and use a healthy comeback line in my response to the racial encounter?"

In this final step, resolution of the racial encounter is the goal. Because a win-win outcome is expected, participants in the racial encounter may not claim sole victory, but instead, should aim for mutual respect and compromise. Certainly, there can be victories in presenting one's argument more clearly and strongly. The key question here is, "Can we resolve racial/ethnic conflicts ethically and with confidence that we've both expressed deep-felt emotions and intellectual arguments, and listened to my partner's views at the same time?"

Role-Play

Acting out racial fears can help in regaining control of one's decision-making under duress. Racial stress undermines self-efficacy or belief in one's potential to create change or speak assertively in the moment of social interaction. Role-playing racially stressful scenarios allows one to recapture the emotional edge and not use the default strategy of being politically correct or stress over avoiding looking like the "angry Black whatever." One role-play example is staging a debate on the verity of stereotypes of beauty and racism for Black girls so they can challenge the implicit messages using language and arguments. Having the participants monitor their feelings, stress levels, and bodily reactions while rehearsing for the debate is a wonderful role-playing exercise. If mind-reading were a skill, perhaps you could know when and when not to appear as the "angry Black whatever." But none of us can read minds. But we can read patterns and see racial dances and choreograph different coping responses to the expected default coping positions. Getting your bold back is the healing dynamic of role-playing. Practicing for an actual encounter can build confidence in assertively speaking up against racial injustice.

This step involves practicing racial negotiation and self-expression skills where success is defined by the individual as not giving up on the resolution of the encounter. The racial conflict could be anywhere, in the classroom, the hallway, or the principal's office. Role-playing is likely to bring about resolution because as each person's framing of the encounter experience is the content of the role-play. Through practicing a variety of coping strategies, individuals can go back to the encounter context and try out the practiced skills taught. Encounter resolution doesn't mean that others in the encounter context embrace your worldview of the problem. It means that your worldview matters and that you can assertively express it, even if it is rejected by others. The resolution of racially stressful conflicts presuppose that it is ethically necessary to teach these skills. These are queries and strategies that are not exclusively usable for teacher inservice training, parent workshops, or educator continuing education experiences. These questions and frameworks can be used for training and evaluating racial literacy for youth as they engage the diverse world through field trips, community service learning projects, athletic events, youth racial equality conferences, and affinity groups. A host of racial stress management and literacy strategies and exercises has been consolidated into a diagram (see Figure 6.1). Think of these issues as curricular and educational where we ask the question, "What educational academic racial stress-reduction skills are our responsibility to teach youth?"

Rewriting Stereotypical Racial Scripts

For me, racial stress provides counselors, politicians, and educators with a practical way to change negative race relations toward healing and competence, primarily because there are so many options for reducing stress. There are fewer tangible ways to stop racism. We've discussed the emotional and physiological burden that individuals, particularly White individuals, feel when unsure about the expectations, rules, and competencies required in cross-racial dialogue and interaction. Theories of interracial anxiety reveal that fatigue from overregulation of one's psychological and physical resources is common, but that racial uncertainty triggers excessive emotional regulation, which leads to greater anxiety—a self-fulfilling prophecy of racial incompetence (Gudykunst, 1995) and potential social rejection (Stinson, Logel, Shepherd, & Zanna, 2011). These theories are helpful in pointing toward solutions that include mindfulness and cognitive-behavioral interventions.

Behavioral scripting has been found to reduce anxiety in Black-White interactions in diverse workplaces where anxiety and interracial conflicts can be high (Avery et al., 2009). Researchers have found that if you planned and practiced the effective behaviors in navigating racial conflicts in interracial interactions, you could reduce the anxiety of White participants and lead to more satisfying relationships. Avery and colleagues propose a study of behavioral scripting with the hypothesis that scripted interactions bring less stress than unscripted racial interactions:

> We propose that the effort associated with negotiating interactions without concrete social scripts should make interracial encounters particularly demanding and, therefore, anxiety-provoking (Blascovich et al., 2000). By contrast, the ease associated with negotiating a role-based script should reduce the psychological demands of intergroup contact, and, therefore, scripted intergroup interactions should be relatively less disquieting for nonstigmatized individuals. In short, higher levels of scripting should reduce the uncertainty regarding how to behave and how others will behave, thereby diminishing anxiety. (2009, p. 1384)

The authors continue by contrasting the use of scripting for a familiar versus a less familiar experience (Towles-Schwen & Fazio, 2003):

> Participants rated their anticipated willingness and comfort engaging in scenarios that had been identified in pretesting as being relatively scripted (e.g., serving a Black customer in a restaurant) and relatively unscripted (e.g., sitting in a crowded library at a table where a Black person is already seated). The more scripted the scenario, the more comfort participants *anticipated* in interacting with a Black individual. Extending these findings, the present work considers how comfortably White individuals *actually behave* during Black–White interracial, compared with same-race, interactions as a function of their roles during the encounter. (p. 1384)

This work is predicated on a host of factors, the most prominent of which is the power of nonverbal behaviors in revealing the discomfort during racial interactions that most cannot express, even if they are aware of them. This research on behavioral scripting has been most pronounced within employment settings for adults (Combs & Griffith, 2007), but I believe it's equally important for school settings, where the most crucial racially stressful encounters are teacher-student and teacher-parent dyads. Rewriting the racial scripts of stress and uncertainty during racial encounters in schools involves predicting and planning for fear reactions, nonverbal hesitance, and spastic eruptions. Moving from involuntary spastic eruptions to literate behavioral, intellectual, and emotional discourse in race relations is the goal of this work.

Racial literacy skills acquisition occurs when individuals are able, through practice, to successfully perform during these encounters. So, not only might parental racial socialization seek to help youth protect and affirm self-efficacy, reappraise racial stress, and negotiate racial conflicts, but it might also lead to the development and acquisition of skills that youth can use successfully in those racially stressful encounters.

CAN WE TALK? PILOTING A RACIAL LITERACY INTERVENTION IN THE CLASSROOM

My colleagues and I created a project called "Can We Talk? (CWT)" (Bentley, Thomas, & Stevenson, 2013). Its focus was to teach Black middle and high schoolers to identify and negotiate racial conflicts in school and classroom by increasing their Black history knowledge, racial stress management, and racial assertiveness skills. We used storytelling, journaling, relaxation, debating, and role-playing of the racial conflicts and their stressfulness as the methods to increase these skills. We found that many of the youth had little Black history knowledge (e.g., Emmett Till) or psychological understanding of that history on contemporary racial identity and politics (skin color discrimination and internalized racialism). But more important, we found that they had rarely or never discussed their feelings about Black history of tragedy (racial violence) and triumph (resilience despite tragedy).

In CWT, we've observed how difficult it is for some African American students in academically talented PWS to become aware of their feelings during cross-racial interactions (Bentley et al., 2013). I asked students to discuss incidents they perceived as racist or discriminatory during school days and in classrooms. The students recounted numerous experiences, and the more students discussed, the easier was the recall for other students present who initially couldn't remember any events. As a result of students' bravery in recounting uncomfortable experiences, I asked them how they felt about these events. Immediately, there was dead silence.

When I asked individual students about the event they described, some would respond as if I had spoken a different language. It took me a while to make sense of this until my colleagues Duane Thomas and Valerie Adams had the bright idea to write feeling words on the blackboard. Talking about your feelings is a language or skill in and of itself. Describing and recounting the racial microaggressions was difficult, but talking about feelings regarding those racial incidents was even harder. The process of talking about an individual's feelings about racial encounters was so primitive that sometimes the high schoolers were helped by simply pointing to or choosing one or two feelings among multiple choices. This process revealed both posttraumatic racial microaggression memory lapse and a racial microaggression emotional aphasia.

As opposed to seeing Black history as simply an information-sharing experience, it became clear that using that history as a trigger for emotionally processing contemporary racial discrimination was essential for addressing one element of racial avoidance—the numbing of one's emotional experience or witnessing of racial trauma. From the history lessons, Black boys and girls were encouraged to tell stories of oppression in their current schooling experiences, which we used to help them identify emotional reactions of anxiety, fear, and anger in their thoughts, their bodies and movements, and their words to each other.

Stress management was another key pillar of the CWT intervention, as students were asked to identify their feelings about racial conflicts (historical or contemporary) and the effects on their bodies, and to use relaxation and breathing to relax those stressed-out bodily effects. The assertiveness training involves having students respond differently in racially insulting conflicts they have shared from storytelling and journaling, by speaking phrases or comeback responses that (1) were not overreactions or underreactions to the insult; (2) demonstrated they understood the racial tension in the conflict; (3) would not put them in greater risk of school failure; and (4) empowered them to defend their dignity from insult.

An example of a resolved conflict includes the following. Let's say a Black female 10th-grader who was failing at French decided to withdraw from the class or disinvest and accept a low grade. She felt the French teacher did not like her because of her race and that this hampered their relationship. The student was also feeling overwhelmed by not knowing or using the language. So instead of asking for help, she continued to fail and withdrew from class and never spoke up. The CWT intervention would be to recall the racial microaggression experiences and process many of her feelings about them. We asked her to get out and say what she wanted to say (appropriate and inappropriate statements) about those different microaggressions. A mildly inappropriate comeback line would be, "I hate the racist look on your face whenever you call on me in class like I'm stupid or something!" The greater use of expletives to demean the perpetrator of the racial insult might constitute more impropriety, but in the name of practice, it's more important to get out honest feelings. An appropriate comeback line would be, "Sometimes it feels like you think I'm not smart enough to be in your class because I'm Black and it makes me sad and want to avoid you and not listen. Is that true?"

After accumulating a list of appropriate and inappropriate comeback phrases, it is important to debate the rightness and wrongness of the feelings that one is having. This helps youth feel empowered that some of their fears are not irrational and in fact have merit and should be protected and spoken. The debating can take the form of challenging the implicit racial slight or microaggression in the conflict or challenging one's own doubt about their right to defend their racial identity in the classroom or school or both. The use of role-playing her conversation with the teacher involves her choosing the appropriate comeback line that fits her style then practicing the comeback responses with boldness, clarity, and with the attitude most comfortable for her. One of my team members would play the role of "difficult French teacher" while the student played herself. For this student, the final step is to conduct the actual conversation with the teacher face-to-face but to do so speaking her concern about the racial slights with a request for help or tutoring in homework and class assignments, and to do so using French. This is an example of how we might move from storytelling to role-playing in helping Black students emotionally connect to the resilience in Black history, use stress management to emotionally process current racial microaggressions in school, and practice healthy comeback lines for perceived and actual racial conflicts in the classroom. With obvious differences in scope, focus, and classroom and school politics, we have conducted similar CWT interventions and racial literacy training in schools for teachers. CWT was an attempt to integrate recast theory, racial socialization research, and racial stress reduction into a classroom based intervention.

Stress reappraisal of a racial encounter can come from self-reflection, but it can also come from peers who self-disclose about similar dilemmas and sharing with youth how to reduce the stress of an encounter. This reappraisal and resolution includes affection (nurturance), protection (monitoring), and correction (accountability) statements from the peers. Often, students described interactions with teachers and peers to explain their disengagement with classroom activities. Here, a 9th-grade boy described his encounter with a White teacher in class (Bentley, Thomas, & Stevenson, 2013):

> *9th-Grader*: Can I give you an example? Like I'll be in class and I'll have my hand up the whole class, and it's like, "Don't look at me."
> *Male Classmate*: Exactly. [As he raises his head]
> *9th-Grader*: And the girl next to me is like, "What is your problem?"
> *Male Classmate*: She don't even have . . .
> *9th grader*: I have no problem; I'm a great man. I'm trying to do the best I can. But if you think I'm gonna acknowledge her or him just

because she is White, whatever. Then whatever. Like, why am I in this classroom? So, I just don't even want—like, so I just . . . that's why I don't even try anymore. . . . [He frowns in frustration as he looks at one of the CWT staff]

The 9th-grader's "giving up" is an ineffective strategy to manage his racial stress and cope with academic pressure. It will lead to failure, apathy, and withdrawal from classroom activities. His response is very common for African American boys who are daily struggling with the invisible social, gender, and racial script expectations of proving worth by feebly "fighting back" against one's public humiliation. He isn't saying, "I'm scared of being rejected by my teacher" or "I was hurt by her rejection of me in the classroom" or "I wonder why she wouldn't call on me when I raised my hand. Did she do that because she doesn't like me or because I'm _____?"

His classmate, Brother 2, corroborated his story ("Exactly") and affirmed his friend's classroom rejection experience. This is very important because there were multiple racial encounters in that one classroom incident. Both boys experienced that moment as stressful. As Brother 1 tells the story of his racial encounter, Brother 2 raises his head to acknowledge the incident happened while he states, "Exactly." He too appears to be reliving the encounter while he is affirming his friend, Brother 1. Brother 1 is feeling rejected and copes with a reaction that ostensibly appears to project strength, dignity, and power. He states, "I'm a great man." This response reveals the gender script demand response when he is humiliated. He is trying to protect his ego and gender identity from insult ("I'm a great man") as if to answer another "elephant" question that no one has asked. Once we ponder what that other racial or gender script elephant question is ("Are you a wimp or a punk?"), then the coping answer to the perceived rejection makes sense.

Yet many might ask why this would be considered a racially stressful encounter and not simply a manhood stressful encounter. One obvious answer to this query is based on Brother 1's response, which is, "But if you think I'm gonna acknowledge her or him just because she is White, whatever." But the other answer is that even had he not spoken it, the script that he is following has gender and racial politics written all over it. His giving up in the classroom is the first step of an invisible and familiar dance between him and the teacher, the classroom, and the school. That is the "when rejected, I withdraw from school to protect my racial and manhood dignity" dance.

These interactions illuminate how gender and racial rejection sensitivity dynamics play out in stressful school encounters. But what happens next after the initial conversation reveals the power of intentionally engaging racial elephants in the classroom, not only by teachers, but by peers. Interestingly, an 11th-grade female student provided encouraging feedback to the 9th-grader as he reported feeling rejected and dejected:

> Don't give up because you can still [catch] up to your homework. You know what I'm trying to say. Like you still go home, "You don't have to answer me now so I'm gonna prove you wrong, like I got everything right." So don't give up, don't. Because then you'll just be like what they expect.

Another female student states, "Sometimes, it's not how you failed, but it's the fact THAT you failed." This statement is to alert the two "brothers" about how the "matrix" or "world of White schooling" works should they decide to follow the script of "whatever." She is racially affirming and protective as she teaches them how to reappraise the academic stress and conflict they face. She is also teaching them how to maintain presence and voice in the classroom. Without an explicit focus on facing racial conflict, these supportive interactions and reframing from peers are unlikely to occur. Further feedback from a college student reappraises the tsunami-level (9 out of 10) school withdrawal stress of the encounter to one of mountain climbing (7 out of 10). A college student continues to chime in:

> At the same time, I think it's just something I just realized this last year. Your grades are absolutely no reflection of how intelligent you are. I think that's something you definitely have to take to your heart and think about real seriously. You should definitely try your hardest to like, do well, I guess academically in that sense, but that. You are clearly an intelligent brother without it.

Sister 1 proposes more recasting and hints at a healthy comeback line:

> But at the end of the day, like they still determine your future, you gotta play both sides. "Yeah, I'm smart. I shouldn't have to prove it to you, but I am going to prove it to you. Because without you, I can't get to where I want."

The 8th-grade boys listen intently to their "oldheads" (older adults or youth who impart knowledge or wisdom and viewed by some youth as having more experience in life) and take to heart what is being said to them. This is evident in their intense focused looks at their oldheads, the nodding of their heads in agreement, and the relaxation and hope in their faces despite a desperately frustrating classroom experience. This is a resolution in that the boys are less tormented by the racial microaggressions of the teacher and have been given a set of coping responses to address this situation should it arise in the future.

In this CWT example (Bentley et al., 2013), we see the potential internalization, countering, rejection, and resolution of a racial inferiority moment for a Black male student in a PWS as peers challenge and help him reappraise his stressful racial encounter with a teacher. Role-playing and rewriting the script of this racial encounter would further this resolution by having the boys replay their roles in this encounter but try different comeback lines (both healthy and unhealthy), process their emotions about those new comeback lines, choose the lines they are most comfortable with, and rehearse them many times.

The first two racial literacy development strategies (storytelling and journaling) are primarily focused on the reduction of stress that occurs after racial encounters, while the latter two strategies (debating and role-playing) are focused on the engagement and resolution of conflicts that arise before subsequent racial encounters. The middle strategy of relaxation must be used before, after, and during racial encounters. These five strategies are meant to help individuals recast racial stress, increase racial self-efficacy, and demonstrate racial assertiveness during racial encounters in school, neighborhood, with family, and at work where relationships are influenced by the stereotypes of racial inferiority. In this case, these strategies are designed to undermine, counter, and reject an individual's acquiescence to or acceptance of the narrative of Black life expendability. Although this work includes mindfulness strategies (breathing and exhaling; focusing on emotions during stressful encounters; observing body reactions), without knowledge and competence about how to negotiate racially stressful matters, mindfulness alone is insufficient. Racial socialization or coaching one through the steps necessary to navigate racial stress and conflicts is a better way of framing this type of practice and triggering one to engage in the following self-talk: "Believing in the narratives of racial inferiority or the inevitable expendability of Black life is someone else's problem and I don't have to accept it for me." Knowledge and competence to resolve specific racial conflicts are necessary. One can't be mindful of stress-reduction strategies and remain clueless about the politics of racial conflicts and expect to make significant changes in how individuals and schools negotiate racial conflicts.

Table 4.2 provides a summary of this chapter's discussion of racial/academic socialization activities and the racial literacy objectives, skills, and socialization contexts where racially stressful encounters occur. It's very important to remember that it's not simply the skills that are produced from completing the practice and rehearsal of these strategies that lead to racial literacy. It's also the resolution of the both-and tension that happens during the exercises where self-blame and self-assertion are co-occurring, where fear and agency are comingling, and where racial stress and relaxation become inseparable.

Now, knowing how individuals can reduce racial stress and choose how to respond to racial microaggressions, what would speaking up against racial bias look like if parents and educators had to practice and teach it to children? How do parents prepare their children to respond in healthy ways to racial microaggressions? What about educational leaders? In the next chapter, I will discuss how parents and educational leaders can promote the development of racial literacy in schools, schooling relationships, and school climates.

CHAPTER 5

Walking While Talking

What Parents and Educators Can Do to Promote Racial Literacy

For so many parents of children of color who worry about keeping them racially safe, their fears are palpable. For so many, their racial histories, both cultural and personal, have been dismembered and are too painful to excavate. Remembering them seems futile and unproductive, or worse—unnecessary. It raises that persistent parental question of "Should I prepare my children for racial challenges so they can respond to injustice and not internalize inferiority or (because of postracial progress) should I keep racial conversations to a minimum because they may create that same racial inferiority we want to prevent?" Similar questions include "Will talking about sex cause my children to have more sex? Will talking about the experiences of gay, lesbian, and transgendered youth make my child gay?" I would answer "No" to all of these questions. I believe the palpable fears of parents to actively engage in racial socialization are not mostly about the risks to their children. They are mostly about the unresolved emotions of parents' past racial experiences. Although teaching children about racial matters is stressful for all parents, there are different challenges for parents of color as their children receive disproportionate negative consequences because of racial discrimination. Thus, there are different levels of stress that these parents experience (Stevenson et al., 2001). Educators' goals of diversity initiatives to teach tolerance may be different than parental goals of diversity initiatives to protect their children from insult and rejection. But how parents and educators work together to match each other's goals and methods is a reasonable outcome to expect.

This chapter will focus on the racial socialization strategies that parents and educators can use to promote racial literacy in youth. The first section will focus on parental challenges and the second section will focus on educational leader issues. To reiterate, racial socialization is *the transmission and acquisition of intellectual, emotional, and behavioral skills to protect and affirm racial self-efficacy for the sake of negotiating and resolving racially stressful encounters that occur in five socialization contexts of information dissemination, relationship-building, identity development, styles expression, and stereotype reproduction.* In a nutshell, racial socialization can be about actions parents and others take to influence racial self-efficacy beliefs or the beliefs that children hold about being able to resolve the racial stressors and conflicts of the world, wherever and whenever they arise. In addition to what parents give, this chapter will explore what youth receive, internalize, and use in daily social interaction.

Racial literacy is the facility of reading, recasting, and resolving racial conflicts in peer and authority relationships anywhere—family, neighborhood, or school. I'm advocating that parents and teachers take a more active role in gathering new knowledge, initiating discussions, conducting practice sessions, and evaluating the benefits of those practice sessions about common racial dilemmas. Several benefits of this racial socialization are expected. Parents and students are expected to improve their

1. accuracy in decoding the intensity and meaning of racial conflicts,
2. effectiveness in altering their perception and experience of highly stressful racial encounters from threats to challenges, and
3. assertiveness in speaking against racial injustice or for racial equity in intrapersonal, social, and schooling contexts.

I will also recommend a more proactive rather than passive approach to racial socialization, specifically in telling youth what to do when they are racially profiled.

THE STRESS OF RACIAL SOCIALIZATION FOR PARENTS

By examining one's history of racial stress and socialization, emotional and behavioral weaknesses and strengths can be excavated. Parents and youth of all racial backgrounds can bring to diversity conversations a story of their own. Instead of feeling helpless on what to do or say when racially stressed, individuals can learn how to calculate, locate, and share their feelings and racialized life experiences while simultaneously reducing their stress levels. Many parents are stressed about their child's potential racial illiteracy or inability to resolve internal or interpersonal racial conflicts he or she may face. This is especially important given the reticence of schools and societal institutions to face racial denial in matters of social, political, and academic functioning. Can my child or student resolve a racially stressful conflict with a peer or teacher in the classroom without undermining his or her academic achievement? Still, there exist multiple strategies for reducing racial conflict. Moreover, buried in one's life story are important lessons about coping with racial stress.

A literacy-driven proactive form of racial socialization involves parents, leaders, peers, media, and other sources of communication sharing psychological worldviews, cultural heritage stories and lessons, historical information, coping suggestions, and future expectations to youth about how to see, respond, and behave when confronted by racial encounters and why. It involves building skills that are specifically effective for the various racial conundrums that students face. Whether verbal or nonverbal, racial socialization is one of the ways parents can increase their children's sense of competence during racial encounters, manage the parental fears, and reduce anxiety about how the world may mistreat their children when they are not there to protect them.

In two decades of conducting basic research and developing measurement or interventions that integrate parent or adolescent perspectives of racial socialization, I have noticed that most Black parents were stressed about talking to their children about race, racial conflict, and what to do about those conflicts (Stevenson & Arrington, 2012). Still, for all of the intervention work I've done with Black parents (Stevenson et al., 2001) and having been raised by an active and conversational mother about racial matters in everyday life, the parental hesitation and refusal to actively racially socialize children continues to surprise me. Parents warn their children of danger all the time. "Don't cross the street without looking both ways." "Don't say everything that comes to your mind." "Don't ever talk about race with other people." One could argue that half of parenting is worrying about what danger lurks for children in the larger world and the other half is telling children what to do to prevent those dangers from occurring. Telling children about potential dangers of racial injustice seems a basic child-rearing lesson in an overloaded cache of parental strategies dating back to the mid-20th century.

It became clear in my conversations with some Black parents in predominantly White public and independent schools that they were burdened to talk about the racial stress that they or their children have endured. At the core of that anxiety was the unresolved shame of Black parents about their own failure at negotiating racial conflicts as well as about enrolling their child into PWS and subjecting them to racial enmity that cropped up no matter how nice the staff and students were. Trying to teach their children how to problem-solve a racial encounter only illuminated their own avoidance and self-blame about what to say and do.

So it stands to reason that White parents would be equally or more burdened to engage in conversations about how to reduce that stress, even as we know the goals and anxieties of racial socialization for White parents are different than for parents of color (Bartoli et al., 2013; Hamm, 2001). There is still the sense of ineptitude about what to say or do, but White parents may more likely see colorblindness as a healthy and desirable goal, while parents of color are more likely to see it as a failure to demonstrate a mature stance on racial politics (Bartoli et al., 2013).

So, whenever I do workshops on this topic for parents or teachers, I start with encouraging participants to forgive themselves for the shame and stress of not knowing how to prepare their children to navigate racial matters. If parents are not given instruction booklets on parenting, then there are certainly fewer or no tools, lessons, or training on developing racial literacy. Guilt and shame almost always block learning, but more important, they distract from the responsibility to take action on these matters. Teaching youth, parents, and teachers to notice how their bodies react and identify the feelings they are having when telling a story about or experiencing racial conflict has become my life's work. Forgiveness is more likely if you understand what you are specifically shameful about or hurt by—not being White enough or Black enough or rich enough or "ghetto" enough is too broad.

The model I've proposed encourages the development of racial stress reappraisal and self-efficacy skills through storytelling, journaling, relaxation, debating, and role-playing. That is, over time, studying how much parents and teachers racially socialize youth and how that socialization is related to youth outcomes became less interesting to me than studying how activist racial socialization skills training might prepare youth to respond to and overcome racial stress in play, work, and school.

Parental Racial Socialization for Students in Postracial American Schools

My mother's story from the Introduction is both unique and common. She endured many stressors, but none of them seem to be as burdensome as the fears about how the world might mistreat her children. Many parents struggle with the stress of parenting children within hostile neighborhoods and surroundings. In *Stickin' To, Watchin' Over, and Gettin' With: An African American Parent's Guide to Discipline,* Gwendolyn Davis, Saburah Abdul-Kabir, and I (Stevenson, Davis, & Abdul-Kabir, 2001) wrote that "parenting is a lifelong acquaintance with helplessness" (p. 22). As soon as we become confident, our competence as parents begins to wane. Still, parenting around racial matters is differently stressful and raises different thoughts, hopes, and fears.

In a volume entitled *Black Educational Choices,* Stevenson, Slaughter-Defoe, Arrington, and Johnson (2012) describe an experience of a parent who struggled with placing her son in a predominantly White school and her stress at making the wrong choices:

"If I don't get him out of this public school, I am going to lose him. I know I am." Two weeks prior to submitting the final draft of this volume to the publisher, one of the editors received a frantic telephone message from an African American mother of an 8-year-old boy asking for financial assistance to get him out of his current predominantly White public school and into a racially diverse private school. "I have no choice but to leave him in the school and he is not advancing." The mother was desperate in her request after reading the research of two of the authors on the emotional experiences of Black students in PWS. Her worry for her and her child's emotional well-being was clear. "There are no choices . . . I can't take it. He can't take it. He is being stifled emotionally, psychologically, and intellectually." Her desperation was evident in her voice and her tearful request to participate in any research studies we might be conducting to help offset the cost of her child's tuition in a better school.

In our opinion, this is not an extreme response. Given the problems facing Black parents who look for better schooling, we argue that for one's precious children, the consequences of poor schooling are dire enough to remortgage a home, move to live in with relatives in a better school district, or simply home school. There is no question that this mother's problem can be looked at from very different vantage points. Still, the question this mother deals with daily and reminds educational researchers, professionals, and policy-makers to address immediately is, "What do we do for Black students who have few to no educational options?" (p. 268).

Clearly, one purpose of enrolling children in PWS is for the expected advantages and greater potential of social mobility and future financial success. But do parents adequately struggle through the disadvantages?

In a chapter about the struggles of parenting in PWS, Edith Arrington and I summarized our research team's interviews with parents (Stevenson & Arrington, 2012). One particular comment from a parent about her daughter struck me at the time and remains a haunting framing of concern that some parents of Black children have when enrolling their children in a PWS. It is a comment about the atmospheric inferiority that is amorphous and unspoken. She states:

> It breaks my heart that my daughter has been the only African American girl in her class since kindergarten and this goes to identity; even when there is a nurturing environment, there can still be a dominant pull. . . . Until we have a critical mass, we will have a different dynamic; it affects not only my daughter but me also; there is a *subliminal attitude postulating failure instead of success.* (p. 72)

Not all parents have to worry whether police officers will view their children as menaces to society because of the color of their skin. The stop-and-frisk policies of police departments in New York and other cities across America represent confirmation that we live in a society where racial profiling is accepted even if it increases excessive and baseless incarceration of Black and Latino youth with no appreciable reduction of crime. Not all parents prepare their children to change their behavior if they perceive authority figures to be threatened by their presence. Not all parents feel they have to manage unconscious bias that comes from very well-meaning and pleasant authority figures, biases that could undermine authority figure relationships that indirectly hamper the achievement and career outcomes and opportunities for their children.

Parenting through racial challenges evokes different reactions than parenting through nonracial challenges. Several aspects of parenting are influenced by racial matters, including racial versus ethnic differences, internalized racialism conflicts, whether or not to discuss racial matters before or after children experience an insult, and neighborhood diversity (Stevenson, McNeil, Herrero-Taylor, & Davis, 2005). There are conflicts in neighborhoods between Black families that are racial in nature as these conflicts focus on superiority and inferiority challenges based on skin color or whether the children go to PWS or neighborhood schools that are primarily Black or Latino. Ethnic differences between, say, Caribbean-born, African-born, and American-born Blacks have influenced how parents talk to their children about dealing with within-group racial conflicts. Racial socialization is vulnerable to diversity composition politics in the contexts that families survive (Stevenson et al., 2005). These and other dilemmas are addressed in my definition of racial/ethnic socialization or the process through which parents teach children to manage the stress of being racially or ethnically different.

Still, there are many more healing and healthy metalevel racial coping responses to counter that nagging inferiority question in parents' daily lives, "Did I make the right educational choice for my child?" Through racial/ethnic socialization and training, I believe these coping responses can become second nature and minimize the negative effects of atmospheric inferiority on the emotional, psychological, and behavioral well-being of all persons, but especially Black students.

The Limitations and Benefits of Racial Socialization as Legacy and Literacy

Although the natural ways Black parents teach their children to survive racial discrimination in schools and society can be influential, they are also insufficient. Natural or legacy parental socialization doesn't usually focus on skills-building and can often leave youth confused as to what to do when faced with a racial microaggression. It's like the difference between parents telling stories about bike riding or fishing instead of going out and showing their children how to ride a bike or catch a fish. Our research found that although Black youth benefited emotionally, academically, and socially from parents who provided more frequent instances of racial socialization, up to half of Black parents didn't talk to their children about racial matters (Stevenson, 1998). I wanted to see if an explicitly taught, frequently delivered, and socially applied form of racial socialization would fare better than a haphazard random parental strategy (when insult happens). One angle on this work was the importance of reviving the emotional effects of struggle in the racial heritage of African Americans and connecting them to contemporary experiences of racial injustice. To what end does it matter that an evaluation and scrutiny of one's personal and racial history can lead to a deeper storytelling experience and initiate a deeper level of racial literacy?

What is an essential healing element in racial storytelling is not simply the rehashing of facts and figures or the retelling of hardships like "walking 10 miles in the snow barefoot every morning to get to school." These are important aspects of storytelling, no doubt. But healing from the shame of racial stress and inequity in individuals requires an emotional engagement with and expression of those historical moments, not simply a recounting. Instead of a "Do you know when I was a kid . . ." lecture that turns youth into stone or triggers them to say, "Oh, my God, not another barefoot through snow story," racial storytelling must connect to the lives that youth experience today.

Parents and educational leaders must be willing to get their intellectual and emotional hands dirty by sharing their own racial stories and asking themselves, "What did it feel like to go through that?" By getting an adult's perspective on those racialized experiences during childhood, families and youth get a chance to transcend time and the "cost of a loaf of bread." What did "the cost of a loaf of bread" emotionally mean to you then? Tell that story, Mom, Dad, teacher. It is how children or I as the child in the 1930s or 1960s or 1990s thought about racial discrimination then and now that constitutes the power of my story, not that my child should feel lucky he didn't grow up then. What better vantage point to understand how racial discrimination and triumph occurs in our lives and affects the emotional and academic well-being of children than through the lens of children? So, the first suggestion I make about racial storytelling is for adults and youth to describe the experience from the perspective of "What was your emotional response at the time that you experienced that racial encounter?" The goal is to get the adult to talk about his or her own emotional experience, not simply to describe what happened. Children need to feel what we felt back then about walking through the snow barefoot, not just hear the facts.

An African proverb, "The lion's story will never be known as long as the hunter is the one to tell it," serves as the thematic cry of my research. How do we learn to tell our own stories that aren't filtered with the stereotypes of lions or the subtle heroic supremacy of the hunter? What if it takes practice for me to emotionally remember, process, and appreciate my own life experiences, both personal and racial? What if I've spent more energy repressing racial encounters so much that it seems impossible to recount them? What if it is too painful to do so? Why do all the hunters get the press coverage and lions live in zoos?

If parents can tell racial stories and the emotional experiences that accompany them, our collective racial group histories can benefit from this emotional reattachment. So while requiring students in high school to take a Black history course is a significant step in the reform of curriculum in urban public high schooling, it nevertheless can decay like other courses that students hope to get through without throwing up. If there is no emotional reattachment to the importance of these historical events, students will not see the relevance to life any more than they will see math's role in making sure one doesn't get swindled by the cashier in the grocery store. Storytelling with the goal of emotional reattachment is a literacy form of racial socialization, not simply legacy.

Parental Counter-Coping Moves in PWS

Many parents of color are often stressed when it comes to enrolling their children in PWS. Although this decision for their children has social mobility benefits, these benefits may not always offset some emotional, cultural, and racial disadvantages. Racial coping can take forms of avoiding or approaching racial stressors, and racial socialization can illuminate which coping strategies are most likely to be affirming and protective. Often, these parents are alone in struggling with these decisions.

For those who find it stressful to be one of the few or the first in predominantly White contexts, there are several coping strategies to alleviate this feeling of racial alienation. One of them is the search for others who are in the same boat, same misery, or experiencing similar racial stress and alienation. Lani Guinier and Gerald Torres (2003) wrote the book *The Miner's Canary*, and in it they discussed how unresolved racial issues underlie many societal institutions and their relationships with people as signs of societal dysfunction. As canaries in the mines of PWS, many but not all Black families look for indications or signs of distress and support. When considering enrolling their children into these schools, many racially conscious parents will scan the classrooms, the office staff, the school teacher corps, and the administrative team to determine if other Black people are present. This is most prevalent for families interested in PWS but the "scanning Blackness" process may be as intense in other school, neighborhood, and institutional settings as well. The same could be said for individuals as they take a new job, join a fitness center, or enter a room. Are there any other canaries like me in this mine?

One element of the "Canary in the Mine" scan is to identify role models of likeness. Implicit in this scan is the expectation that the presence of someone who looks like me means my child is not alone. To see a Black teacher, principal, head of school, director of admissions, for many parents is a first. To see more than one other Black student in a class or more than three is a first for many students in PWS. These firsts are often thought of as "progress," "safer," "diverse," "open," "progressive," or "better" by many. The power of "first" may mask the fear of being the "only." I would say that all parents regardless of their racial backgrounds are looking for markers of safety when they visit schools, and some of these have racial underpinnings and some do not.

The next level of scanning involves judging if those people of color are allies or not and whether there is a match in worldview with regard to racial identity, politics, and communication. In relieving a key element of parenting stress, the primary question to allies is, "Have there been other Black children like mine who have struggled with the stress of racial difference and are they still at the school? Can they or will they be able to help my child through any racially difficult experiences?" I'm interested in what parents, students, teachers, and administrators in schools do with the stress of these racialized assumptions and perceptions, or "elephants in the room," and how we can help them face these elephants directly.

Why would scanning be a necessary racial coping strategy for some Black families? It's about stress relief. This "Canary in the Mine" scan may be conscious or unconscious. There is an implicit assumption that "if I can find someone Black in a position of power in this school of predominantly White authority figures, perhaps my child's behavior, personality, smartness, feelings, identity, and style will not be misunderstood, or worse, mistreated." Now, this assumption could be completely wrong, but if it is there, then many questions about whether the school climate is safe may get answered or fears of cultural alienation may become less emotionally burdensome to parents of students of color, especially. The expectations of a "good education" are often coupled with the expectations of a "bias-free" or "bias-light" schooling experience. "Perhaps as a parent, I can be relieved from the fear that my child's battle scars from unconscious bias will be plentiful." For some parents, if that is true, we say, "The presence of other canaries means my child will not be alone and that my own stress of placing my child in this experimental racial pressure cooker will subside."

Parental Hesitance About Racial Socialization: Healthy or Unhealthy Racial Paranoia?

It is clear that not all parents are stressed by being in PWS, and so many of these strategies may seem irrelevant. I am writing mostly for those who find it relevant to ask these questions. I am writing on behalf of families and students who see or feel the stress of racial discrimination as they navigate schooling. These students, parents, and teachers often struggle with being among the few who, like canaries in a mine, are the most sensitive to the poison of racial enmity or isolation and the first to bear the burden of being different. But not everyone is on board with early preparation and direct confrontation when it comes to racial coping. Many questions are raised. What if no one behaves differently toward us because of our racial difference? What if those racist attitudes don't happen? Some parents reason that talking about these distressing matters could bring distress to youth unnecessarily and "put ideas into their heads."

Should we talk directly to children and youth about racial politics, and if so, how do we do it? Will the students become paranoid and overrun with political correctness? Will they obsessively look for racism everywhere and get distracted from successful achievement? Some paranoia is healthy, especially if it is verifiable, as Grier and Cobbs (1968) made clear several decades ago. But what if the problem is not racial paranoia but failure to see the microaggressions?

What I am talking about acknowledges what the anthropologist John Jackson (2008) describes as "racial paranoia and the unintended consequences of political correctness" where racial thinking is defined as a phenomenon that "inhabits the gut, not the mind. It is a hunch as much as a proven fact. It is a rapid-fire assessment that can hardly be dispelled with recourse to claims about contrary evidence or logical analysis" (p. 18). I see racial paranoia slightly differently, and in a both-and sense. It is both constructive and destructive. In the sense that paranoia is not a healthy thinking process, it is defined as imagining events to occur that in actuality do not. It affects one's sense of support and leads to distrust of common interactions and relationships. Jackson suggests that this paranoia is based on unsubstantiated but deeply ingrained beliefs and myths about a racialized world of social interactions.

But paranoia in my opinion is not insidious simply because of the fact that one might imagine events and conspiracies to exist when they do not. It is most problematic when those "distorted thoughts" influence behavior. So it is more of a psychological experience, although one can see both anthropological and sociological consequences of distorted racialized worldviews by groups over time. But racial paranoia is a matter of the mind first, then the gut, then the action, and that process makes it much more of a learned process. That is, paranoia can be taught and unlearned even in our psychological defining of it. Facts about the painful reality of racial profiling in public schools are more than enough to justify healthy suspicion among Black parents about whether their children are being treated fairly. That racial maltreatment cannot always be verified is not an argument for suggesting it is not present.

The realities of racism in our world are sometimes hidden and thus not always open for investigation (Feagin, 2009). Ironically, the racially paranoid among us may be accurate in their suppositions that danger lurks craftily but unable to prove it because they either do not have the tools of deconstruction or they fail to see the tools. Still, I would argue that the most detrimental part of paranoia is not just that one can prove or disprove his or her position, but how it leads one to think and behave in self- or other-destructive ways. The primary tragedy of any paranoia is not just the distorted thinking (because it may not actually be all wrong), but how it leads one to turn friends into enemies and enemies into friends. In either case, I would argue from an emotional standpoint, underreaction to racial injustice is just as unhealthy as overreaction and speaking up about an alleged infraction can ignite dialogue where the matter could be clarified.

Some would argue that talking about race to address racial conflicts only "makes race relations worse" (as many conservatives asserted when President Obama discussed the Trayvon Martin murder and suggested he could have a son who looks like Trayvon). A better approach would be to ask and predict, "For whom might race talking make matters worse? Are there racial insults in the world worth any attention? If so, how should we attend to them?" I would agree with Derald Sue and others that these minor racial insults add up over time and without a psychological defense and offense, youth are vulnerable to internalizing these negative insults as being about identity instead of about the atmosphere that surrounds them. Perspective is important.

So what does a parent say to protect his or her child from the harmful effects of racial discrimination, perceived and actual? In February 2012, Trayvon Martin, a 17-year-old boy, was killed by George Zimmerman as he was walking home to his father's girlfriend's house from a grocery store. In an essay about this experience, I wrote about what parents could say to their children before they leave home to face a world that often views them as criminals. I struggled a lot with his killing, as my own fear of my two sons' risk of being racially profiled became overwhelming (like a 7 or 8 on the stress scale from 1 to 10). My conversations with my sons about how to deal with racial antagonism only made me more helpless as I slowly realized, again, that I couldn't be with them 24 hours a day. My older son was just turning 21 at the time and racial profiling of him kept me up at night while my younger son was approaching preteen years and his looming adolescence gave me nightmares. I wrote about the challenges of giving my oldest son "The Stalking Talk" when he was 8 years old (Stevenson, Davis, & Abdul-Kabir, 2001). "The Stalking Talk" is that conversation many Black parents have with their Black children at a certain age regarding what to do should they face racial hostility from police, other youth, or authority figures. In the essay entitled, "What If Trayvon Came Home? Giving the

Stalking Talk to Black Males" (Stevenson, 2013), I wrote what I or parents might say to our sons, everybody's "Trayvon," about what they could do when they are racially profiled despite the surreal, absurd, unpredictable, and unstoppable nature of this form of racial terrorism. What should be included in that conversation about racial profiling?

WHAT PARENTS SHOULD KNOW TO PROMOTE RACIAL LITERACY

So there are several "wake-up" points or lessons for parents that I propose. These wake-up points are meant to shake parents from their denial and avoidance to address racial matters in their own lives and instruct their children in navigating an unpredictable racial conflict.

1. Know That Racial Shame Undermines Parents' Explicit Teaching of Racial Coping

There is nothing wrong with talking to youth about racial conflicts and what to do. In fact, to not explicitly teach students about negotiating racial stress could constitute parental neglect or incompetence if keeping children emotionally safe from racial rejection is the goal. Black students and students of color experience more racial threats (racial profiling, low expectations, academic tracking, disproportionate and inappropriate discipline from pre-K to college) to their academic and social identities in schools than other students. Any hesitancy or failure to recognize the threat disparity and directly block these threats also prevents reduction of racial disparities. Conversely, when the tragedy of these racial threats receives inadequate attention from educators and other authority figures, parents must through social advocacy confront any interactions that minimize the expendability of Black safety in schools.

The shame of racial conflict should not drive the response to the injustice. The shame that comes from talking about race can be addressed through therapy to prevent it from slipping out in observable, politically correct missteps (mistaken and awkward use of racial comments, spastic body reactions to racial conflicts, distorted self-talk and rumination about meaning of racial missteps, and obsessive-compulsive screening of racial thoughts) during social interactions with others.

Often, parental racial shame includes the fear that your child might be unconsciously treated differently by teachers or peers because of his or her racial background. Not facing this fear can leave some parents to feel more helpless and ruminate about what they can say or do about it. Eventually, it is not uncommon for some to encourage children to "prove others wrong" or "reject racial reasoning of any kind" or believe "competition cures all discrimination." Racial shame of parents can also represent regret after an incident and can include the anger over not protecting children during a racial encounter that we could have seen coming or that we failed to prepare our children for. The remedy for this shame is to reject the narrative of Black expendability within our parenting and speak openly to our children about our concerns and expectations in ways they can developmentally understand.

2. Prepare for Racial Threats Like Other Threats to Child Safety by Telling Stories

Based on my work on racial socialization over the past 2 decades, I am firmly in favor of preparing for potential racially discriminatory incidents, even if they don't occur. Nevertheless, when I do public speaking about racial socialization and literacy, I have to prepare for questions that suggest the very mentioning of racial dangers and threats is "racist" and is the real problem. Talking about racism is not a disease. If talking about cancer could give people cancer, then many research scientists from the National Institutes of Health and Centers for Disease Control would be suffering greatly and would show the highest incidence rates. Still, I get asked the following questions of doubt often:

- By talking to children about racism, aren't we teaching the children to hate?
- Doesn't this talking make our children, our world, racist?
- Won't bringing up racial matters teach children to feel bad about themselves?"
- Don't you think that bringing up racism to your children is like setting them up to overreact to something that will never happen?
- Isn't it like putting paranoia in a child's head about racism when they aren't even thinking about it?
- If racism is so stressful, why would you talk about it?
- Racism doesn't exist like before, so why talk to your child about something that happened decades ago?

I say "No" to these questions because we prepare members of our society in workplaces and transportation to endure a host of public tragedies that may rarely occur and that have a low probability of survival. The chances of experiencing an earthquake are slim, but that doesn't stop Californians from learning what to do should one occur. Airline passengers are notorious for not listening to the flight attendants who demonstrate (in perfect unison with hand gestures and smiling on cue) what to do in case of an aircraft emergency before every flight takeoff. Many passengers bristle at the disturbance that this "same-old" ritual causes us as we are desperately trying to go to sleep or pine over the gifts in the airplane gadget catalog. Few of us have experienced an airplane crash (and lived to tell of the enormous importance of the flight attendant's lesson), but airlines still provide the training. (In hindsight, perhaps it would increase passenger attentiveness if each aircraft emergency demonstration was accompanied by an airplane crash survivor who could give testimony and gratitude to the flight attendants). Are we saying that it makes sense to prepare for an aircraft emergency where the odds of occurrence is small and the odds of survival are smaller, but no sense to prepare Black boys and girls for the potential detriment and risk of racial profiling, which occurs more frequently?

Parents talk to children all the time about dangers that have a low probability of occurring without invoking the danger. Parents don't seem to have as much hesitation to "talk" to their children about other social challenges. Parents prepare their children for "strangers who might talk nicely to you and try to get you to go with them" or "friends who might bad touch you in ways you don't want."

As parents, many of us dread the discussion about where babies come from when our children are small or about sex when our children and teens get older. When youth are pressured to have sex prematurely or take drugs in their teen years, we might criticize a parent whose only response is to state, "That shouldn't happen." We dread the parental discussions with our children about avoiding drugs and peer pressure. Yet when it comes to the parental discussion about healthy responses to racial or ethnic intimidation or derision, many parents are more stressed than when talking about sex or drugs. For the same reasons we want children prepared to cross the street, ask for help, not play with fire, or not choose friends who might hurt them, we should prepare children for racial hostility or rejection from others. Just because children rarely run out into the street and get hit by a car or rarely play with matches and burn down houses does not deter the parental lesson. So while it is important to discuss sex, drugs, and bad relationships with youth, so too is it vital to discuss matters of racial tension. Although the prevalence of racial threats is frequently unknown and underestimated, why should racial dangers—whatever their probability—receive any less attention?

Now, racial insults can come from those who are from within our racial communities and from without. This raises a host of different types of racial conversations with youth that many parents never bargained for. Both cross- and within-racial/ethnic conversations can be stressful. Although I believe this is necessary for all children, it is particularly children of color who cannot hide their difference and who receive disproportionate negative reactions from key power brokers in the world. All students are affected by bias, but youth of color are affected disproportionately.

A serious preparation for social insult and injustice has to specify what to do, what to say, and how to think about yourself as you respond to the pressure. One aspect of preparation for racial injustice is to expect it by talking about it using developmentally appropriate examples and language and by telling stories about one's racial history for pride and protection and relevance to contemporary racial politics.

Teaching Black history is invaluable in revealing how racial hierarchy has for centuries promoted racial humiliation in public racial discourse and identity development. Parental instructions should first challenge the racial supremacy paradigms and the inherent assumption that Black life, humanity, and culture of any kind is inadequate or expendable. Learning about and discussing Black history is important for identifying how racial hierarchy has been a unique American phenomenon that influences how people from different racial groups think about Whiteness and each other. There are two types of Black history to be taught here. One is the more common *cultural Black history* and the other is the *personal Black history*. Cultural Black history includes the struggles and triumphs of Black people and their contributions to American and world culture, knowledge, worldview, and progress. Personal Black history is about an individual's experience of being Black or a member of a racial group across a lifetime. Lessons from these experiences deserve excavation, as they can be used in teaching youth. But the most important aspects of these stories is not the facts, but the emotional reconnection that can occur to these events as they are found to be relevant as tools for surviving contemporary racial problems.

3. Healing the Feeling of Racial Trauma Outweighs Protest and Political Correctness

While racial justice protest is essential in any social change initiative in American society, most protests are often adult-focused, driven by changing laws, and less instructive on face-to-face emotional conflicts. Teaching children and youth to emotionally navigate racial injustice will lead to resilience coping skills they can use for social interactions in schools that undermine achievement. Public protests are not as useful as racially literate relationships for resolving racial trauma. In developing racial literacy, parents are encouraged to apply affection, protection, and correction approaches to reflections of past racial experiences, but also in the telling of their stories or in providing explicit feedback to youth.

Affection or nurturance applied to one's storytelling for self and children would include

1. forgiving oneself and others (family, neighborhood of origin, America) for being stressed and incompetent at racial knowledge, conversations, and social interaction;
2. showing empathy to oneself and others for the stress and trauma of experiencing racial rejection; and
3. giving physical nurturance when racial insults occur because wanted positive physical touch addresses trauma more powerfully than words.

Protection or monitoring applied to racial storytelling for self and children would include

1. practicing storytelling in a safe place (with oneself or a trusted friend) before disclosing painful racial trauma to others;
2. preparing a lesson that conveys the meaning of that story to the storyteller and that could instruct others in coping effectively with racial encounters; and
3. assessing how often one's children are exposed to racial rejections and microaggressions in school and public.

Correction or accountability applied to racial storytelling of self or children includes

1. assertively speaking up against racial injustice or incompetence or for positive racial coping that occurred in one's past or present (even if that speaking up is included in self-talk: "Even though I was a child, the police officer had no right to treat me as if I was a criminal when I was simply standing on the corner laughing with my friends"); and
2. decisively acting to challenge racial injustice or incompetence through social advocacy and community building (start an affinity group for African American students for support for racial literacy training and protection against racial rejection at school).

4. Racial Literacy Requires Practice with Managing Stress

Emotionally processing racial trauma and its intensity can be much more useful for one's health and lead to greater anxiety reduction and competence than a social protest. Parents must tell and process their own stories of racial conflict (including rejection and acceptance) from their childhoods before having racial conversations with their children. In racial storytelling, parents must practice the coping strategies of affection, protection, and correction while they practice answering racial literacy questions and objectives, including

1. racial stress appraisal ("While telling the stories, how stressed am I and what do I notice about myself through calculating the intensity, locating any bodily reactions, and communicating my appraisal to self or others?);
2. racial stress reappraisal ("Can I begin to view the intensity of this stressful encounter as modifiable from being a threat to becoming a challenge?");
3. racial stress relaxation ("Have I used relaxation strategies like breathing to manage and change my in-the-moment [ITM] anxiety from a threat to a challenge?"); and
4. racial stress engagement and resolution ("Have I faced the racial conflict directly to understand its history, novelty, and impact on school climate before I devise a solution to address that impact?").

Parents must consider child development when instructing about racial dangers and not allow the racial conflict to overshadow the emotional needs of the students. The political challenges presented by potential public humiliation and stressful overreaction to the racial conflict by some should be prevented from driving the racial conflict resolution more than the healing and resolution of the emotional needs of the child. Racial encounters are potentially traumatizing for youth and adults. Schools are the safest places for children to learn, but racial tension undermines the safety of school climates. Parents must learn to anticipate these events before they happen by reviewing their personal racial histories. Hoping and praying that these events don't occur is avoidance coping that can leave students unprotected.

WHAT IF TRAYVON CAME HOME? GIVING "THE STALKING TALK"

At no other time in American history have our children needed "The Stalking Talk." No action recommendations on preventing the tragedy of racial profiling Black youth can capture the pain of a parent's loss of a child who has been mistreated or murdered because he or she was Black. Still, facing this tragedy is hard. I've spoken to so many parents and educators who would rather face a hurricane than talk to their child about racism. In their eyes, there appears to be this yearning question of "Why does it have to be this way?" or "Tell me it ain't so" or "Why can't I make sure my child receives the best the world has to offer, not the least, without bringing up racial matters?"

Still, I believe it is at our children's emotional peril for parents not to face the racial pain in their past. These histories of racial distress do not go away. Some parents and activists disagree with my direct approach to racial socialization with the question of "Why must children bear the burden of resolving racial inequality rather than the discriminatory systems and adults who deliver this injustice?" Implicit in this question is the "belief in a just world" and the desire for a world without racial discrimination. Or it is a question that reflects a strategy to blame others for racial inequality. It is a faith in a dream where one's child *shouldn't* have to worry about being mistreated because they are Black- or Brown-skinned. But "shoulda," "woulda," and "coulda" don't pay the bills; don't turn the lights on; don't drive the car; and don't stop the rain of racial indignity and impropriety in the setting we should expect to be the safest for our children—school. My answer to the question is, "Because the children pay the most for the racial ignorance and lack of social action." Of course, I think it's best to do both—work with youth to prepare them for racial injustice but also challenge institutions and systems of threat to change their policies. But given what history has taught us about the time it takes for and the high levels of resistance to racial progress, I put more faith in the former.

Parents don't have time to protest systems and care for children without sacrificing one or the other. Besides, if daily your children could be held hostage through racial profiling, low academic expectations, and premature expulsion from school simply for being different, why wouldn't the best parental response to the ransom request be to teach them how to "say no to strangers" or "identify kidnappers" or "see racial elephants" instead of demand that the different institutions change their policies? You wouldn't send your child into a cold winter's day without a coat, right? Perhaps the hardest pill to swallow or scariest thoughts to fathom as a parent of a child of color in a PWS are implicit in this question: "Having seen the presence of sand and thinking I was sending my child to the beach (a school of immense resources, safety, and stimulation), have I inadvertently sent them unprotected to the desert (a school of promise accompanied by a disengaged, barren, and life-threatening climate) instead?" Then there's the option of how parents, along with school leaders, might either prepare their children for the desert or modify the school climate to be supportive of healthy racial identity development for all of their students.

RACIALLY LITERATE LEADERSHIP: WHAT EDUCATORS SHOULD KNOW TO REDUCE RACIAL THREAT

So how do educational leaders begin to resolve racial stress in schools? How do we translate the abstract problem of racism in societal systems so clearly that it is interpreted as relevant within the daily lives of students, teachers, parents, and educational leaders? This section will provide examples of healthy responses to school-based racial encounters. These encounters are not exhaustive but might help answer the question, "For what kinds of stressful situations in schooling relationships would the development of racial literacy be useful?"

Educators need to understand the literature on coping with racial conflict for youth and for adults and develop professional development opportunities that embrace this literature. Racial literacy will require the processing of difficult feelings but leaders can ease these experiences by developing action plans that reward racial risk taking. Being aware of one's feelings during racial encounters is difficult (Word, Zanna, & Cooper, 1974). Educationally speaking, it's a foundational skill for a variety of achievement outcomes. This is true given that we know individuals can become so alerted to their racial discomfort that they deny any anxiety and exert effort to cover up observable nonverbal behaviors (Dunton & Fazio, 1997; Plant & Devine, 1998). There is a threat to being "found out" to be uncertain about what to say or do during a racial social interactions. This threat is nothing to diminish or ignore, as it lies at the center of racial tension in schools.

Conversely, students, teachers, and parents of color may become anxious when faced with racial inferiority assumptions that others in school may have of them. Some research has found that African Americans may not rebut racial bias if they have internalized beliefs of fixed intelligence ("like you're either smart or you are not") because they feel it is a waste of time to change or challenge that bias (Rattan & Eberhardt, 2010; Rattan, Levine, Dweck, & Eberhardt, 2012). In one respect, this can be positive because it prevents individuals from wasting emotional resources and draining energy away from other self-development activities. In another respect, this lack of faith in one's ability to change has been linked to the development of discriminatory educational policies (Rattan et al., 2012). Specifically, believing that people do not have the potential for greater intelligence is related to one's opposition to social policies designed to remediate inequality (Rattan, Savani, Naidu, & Dweck, 2012), support for extreme punishments for juveniles who have committed crime (Rattan et al., 2012), and hesitancy to confront racial prejudice in social interactions (Rattan & Dweck, 2010). Conversely, those who believe in a mutable intelligence not only stand up for themselves, but they are more psychologically healthy as a result.

The research on worldviews and beliefs in potential runs solidly in line with the research on how distressful nonverbal behaviors are evident in cross-racial interactions (Ambady, Bernieri, & Richeson, 2000). If we can change the negative expectations of Black students and other students of color in schools, we may be able to change the racial climates in schools. Still, it may require educators to move beyond flowery words of social justice and diversity and begin teaching students how to demand respectful behavior from each other.

Talking the Talk: Educational Leader
as Revolutionary, Teacher, or Reticent Politician

The rhetoric about eradicating racism's effect on American culture and social systems is a familiar cry in progressive schooling. Still, racial stress in daily face-to-face relationships is revealed in the ways schools reflect, plan, obfuscate, and take as mission the programming of diversity. To many PWS, using the word *diversity* is an accomplishment. To many, defining diversity is a nightmare as the agenda becomes too vague to reflect the identity and missions of the schools. Teachers, parents, and students are often beholden to educational leaders who seek to appease all constituents. Under fearful leadership, actualizing change to reflect diversity positively in all aspects of schooling may be experienced often as an impossible task.

The heads and principals of schools who've appeared to be the most stressed were those who had no diversity plan they could personally defend. I will call these leaders *The Reticents*. The Reticents are trying not to appear hostile toward diversity efforts while being unable or unwilling to provide adequate support for these efforts to grow. This hesitant coping leadership style often signals to staff and teachers and parents that diversity programming is a disaster waiting to happen. Open expression of racial conflicts are perceived as leading the school into chaos. Unfortunately, without racial literacy that contributes to healthy racial dialogues, any racial conflict may be experienced as a crisis waiting to happen. Hesitation and caution is the hallmark style of Reticent leadership and the fruit of these approaches can be observed at the institutional level in school diversity mission statements, in spectacular brochures with more pictures of people of color than exist in the school, and in little integration of problem-solving racial dilemmas in the curriculum.

Attempts to make the climate of PWS safer for students of color or Black students is long and painstaking. Without leaders who emotionally and intellectually understand the history, power, and relevance of racial resistance of the school and the nation; who can devise a plan that integrates this history as central to curriculum; and who can communicate a story for endorsing racial literacy as an academic objective to prepare students to tackle the complexity of racial politics as interpreted by different racial groups within an expanding racially diverse world, a safer school climate is more of a dream than a reality.

When educational leaders can't take a positive, assertive, purposeful, and specific stance on behalf of racial equality or diversity in mission or practices, then students and parents and teachers are left helpless to create their own rules and rituals to develop safety when racial encounters arise. My work on racial socialization as intervention to buffer racial insult and affirm racial self-efficacy is rooted in the consistent failure of institutions (education, justice, and health) to provide emotional and intellectual cover for children and families of color. The limited body of work on racial social-ization in White families is an attempt to address the equally tragic failure of what institutions teach about the negative effects of Whiteness privilege on their emotional, behavioral, and intellectual well-being (Bartoli et al., 2013; Hamm, 2001). In schools that don't question Whiteness and privi-lege in their policies and curricula, affinity groups or student special interest groups (African American student union; Gay-Lesbian-Transgendered Stu-dent Club) become more important for youth to find safe spaces to express their difference. Educational leaders, despite their ignorance or reticence, still have the power to encourage the school to condone or block acts of climate safety making.

But at best, affinity groups represent temporary shelter from colorblind-ness and racial hostility and are only as protective as the foundation of the school that upholds their existence. Without the school sanctioning with-in-group racial membership and collective gatherings from an intellectual pedagogy, racial resistance will continue to be a frequent both-and-coping response that is healthy and unhealthy (Ward, 1996). Without leadership, there will always be a need for racial socialization to take place within natu-rally occurring "racial safe spaces" where students and parents and teachers will share their views and "walk the talk" of facing and problem-solving racial anxiety and dilemmas in schooling.

Leader Reticence Toward Diversity: Politics as Usual or Purposeful Education?

Should educational leaders of PWS be responsible for relieving the ra-cial stress of their students and teachers and training their personnel to al-leviate the racial stress of parents and students such that it becomes a central part of the educational curriculum? Yes.

Constructing a "national" definition of diversity won't help the lo-cal leader if he or she hasn't emotionally, intellectually, and interperson-ally worked out a definition worth fighting for. Hopefully, it is a definition relevant to and integrative of their schools, the neighborhoods that sur-round their schools, and the culture of the people who inhabit their schools. Without strategies and skills in racial encounter awareness, stress appraisal and reappraisal, engagement and resolution, educators become politicians, not educators. Educators teach, illuminate, and lead through the dissemina-tion and explanation of knowledge. In the world of the Reticents, diversity agendas become symbols of racial progress rather than racial literacy lesson plans to be taught and evaluated.

When Racial Opinion Is Misconstrued as Racial Knowledge

Perhaps the most disrespectful act of Reticent leadership is to assume that diversity is an opinion-laden tension, dynamic, or discourse instead of a knowledge-based intellectual, educational, or curricular tension, dynamic, or discourse. The research on racial negotiation can inform school planning on the prevalence, character, and resolution of racial conflict (Comer & Emmons, 2006; Gordon & Bridglall, 2007). Educational leaders who don't know this research are most likely blind as to how to bring diversity agendas to their schools and will find it difficult to address the emotional reactions that students, parents, and teachers will have about that diversity.

It's not that educators have to eradicate racism as much as see racial microaggression and their effects on schooling relationships. The role of institutional influences ("What is this school going to do about racial micro-aggressions in the school culture and climate?") may have greater sway in diversity planning even though microaggressions in relationships are more common in the daily experiences of students in schools ("What can students, teachers, parents, and leaders learn to say and do when faced with micro-aggressions during school or outside of school?" "What are the curricular strategies and citizenship goals implied by an education that understands that diversity skills will be essential for success in a country populated with people from racially diverse backgrounds by the year 2050?").

Racially literate educational leadership not only sees the racial conflicts in schools, but attempts to address those conflicts in the classroom, the hallways, the athletic teams, the curriculum, and the mission of the school with a sense of vision and purpose, not hesitation. But the wise leader will use racial knowledge and research for racial problem solving, not simply as a symbol of charismatic idealism, personal goodness, or moral imperatives, but as a meaningful way to reduce the achievement and resource gap. The knowledge is available, but leaders who have not read about or are unaware of this knowledge are simply incompetent, regardless of the enthusiasm of their racial idealism. It is refreshing to see educational leaders who understand the limitations of their symbolic power and who become direct and strategic in confronting racial stereotypes and inequity. Racially literate educators must gather and review their schools' data on racial climate and relationships, not simply achievement differences. Racially literate leaders gather and review the history of racial conflicts within their schools and construct case studies in which "What if?" and "We need a do-over" scenarios can be analyzed. It's a school racial storytelling initiative, of sorts. These case study sessions involve leaders engaging different personnel, students, and parents to give their feedback and vantage points about the best ways to problem-solve these conflicts. Through the case study review, teaching

about diversity and its importance to the school will have historical signifi-
cance. Nevertheless, programming diversity and racial literacy for the future
requires rationales and theory within which curricula, lessons, and praxis
produce racially competent schooling relationships. Given that competence,
not character, is the goal of racially literate education, how does the training
of racial literacy begin?

The skills to reject the narrative of expendable Blackness and heroic
Whiteness are lacking because schools mostly teach racial stress and stereotype avoidance, not racial negotiation. Most people learn stereotype rejection skills by accident. Still, this level of competence is basic, not useful
when conflicts become complex. Knowing how to hook your light switch
up to electrical current doesn't make you competent at rewiring your whole
house. You might want to get some training in that or pay someone to help
you with that problem.

It's funny to me that when it comes to racial matters, educational leaders
and politicians, parents, and any dude on the street can somehow think their
opinion or their good character should suffice as a "Get out of Racial Jail
Free" card. It's like this card comes with undeniable benefits. Not only might
you believe one can get into the most swank, racially intense nightclubs, but
one might get to talk freely about any racial topic without debate or question
or dispute. We believe we can speak on, lecture about, consult on, advise on,
ignore, dismiss, cajole, and deny racial knowledge, attitudes, and skills without reading articles, knowing the latest research, asking for help, practicing
the skills, or getting expert supervision. That's hilarious and tragic to me.
It shouldn't be so easy to dismiss the racial elephants in the classrooms of
American education as if they are watercooler topics of banter.

So how do educational leaders and parents fighting for racial literacy in
schools avoid developing ulcers, racial reaction formations, racial anxiety
disorders, or leaving the country to retire? I'll cover those issues in my next
book. Nevertheless, I believe racial literacy in schooling requires practicing
courageous leadership. In the next and final chapter, I will focus on how
leaders, educators, and students can practice racial literacy and assertiveness
at school. Practice? Are we talking about practice? Yes, practice.

CHAPTER 6

Racial Literacy as Civil Disobedience

Practicing Racial Assertiveness in Schools

> Movement encourages movement. In this respect also the Algebra Project was echoing the work in Mississippi and throughout the South thirty years before. As I have tried to emphasize, the civil rights movement of the 1960s was less about challenges and protests against white power than feeling our way toward our own power and possibilities—really a series of challenges by ourselves, and our communities, to ourselves. (p. 125)
>
> —Moses & Cobb, *Radical Equations* (2002)

> So don't hate the player or
> the shame that the racial blame keeps wreaking.
> Hate the racial game.
> 'Cause it's way too insane if you keep sneaking and freaking about
> every time the elephant wants a shout out.
>
> —Stevenson, *Elephant Attention* (2012)

Using the slogans and philosophy of the 1960s civil rights protest, Robert Moses, a civil rights advocate, created the Algebra Project. The Algebra Project was designed to increase the knowledge of algebra to all middle schoolers by framing it as a right, like the right to vote. As technology has replaced American industry as the main source of employment, knowing math will be essential for youth to be successful in the future. The point of the first quote above is that rather than seeing racial protest as a statement to illuminate the failures of the existing leadership, let's view it as an opportunity to cement self-determination. This chapter summarizes the recommendations for educational leaders and schools to develop racial literacy for teachers, parents, and students by describing teaching and training processes, activities, and expected outcomes.

GOT SKILLZ? RECOMMENDATIONS FOR ASSERTIVELY ENGAGING AND RESOLVING RACIAL STRESS IN SCHOOLS

The ideas, exercises, stories, and recommendations in this book are a compilation of over 20 years of watching and listening to hundreds of students, educators, and parents as they engage daily social rejection and experience academic underachievement within schools. Exercises specific to racial literacy development can be found in this chapter. I am not advocating these strategies and models of racial stress and coping to ignite racial chaos in schools. My experience has suggested that programmatic attention to racial equity is met with intense resistance.

If two decades of being a fly on the walls of public and private schools has taught me anything, it's that the racial chaos is already there. For every racial justice action, there is an equal and opposite racial justice reaction. That antiracial justice reaction is too often invisible and most schools work hard to keep these elephants asleep. Still, I am more hopeful than not about the potential for change that teaches youth to competently resolve conflicts in a tomorrow that will be more racially contentious as it becomes more racially diverse. The need for racial literacy from the cradle to the grave is greater now than at any time in America's history. That hope in racial conflict resolution is rooted in witnessing unbelievable change in people who were never expected to change, from seeing families and relationships torn by years of trauma, and from living in neighborhoods impoverished beyond any metric the World Bank could calculate.

Perhaps the most salient aspect of racial literacy training is its' support of emotional processing to instigate self-affirmation and self-efficacy during encounters of racial stress. Self-affirmation is a resilience construct found to positively influence coping with social rejection and life hardships (Stinson et al., 2011). In my view, recasting racial stress has the potential to elevate racial self-affirmation. Moreover, we should expect to observe the growth of self-affirmation in one's behaviors, thoughts, and emotions. Specifically, as individuals use mindfulness and stress reduction breathing exercises in the moment of the racial conflicts they anticipate, engage, or ponder, self-affirmation is an expected outcome. Several recommendations for developing racial literacy and self-affirmation in schools include the following:

1. Reject postracial rhetoric as catalyst for equity in education.
2. Integrate racial literacy as a core mission of smart schooling, not just ethical civility.
3. Don't believe the hype of racial fear: "Just say hello" to racial conflict.
4. Believe in your "right" to "choose" to speak up about racial incompetence.

5. Teach and practice racial literacy as skills for specific contexts, not general ideas:
   a. Reduce anxiety, build self-affirmation, and rehearse speaking up before and during racial conflicts.
   b. Teach youth racial hardiness to assertively confront racial blindness.
   c. Reward racial self-affirmation and literacy in behavior and voice.

Reject Postracial Rhetoric as a Catalyst for Equity in Education

Postracial rhetoric may best assuage the anxieties of individuals who feel incompetent to navigate the obfuscation of racial injustice. Unfortunately, that diversity agenda is another case of the racially blind leading the racially blind. Along with the hostile racial resistance of Orval Faubus and the heroic struggles of the Little Rock Nine, some could argue that the Reconstruction period of the late 19th century was another form of "postracial rhetoric and fear" run amuck. But neither anxiety nor fear about the future of race relations should drive a racial justice initiative. Taking a human life-span developmental look at Black civil rights and race relations protest in American society, I would argue that the African enslavement resistance, Reconstruction of the late 19th century, and the civil rights movement of the mid-20th century represent the infancy and toddlerhood events of Black protest and maturity. More protests and rebellions are necessary to prepare and instruct Americans about becoming skillful at seeing and curing racial blindness. But that protest will need to become psychologically meaningful to its participants and begin locally within individuals and in-groups before they are ignited nationally.

That is, maybe our protest should not take place solely in large public demonstrations but in private, familial, and relational self-reflection for the purpose of safely restructuring our roles and social interactions during racial encounters. Maybe racial protest will take root if we heal from the trauma of racial stress before we take on "the system." The fear of humiliation in front of large audiences is too great, as is the temptation to avoid these moments. Despite our best efforts and the best promise from desegregation in making schools equitable, racial and class segregation remains—perhaps is worse. Some might argue that racial equity advocates have lost the war on desegregation despite several battle victories (Schofield & Hausmann, 2004). I am not advocating the cessation of public protest or desegregation efforts, but I believe we need to be aware of the racial resistance right in front of us. As we move forward, let's integrate the power of Stephen Biko's eloquent saying into a psychological protest strategy—that is, "the greatest weapon in the hands of the oppressor is the mind of the oppressed."

One weak pillar of the postracial ideology argument is that the civil rights movement and its symbolic "Firsts" were powerful enough to eradicate the systemic and psychological pervasiveness of racism. This premature claim of victory disregards casualties of lost financial investments and lost lives of poor families from various racial backgrounds, and Black and Brown families, specifically. There was also the racial backlash that accompanied those victories (busing, school desegregation, and health-care reform) and the traumatic effects on the children. Intensive protest for the community cannot be successful if it neglects the affection, protection, and correction of its most vulnerable members. Our energy will be judiciously spent fighting the civil rights battles if leaders build action plans that attend to the emotional needs of the children, preparing them for a world poised to ignore daily racial injustice. Parents and leaders need to teach why the protests of the "preracial" America were being waged and the roles children can play today.

We can and must psychologically prepare children and youth for the stress that comes from being different. We cannot maintain a social justice movement that battles the legal barriers to equity without simultaneously preparing our children for the psychological effects of racism and inequity that persists despite equity laws. School is the most relevant and frequented stage where the psychological politics of race are played. On this stage, we can teach youth and families to respond in healthy ways to racial backlash or to the resistance of many against "Racial Firsts." The legal and educational blockades to racial justice remain to this day and these barriers ultimately influence social mobility. They require countermeasures that include emotional and relational skills. B. B. King used to sing a song, "The Thrill Is Gone." Well, the work of declining equitable education is suffering not only from a lack of passion, but also a lack of resolve (Garcia & Stigler, 2011). "The Will Is Gone" is a better motto for the current concerns about racial equity in American schooling. We need a psychological and emotional response to these "racial elephants" that localizes protest in our relationships as much as in societal institutions.

Parents must recognize that no cavalry of racial equity fighters is coming. The public resources to support equitable schooling have dried up, by hook or by crook. In segregated schools, Black and Brown and poor White parents and family members will have to become teachers of math, science, and reading at levels not seen since before integration. "Home schooling" plus public schooling could become a mainstay for Black and Brown children to have a better chance for achievement.

Schools with fewer quality teachers are not going away. Education dollars spent for children are not going to increase anytime soon. Educational entrepreneurs are waiting like vultures for public schools to die. Drool from the salivation of the prison industry covers the sidewalks outside school doors, waiting for dropouts and kick-outs (Sentencing Project, 2012). Black parents are going to have to be present at schools to demand the same curricular attention to their children as other parents do. But there will be a need for racially literate schooling after the school day is over if youth are to avoid miseducation. Families will need to depend on other families to collectively address these challenges and help each other.

While it takes a village to raise a child, what does it take to raise a village of racially literate students and educators? Black and Brown and poor White families will have to pool their emotional, psychological, intellectual, and cultural resources to socialize their children so that they can get the most out of their schools, but as better players in the racial game of schooling, not naïve, helpless, and empty vessels. Racially literate villages will have to teach youth and parents that they are the ones that conservative and progressive middle- and upper-class families are running from to get a better education. They will have to teach their children to reject the racial inferiority that assumes predominantly Black schools or the few Black students in PWS are interminably less capable and can't or won't achieve. They must be taught to see, engage, debate, and conquer Black expendability and racial stereotypes in self-talk as much as if not more than in conversation with others, in curriculum development dialogues, or educational policies. Preparing villages of committed families is racial literacy, too. But in PWS, Black, Brown, and White students can use these same racial literacy skills to discover and reduce racial disparities in education, despite the emptiness and blindness of postracial rhetoric. How do students, parents, and teachers mobilize together should schools, school leaders, or politicians refuse to agree on how to navigate thorny racial dilemmas that lead to unconscionable racial disparity? Create villages of racially literate families and communities.

Integrate Racial Literacy as Core to Smart Schooling, Not Single Acts of Ethical Civility

Educators are ethically bound to know better, see better, and do better, for the sake of children's learning. That said, I fully appreciate how painfully difficult it is to address racial conflict. But that explains racial gridlock. It does not exempt educational leaders from addressing racial dilemmas in schooling, particularly as they are so central to achievement. Educational leaders cannot make stump speeches at bully pulpits about racial equality and progress and yet allow fear to paralyze them to avoid addressing racial conflicts in their own schools. They can't avoid resolving racial conflicts, produce students who remain uncertain how to resolve racial conflicts, and still claim to be ethical educational leaders. Educators, counselors, politicians, and parents can't have it both ways. Something has to give because the learning of children is at stake, and so is the racial self-efficacy or confidence necessary to usher that learning into creative spaces.

Solutions to racial matters are hard to come by. Given the difficulty of getting society to see the racial elephants, it's enough for any activist to give up and retire in Africa or simply walk the earth. So let's stay away from "world peace" for now and focus on change we can see, feel, and touch. The racial progress needed to reform the racial climates of PWS is more relational than symbolic, more face-to-face than systemic, more applied and skills-based than sermonic, and more verifiable and observable than opined or hoped. Racial progress is more than ideas. It takes teaching one child, one teacher, one parent, and one classroom at a time.

Racial civility is demonstrated through voice, tone, mannerisms, body language, and as a way of relating. I have observed that civility in many PWS is often reflected in a cultural embracing of "niceness." There are a lot of complex rules and values implicit within the cultural niceness, including rules about how to avoid racial conflicts. Racial civility within this culture often becomes a choreography of avoidance where folks avoid stepping on toes to prevent public humiliation about their racial incompetence. Everybody is talking about and looking for racial equity, but the fear of what to do about it makes its reality improbable. Consequently, since the 1960s, political correctness has become the safest response to the stressfulness of racialized social interactions. Niceness is often seen as the best remedy for this scattered reaction, in the absence of other specific racial coping skills. We can do better.

If racial matters could be solved competently with goodwill and social courtesies, race relations would not remain as the most vexing social interaction of our lifetime or the most challenging civil rights dilemma in K–12 schooling. The reason "being nice to everybody" is insufficient is that our human tendency to avoid interpersonal conflict leads to distancing rather than closeness in relationships. As a society, we continue to increase our openness to mindfulness and meditation strategies but still find it emotionally difficult to ponder, reflect, or listen thoroughly to others' racialized emotional experiences. Seeing and engaging uncomfortable racial conflicts in the classroom are not easy tasks. Given this difficulty, the question that must drive educational leaders and families as discussions of school mission and strategic planning are initiated is, "What are the solutions to racial stress in everyday lived experiences in society and schools?"

Don't Believe the Hype of the Racial Fear: "Just Say Hello" to Racial Conflict

In this book, I have proposed in vivo (in-the-moment [ITM]) stress management as a different way to assess and resolve racial conflicts in relationships found in school and public spaces. Schools may best view the politics of American race relations as resolvable if administrators, teachers, students, and parents can apply stress-reduction strategies during a racial encounter. Rather than simply focus on strategies that work to hide or deny racial conflicts in schools, what tools can we develop to become better educators who demonstrate through hope that racial conflicts can be resolved?

By denying that racial stress exists within schools where students of color are judged academically and intellectually, schools, parents, teachers, and students collude in a dance that harms those who see the racial elephants in the room and refuse to dance. To be clear, the elephant is the racial stress or conflict and the fact that some do not experience it is simply a statement of the diversity of appraisal and coping experiences among the persons in the classroom context. It is one thing not to see obvious racial stress or conflict. It's another thing to see racial stress as a monster to run from. It's yet a very different thing to consider racial stress to be a noxious and powerful foe that can be minimized through engagement. The prevailing theory on avoidance of fearful events and persons suggests the more you run from fear, the greater your perception of its awfulness becomes. Instead, engaging the fear is your best chance to ascertain its dangerousness.

Not all reactions to racial stress are the same. This diversity of reactions is helpful in showing that for some, this stress represents the monster, and for others it's an annoying disturbance. R/ES processes illuminate individuals' appraisal of the dangerousness of racial conflicts. R/ES processes involve what our families and society taught us through verbal and nonverbal communications. In essence, that teaching involves whether to run, fight, or make like a deer in the headlights.

I seek to illuminate moments, rituals, interactions, and traditions of racial hegemony, both subtle and blatant, which directly and indirectly trigger the stress and shame for students, teachers, and parents. Try as we might, the elephants of racial/ethnic conflict never really stay silent in the corner. Although the metaphor of race relations as a safari is not new, it alludes to a both-and worldview perspective, namely, the excitement and danger of taking an unpredictable journey. When I think of elephants and safaris, I think of the duality of life's experiences and how opposing tensions coexist within relationships between humanity and nature, parent and child, teacher and student, and between racial groups. We may not be that different from each other, but any difference should not be hidden like a sore, for the sake of "all getting along." Opposing tensions of interest in racial encounters include "hardship and survival," "harsh brutality amid panoramic beauty," "thoughtful reflection and decisive action," "raging rampage and gentle spirit," and "falling rains that accompany peaceful serenity and growth." Recasting racial stress in the moment of a conflict can reduce irrational fear reactions. The reduction of stress encourages hope because successful racial conversations and actions can become skills-based programming initiatives rather than a list of nonactionable principles and ideas that can't address irrationality or modify racial conflict avoidance coping in the climates of PWS. Racial tensions are necessary ingredients for helping us to face our relational shortcomings.

Believe in Your "Right" to "Choose" to Speak Up About Racial Blindness: "It's Not About the Blame"

As a student of racial social interaction, I find it compelling to predict how folks will react when a racial encounter moment arises. Unspoken racial dialogue between two people can sometimes become painfully situated around the anxiety of "what others will feel" rather than on some mutual interest. So efforts and energies are wasted on minimizing the feelings of racial blame that participants in the encounter might feel. By buffering this blame, we are inadvertently enabling racial blindness. Often, these guilt meltdowns demand a comment from a Black authority to allay the fears and reassert the "other's" racial competence. These interactions are stressful because mutual dialogue fails. But if resolving racial conflicts is "not about the blame," what do educators do? In face-to-face racial encounters, both parties must agree to use avoidance to manage the tension. If these encounters are like dancing in that there is reciprocal movement, then shifting one's role or avoidance response in that dance can be disruptive. Just as in family interactions, there is a homeostasis or balance to this emotional reciprocity that maintains the tension at a workable level; where avoidance of the conflict (racial inferiority, blame, and humiliation) becomes a strategy for keeping the dancing alive.

So each of us has to ask whether we create more racial stress by speaking up about this dance, or are we left helpless to swallow the stress of repetitive and predictable trauma like Bill Murray in *Groundhog Day*? To rescript the racial conversation of avoidance, some disturbance of the balance of racial hierarchy and fear of blame has to happen. So yes, speaking up about the rituals of racial absolution or problematizing Blackness is a basic requirement of racial literacy. Better yet, just speaking up about the racial disparities that individuals witness or experience daily can be an amazing act of civil disobedience because it disrupts the balance of stagnant race relations in school and society.

The revolutionary Caribbean psychiatrist Franz Fanon (1967) once stated, "I find myself suddenly in the world and I recognize that I have one right alone: that of demanding human behavior from the other. One duty alone: that of not renouncing my freedom through my choices" (p. 229). Racial literacy is essential for teaching individuals and groups to make choices in racial encounters that do not put their lives, their dignity, and their freedom in jeopardy. In Fanon's quote is another clue for unlocking the door of racial intransigence and reticence in relationships, in face-to-face encounters, and in PWS. It is choice that matters in racial political encounters, particularly the choice to refuse to respond to that awful question of inferiority. Without the choice of coping or answering or not answering racial conundrums based on this awful question, we can't construct meaningful solutions for resolving racial stress and conflict anywhere, least of all in predominantly White educational systems.

Most of the poetry and essays on combating Whiteness and racial stress I have written in private have been healing. Because it's slightly delusional to think I can change someone who is afraid of my Black presence, I have focused more on my reaction to that fear. Racial stress in others is not something one can control, ultimately. Perhaps by speaking in a certain voice, walking slowly around crowds of people, or saying "excuse me" all the time, you may convince yourself that you are able to reduce some stress. But it is a lie. Walking slowly can be seen as creepy as and scarier than simply being Black and still. And yet to others being Black and still is a nightmare. Ultimately, as Catch-33 dynamics go, Black people may have to face the reality that our very presence is scary, whether we open our mouths or not. Still, whether it is better to speak up and out or be silent, the key is being able to choose your response to that eternal Duboisian query, "How does it feel to be a problem?" The saddest part for all people in school and out would be having no healthy comeback lines and having nothing to say, thus making choice impossible.

Racial assertiveness and literacy involves not only choosing to speak up. It begins with nurturing racial self-efficacy and believing you have the right to choose to speak up against racial incompetence. It's the freedom to choose what one wants to say or do in any given moment, so that you don't pretend to feel unharmed by racial microaggressions or rationalize them as common and unintentional or by telling yourself "I'm being too sensitive." Writing down my *stressful reactions to racial encounters, planning multiple coping responses, practicing healthy comeback lines,* and *communicating these responses and lines* allow me to embrace choice as the key to stress reduction and heal from the rejection over and over again.

Teach and Practice Racial Literacy as Skills for Specific Contexts, Not General Ideas

First, it is important to note that without the presence of affection, protection, and correction in the climate, facilitator styles, teacher-student relationship, and overall training experience, racial literacy skills are not easily taught or learned. Relative balancing of safety and risk taking in trying racial literacy strategies is essential, and the more educators communicate this balance and praise efforts at risk taking, the more likely participants will internalize the skills. Communicating and explicating the benefits of racial self-efficacy that were discussed earlier is one way to promote affection, protection, and correction interactions and illuminate the potential of risk taking for the racial literacy training. Cooper's (2012) notion of creating a critical third space is another way to support the membership challenges of Black students in PWS.

Second, racial literacy skills require specific practice for reducing stress within each of the five socialization contexts of information dissemination, relationship-building, identity reconstruction, styles expression, and stereotype reproduction discussed in earlier chapters. As such, I would see the integrated usage of these skills of racial self-/other observation of racial stress, self-/other racial stress appraisal, racial stress reduction, racial self-control, and racial assertiveness in these five contexts as an advanced form of racial literacy. Racial encounters within *information* social contexts are different from racial encounters within social contexts that require communication through *relationship-building, identity, style, or stereotype*. These advanced skills can be taught and observed over time as participants practice, rehearse, and apply the skills in real-world encounters using racial literacy curricula (see Figures 6.1, 6.2, and Table 6.1).

Reduce Anxiety, Build Confidence, and Grow Self-Affirmation Before Engaging Racial Conflicts

Given that the anxiety in interracial interactions is so disruptive to positive social discourse, positive behavior, and common social civility, how can educators help make these interactions less difficult for all students? Reducing racial anxiety is one important aspect of building racial literacy. Another is increasing racial self-efficacy, or the belief in one's capacity to resolve racial tension wherever they arise. A statement of self-efficacy would be, "I believe I can respond in a healthy, respectful, and competent manner during a racial encounter by identifying the stressors and their effects on my body and reducing that stress in ways that increase my focus on the matters before me." It is a confidence in one's potential to negotiate racial tension. Racial coping self-efficacy beliefs grow when individuals receive direct racial communication about the meaning of racial political discourse and through a review of one's past successful or unsuccessful experiences with a racial conflict. Ultimately, I think of these beliefs and actions as skill sets that can be taught. The training of racial literacy must instill in every person the belief that one can change one's appraisal of and approach toward racial microaggressions, racial malapropisms, and racial encounters of the most unusual kind.

The specific strategies (storytelling, journaling, relaxation, debating, and role-playing) to develop the racial literacy goals and skills in individuals

FIGURE 6.1. Recast Curriculum Sessions

R/A Encounter Awareness—Observing the Behaviors of **Self and Others:**

> 1. Encountering Elephants: Mind Control and Reading My Emotions
>
> 2. Encountering Elephants: Game Control and Reading Others' Emotions

R/A Encounter Stress Appraisal—Appraising the Stress Reactions of **Self and Others:**

> 3. Managing Racial Stress: Breathing and Exhaling While Black
>
> 4. Managing Gender Stress: Man/Womanhood Breathing and Exhaling

R/A Encounter Stress Reappraisal—Caring for Self and Modifying Maladaptive Coping Stressful Encounters :

> 5. Managing School/Neighborhood Stress: Breathing While Talking to Teachers and Police

R/A Encounter Engagement—Controlling and Regulating Emotions During Conflicts:

> 6. Debating Racial Stereotypes: Is N-word for Friend or Foe?
>
> 7. Debating Gender Stereotypes: Never Let Them See You Sweat
>
> 8. Gaming the Game: Retaliation Is Incarceration

R/A Encounter Resolution—Racial Competence and Assertiveness:

> 9. Word Up: Creating Healthy Comeback Lines for When I'm Disrespected
>
> 10. Game Over: Being Smart While Looking Cool in School

FIGURE 6.2: Healthy Racial Coping Comeback Lines: A Checklist

- Racially stressful encounter?

- Feelings about it

- Inappropriate or unhealthy statements or comeback lines I want to say in response

- Feelings about the inappropriate or unhealthy comeback lines

- Do any of the unhealthy comeback lines reduce the racial stress of the encounter? If so, how?

- Appropriate or healthy statements I want to say that preserve dignity but don't lead to unjust incarceration

- Do healthy comeback lines reduce racial stress and how?

- Practice the healthy comeback lines while breathing and exhaling until it becomes habit

Table 6.1: Diversity Stress Appraisal, Relaxation, and Resolution

Diversity Experience or Context	What type of diversity encounter? (Racial, gender, class, age, sexual orientation)	Will/did I have an encounter? What stories can I tell?	How stressful was each encounter? 1—5—10?	How well did I use relaxation strategy when stressed?	Did my stress level increase or decrease?	How well did I engage or re-engage the encounter?	Did I practice (using debate or role-play) any diversity skill?	Was any aspect of the encounter resolved?
POCC Students/Faculty/Chaperone								
Black Boys/Girls Group								
Affinity Groups								
Diversity Day								
Diversity Committee								
Teacher Prof Development								
Parent Groups								
Athletic Teams								

are based on a long and reliable research history of effective psychological strategies, including

- cognitive-behavioral management strategies and mindfulness;
- in vivo (in-the-moment [ITM]) emotional processing where individuals learn to reduce their stress levels during conflictual social interaction;
- stimulation of emotional intelligence, self-affirmation, self-observation, and self-control around racial encounters that students, parents, teachers, and leaders have experienced; and
- developing culturally relevant pedagogy for in-classroom curricula.

Storytelling is the beginning of racial literacy. So how do we begin to get parents, students, and teachers to talk about how fearful they are about racial encounters? Storytelling. Storytelling is an important first step in identifying one's racial stress appraisal, socialization, and self-efficacy regarding past and current experiences. Storytelling levels the playing field and hierarchy of race relations. What did our families teach us about avoiding these discussions? Stories allow us to see our past and present. They empower, as the storyteller chooses how much or how little to share. Choosing ignites a form of racial self-efficacy that avoidance or denial cannot.

If seeing colorblindness "is believing" and storytelling is a vehicle for self-observation, then storytelling will illuminate the relationship between racial stress, self-efficacy, socialization, and coping. I'm hoping the emotional and therapeutic benefits of telling and retelling one's story of racial conflict and triumph will become visible. In turn, I am challenging educators, politicians, and parents to engage in the same risk taking of storytelling on behalf of stress reduction in schools across this country. It is what I ask from my students and colleagues. When you think of the elephants of racial hierarchy from your childhood, from your workplace, and within your collegial relationships, what feelings and thoughts do you observe within you? Better yet, as you become mindful of taking the safari into the jungle of racial politics, what images do you see and what stories would you tell?

Behaviorally and mindfully *reappraising* racial stress from being an insurmountable experience to one that can be transcended is difficult enough to accomplish. But the fear of taking risks during racial encounters is a more challenging hurdle to leap. How then do we strengthen educators' resolve to believe they can engage racial conflicts without running?

It takes practice. I know what you're saying: "Practice? Practice? We're talking about PRACTICE?" Yes, repeated practice of actively rejecting the emotional, cognitive, and behavioral expectations of racial inferiority that are implicit within predictable stressful racial encounters. In particular, racial literacy requires the ability to be mindful of racial conflicts while monitoring one's racial stress. Moreover, it involves speaking up about one's experiences. Appreciating and listening to the resistance and stress in the stories and experiences of students and parents of color are two of the most important goals for diversity agendas in PWS.

Teach Parents and Youth Racial Hardiness to Assertively Confront Racial Obfuscation

We don't need to wait for another commission report on the state of Black and Brown life in America. Time is up, and serious change in how we approach race relations must *first* challenge the expendability of the Black humanity narrative. This narrative is all-encompassing and persistent, but our response to it must be equally persistent. In addition to disaggregating data on racial hardship, school leaders need to teach parents and youth about racial hardiness. Hardiness is the ability to endure difficulty and stressful events in one's life. Studies show that individuals who develop hardiness or self-discipline are more successful in life, view obstacles and failures as challenges rather than statements of worthlessness, and enjoy life more (Duckworth, Quinn, & Tsukayama, 2011; Romer, Duckworth, Sznitman, & Park, 2010). Racial hardiness would represent facing racially stressful encounters with a sense of hopefulness and tenacity, rather than doubt, shame, avoidance, and fear. The existence and humanity of Black life is not on the table for discussion. It's a given. Racial hardiness would allow individuals to reject the expendable Black humanity narrative as a predictable irrational fear reaction that individuals could reframe as incompetence masquerading as intelligence and choose to debate or not waste any psychological energy to consider.

Racial socialization in the 21st century takes place through symbols and stereotypes that are mass-produced and funneled through multiple communication sources (Adams & Stevenson, 2012). But rarely is it sophisticated, historically accurate, and socially and ethically instructive. Relying solely on symbols of racial progress will keep us illiterate. Today more than ever, youth need both hardiness and empathy toward racial injustice. Each requires racial literacy training to psychologically and emotionally cope with and navigate racial hostility and illiteracy in the space where all youth spend most of their waking hours of childhood and adolescence—schools.

Like a herd of elephants in the mist, we question whether racial conflict is real. Did we see it or was it a figment of our imagination? We would rather comment on the mist. "Wow, look how foggy it is today!" The few and the only Black students need much more than obfuscation or speculation about why they get expelled from school more often than other youth for no greater acts of misbehavior. They need more than political opinion masquerading as racial discourse. Our students need prizes now for their ability to navigate neighborhood trauma and still attend school. They need good schooling yesterday. They need schools that teach them to see through the fog of racial inequality and reduce the racial, gender, or class stress in relationships that touch, teach, ignore, suspend, and expel them—today.

Whose job it is to teach these racial hardiness skills? Churches? Schools? Media? Families and parents? Who has historically been known for translating complex life experiences from symbols and stereotypes into daily lessons of coping, survival, and self-actualization? All of these institutions. And that's where we will begin discussing the importance of socialization—racial socialization—in the development of racial coping skills for Black youth. The teaching of these skills was much more prevalent in the first three-quarters of the 20th century because Black families couldn't trust public institutions to communicate cultural traditions of survival and coping. Parents and families were the only entities to transmit knowledge, history, and stories of survival. This lack of trust of social institutions and their leaders and workers was especially true after integration.

This is one of the recasting functions of parenting—to racially socialize and prepare youth to become healthy, competent, and contributing members of society. But how do parents prepare youth for a world (or classroom) of racial stigma when a postracial America makes such recasting seem outdated or, even worse, racist? Now more than ever do children of color need racial socialization to negotiate the old-school nature of the new-school racial inequality.

Being racially assertive is not like other types of assertiveness, because one can lose friends, colleagues, and access to the social and economic capital that comes from being a race-less or race-neutral team player. But in essence, if schools or educational institutions choose silence or race-lessness as a political strategy, students of color will bear the brunt of social rejection that we know influences their academic and social progress. They attend and learn in school with little protection from the insult to their racial difference, and through silence, schools inadvertently condone and protect racial rejection. Despite the silence of systems about racial conflict, it is equally true that any person who could speak up against racial injustice during these tense moments risks becoming a racial elephant.

Look for Racial Self-Affirmation and Literacy in Behavior and Voice, Then Reward

What would we expect to see in school curricula, student learning, and teacher teaching that would represent racial literacy? These criteria would be useful for evaluating the competency of each student, parent, teacher, and professional to resolve racial encounters in daily social interaction by appraising and relaxing their minds, body, and heart. The following list includes racial coping skills (behaviors and actions) that increase racial self-efficacy and self-affirmation. The goal of racial self-affirmation will be reached if the skills of storytelling, journaling, relaxation, debating, and role-playing are practiced using experiences that individuals perceive to be stressful racial encounters. In general, the goals for racial literacy training include the ability to do the following:

- Tell a story and self-reflect on one's past and present experiences with racial/ethnic tension, triumph, and potential.
- ➢ Become racially self-reflective and -evaluative during racial conflicts by
  - ✓ Taking time to ponder immediate experiences of racial discord and unity.
  - ✓ Being mindful of or writing down one's immediate *physiological* reactions (sweating, anxious movements, uncontrolled breathing, stuttering, and racing thoughts); *emotional* reactions (feeling anger, sadness, shame, excitement); and behavioral reactions to stressful racial interactions.
  - ✓ Calculating the intensity, locating the bodily effect, and communicating the stress level during a racial encounter.
  - ✓ Being mindful of barriers to listening clearly during racial conflicts.
  - ✓ Reading books and research about the negative effects of racism on well-being.
  - ✓ Promoting the transmission and acquisition of racial/ethnic intellectual, behavioral, and emotional skills.
  - ✓ Acknowledging the presence of blame but identifying its detriment in resolving the racial tension.
  - ✓ Critiquing knowledge and information in classroom lessons, media portrayals and information, and societal political and public discourse about racial politics.
  - ✓ Knowing what the current state of progress or regression of the educational welfare and potential of different racial groups based on reliable data, not simply personal interest.
  - ✓ Reconstructing your racial/ethnic identity as your life experiences dictate.
- Reduce racial/ethnic stress during encounters that occur in different social contexts (information dissemination, relationship-building, identity reconstruction, style expression, and stereotype reproduction).
- ➢ Be able to engage relationships with persons who are racially different without

- ✓ Changing the conversations about remedying racial injustice to conversations about managing White guilt, absolution, or blame.
- ✓ Leaving the relationship once racial politics and accompanying tensions are raised.
- ✓ Leaving the relationship when a person strongly disagrees with your racial beliefs.
- ✓ Having more than one friend of color who can challenge and debate your worldview about racial matters.
- ✓ Using relaxation and breathing management.
- ✓ Monitoring and modifying underreactions or overreactions to a stressful racial encounter.
- ✓ Self-correcting by forgiving, reflecting, and reengaging when underreaction or overreaction occurs.
- Teach and practice the awareness, appraisal, reappraisal, and relaxation of racial/ethnic stress unique to each of Information, Relationships, Identity, Style and Stereotype (IRISS) contexts.
- ➢ Be able to express and adjust your cultural style in a variety of public settings.
  - ✓ Be able to try out different styles until comfortable.
- ➢ Be able to counter stereotypes in school, neighborhood, home, and media with knowledge and information.
  - ✓ Be able to research existing knowledge on racial politics and stereotyping.
  - ✓ Be able to clearly communicate and explain these issues to children and adolescents and peers.
  - ✓ Be able to regulate emotions in racially stressful situations.
- Teach and practice the engagement and resolution of racial/ethnic conflicts (through debating racial stereotypes and role-playing racial encounters) in schools, neighborhoods, and homes.
- ➢ Be racially assertive during racial conflicts by
  - ✓ Sharing stories about racial indignity or injustice that you managed effectively and one you managed ineffectively.
  - ✓ Raising a concern about racial injustice at school, work, or neighborhood that you have practiced and role-played.
  - ✓ Challenging and debating a controversial racial matter in a public meeting.
  - ✓ Sharing or writing down a moment when you were tempted but instead resisted the urge to suppress your verbal disagreement with an observed racial injustice.
  - ✓ Initiating difficult racial conversation without changing the subject.

✓ Being able to debate, speak assertively, and challenge the reproduction of these stereotypes with students, clients, colleagues, family, entertainers, and politicians in public competitions and private conversations.

✓ Debating and challenging stereotypes in classroom, research, political, and important decisionmaking setting (courtroom, jury, school board, campaign) using knowledge and data.

✓ Asking a trusted colleague or expert for help to resolve a racial conflict you feel overwhelmed by.

This list is not exhaustive but these behaviors are most likely to develop in safe contexts that don't exacerbate the fear and stress of humiliation and ridicule; exclusion from resources or potential career advancement opportunities, rejection of potential or expectations for success, and loss and alienation of humanity *during racial matters*. Now, learning to use most of the skills on these lengthy lists will take work, but participants must be rewarded when they use these skills as they stave off the doubt and bolster confidence. Prompting the development of these skills and others can begin with a set of questions to guide teachers, parents, students, and educators about the kinds of outcomes we expect to see among racially literate persons, curricula, and climates. Figure 6.3 is a diagram of activities that can be used in racial literacy training to develop, deepen, and evaluate social interaction skills during racial encounters.

THE STORYTELLER'S DEMISE:
THE POSTTRAUMATIC STRESS OF RACIAL ASSERTIVENESS

Despite the enormous benefit of racial conversation, racial conflict resolution, and racial literacy skills-building, raising, asserting, or confronting issues of racial stress in schools, public spaces, and family can often feel overwhelming. The storyteller is usually the first one to get shot in the world war of conflict-phobic race relations. After 20-plus years of teaching about diversity and racial injustice and how to face it, I often feel drained. Some call it racial battle fatigue (Nauert, 2011; Soto et al., 2011). The level of vulnerability it takes to teach this work is enormous, about an average stress level of 7 most days. And if you're asking, it would most likely be felt in my stomach area, a certain degree of queasiness when I'm talking to a crowd that is silently gnawing. When I'm here I usually breathe and muster any joke that fits the moment so I can laugh, relax, and breathe without looking too obviously stressed.

FIGURE 6.3. Techniques and Strategies for Recasting Racially Successful Encounters (BE-Breathe/Exhale)

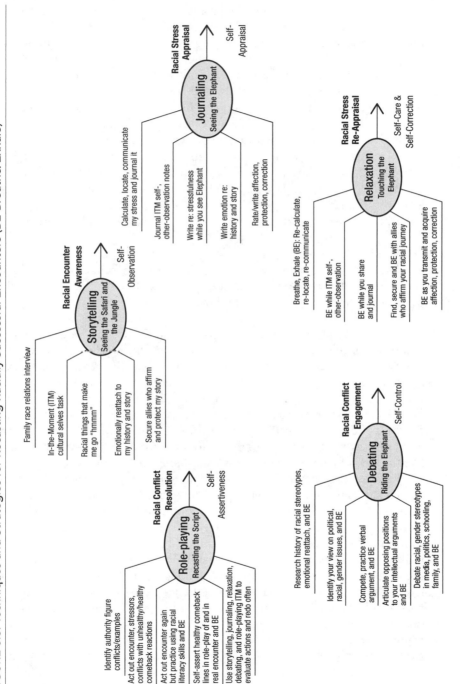

Despite my insistence that racial literacy is not about blame, my students will still feel responsible for racism. Once one feels responsible or blamed for racism, one usually gets angry. Once one gets angry about feeling blamed for racism, one becomes indignant and self-protective ("How dare you blame me for being racist?). And once one becomes self-protective and defensive, one tunes out, snarls, and lashes out. Once one snarls, other people will look at the person and call him or her racist. Once others call one racist, everyone becomes silent. Once everyone becomes silent, I get stressed and tell a joke. Then there is no telling what happens next. It's up to the gods, or left to whatever poor sap does the next diversity workshop. This is just a nightmare I have every now and then called "What if my 'Diversity or Racial Wake Up and Smell the Coffee' workshop goes badly?" The torture begins with giving a mouse a cookie or, in this case, giving an elephant a muzzle. Inciting my students to self-reflect about their racial challenges can be wonderfully positive and life-changing or it can lead to perpetual guilt-tripping.

Integrating racial literacy into school curricula can be a challenge of leadership in that this work often feels like taking one step forward and two steps backward. The resistance is high and the progress is small. I often experience vicarious trauma from witnessing stress in the countless faces of diversity coordinators around the country I visit. I see it in the eyes and attitudes of the first or few faculty of color or who are White in elite academies and want to speak up about racial conflicts but are too afraid. I see it in the voices and stories of the few educational leaders who embrace racial literacy as a meaningful educational goal. The burden of bringing awareness and attention to the racial elephants in schools has its triumphs because I see relief and purpose in the faces of those who speak up about the elephants of racial conflict. But on many days, racial progress feels tragically stagnant or worse—it feels painful, like the kind of pain one has after getting stampeded by the herd.

Because reducing one's stress about matters of racial indignity can bring a keen sense of empowerment, I feel hopeful. But it's the refusal to take risks that triggers the stampede, in my opinion. Support from one's allies helps to heal the wounds, but one feels often like a nagging prophet who stands on the corner predicting the end of the world. I often feel like folks look as if I'm messing up their happy situations or exaggerating conflict for the sake of "bringing the pain" and making them feel guilty on purpose; like my goal in life is to make people dredge up past trauma. Perhaps the most troubling reaction to my work is that bringing up these issues is about teaching hatred. Nothing could be further from the truth. Still, rather than framing racial literacy advocates as prophets of doom, I would see them as storytellers or griots. Still, being a storyteller has its risks, the least of which is alienation and depression.

The posttraumatic stress of it is that you keep reliving the nightmares of being ostracized for saying the "racial" thing. Or it's the rumination of doubt about how you could have said that racial thing much more softly or more strongly given the responses of your colleagues. Posttraumatic stress in the racial literacy struggle is very different from not seeing the light in the tunnel or the daylight outside the tunnel. It's about the inability, refusal, or paralysis of leaders to take that last risky step out of the tunnel into the daylight, like challenging discipline policies in schools are racially biased. It's about so many leaders and teachers and parents who feel the tunnel is a haven, a safe room of sorts from racial conflicts.

My mother's way was to frame the context and provide her children with the behavioral and psychological skills to cope well within contexts where many hostile incidents could occur. My father's way was to focus on the incidents as less important than our souls' salvation, which were under the jurisdiction of God. As long as our souls were right, then the incidents of injustice would have no power over us. Sometimes you push and sometimes you pray. All of these racial coping strategies had a common theme— "the problem of racial inferiority is theirs, not yours." There remain clear reasons to speak racial truth to power that go beyond political correctness, political party affiliation, cultural tradition, sour grapes provocation, and scorched-earth trauma, and that are for the sake of the great spiritual beyond. Racial hostility hits people daily where it hurts—existence. If nothing else, what I learned from my parents' contrasting racial coping approaches was Fanonian in essence—that even if it was stressful, my humanity deserved to be protected and affirmed, as was my right to be.

So when I speak to young Black boys and girls in schools who notice that many students or teachers or police fear, harass, or avoid them, I see it as an opportunity to teach healthy comeback lines. My colleagues and I teach them that reacting angrily to those moments is not a choice if they do so out of anger or humiliation from the disrespect. If it's your only reaction and you use it most of the time, then it's not really a choice. It's part of a scripted role you play or stereotype you live up to. I respectfully argue with them (debating) about how they are simply actors in a play where they are expected to retaliate when disrespected because of their manhood, their Blackness, or their station in life. I tell them that the justice, health, and education systems are prepared to humiliate, then punish them the moment they play the role of "Retaliator" aka "Villain" aka "Criminal" aka "Dogg" aka "Nigger."

I intentionally argue with them and teach that they can choose a number of behaviors that heal them, keep them safe, and outmaneuver the feeble fears of others about Black boys, girls, or people. Our boys and girls are under intense racial and gender profiling and without an awareness of this dance, they are vulnerable to being ensnared. Most public health systems have become institutions of "system threat" for youth of color. Increasingly, given the way youth are arrested in schools, schools may be the most powerful perpetrator among these "threat systems."

But our ability as a civil society to address racial disparity in schooling is not solely predicated on whether we eradicate and heal from difficult racial conflicts or elephants. Reducing racial disparity and inequity in schools begins and ends with whether we believe we can. It's mostly about the racial self-efficacy, the will, the courage. Can we talk about racial stress, conflict, and disparity in classrooms across America and walk through that jungle of racially blind bones? Yes, of course, but will we take the risk to do so? That is the question.

If only elephants could talk. Frankly, I haven't seen it yet. While I'm both doubtful and hopeful that educational leaders and politicians can demonstrate enough civil disobedience and courage to engage the racial conundrums in American schooling, the proof will be evident in the classroom, not the Congress; in proximal face-to-face relationships, not distal virtual or societal ones. I'm more confident that students, parents, and teachers can learn, embrace, and teach racially literate and healthy coping responses to racial stress whether schools, leaders, and politicians decide to change or talk or not.

> **Just say hello** and ask if he wants to stay or go
> and then we'll all know whether it's okay to mention the racial tension
> or find the right intervention for our negative emotions.
> Because ignoring the snoring in the corner gets boring
> and elephants won't leave without attention.
>
> — Stevenson, *Elephant Attention* (2012)

References

Adams, G. (1978). Racial membership and physical attractiveness effects on preschool teachers' expectations. *Child Study Journal, 8*(1), 29–41.

Adams, V. N., & Stevenson, H. (2012). Media socialization, Black media images, and Black adolescent identity. In D. T. Slaughter-Defoe (Ed.), *Racial stereotyping and child development. Contributions to human development* (Vol. 25, pp. 28–46). New York, NY: Karger. doi: 10.1159/000336272

Advancement Project. (2005). *Education on lockdown: The schoolhouse to jailhouse track.* Washington, DC: Advancement Project.org

Aleman, E., Salazar, T., Rorrer, A., & Parker, L. (2011). Introduction to postracialism in the U.S. public school and higher education settings. The politics of education in the age of Obama. *Peabody Journal of Education, 86,* 479–487.

Alexander, M. (2010). *The new Jim Crow: Mass incarceration in the age of colorblindness.* New York, NY: New Press.

Ambady, N., Bernieri, F., & Richeson, J. A. (2000). Toward a histology of social behavior: Judgmental accuracy from thin slices of the behavioral stream. *Advances in Experimental Social Psychology, 32,* 201–271.

American Psychological Association, Task Force on Resilience and Strength in Black Children and Adolescents. (2008). *Resilience in African American children and adolescents: A vision for optimal development.* Washington, DC: Author.

Amodio, D. M., Harmon-Jones, E., & Devine, P. G. (2003). Individual differences in the activation and control of active race-bias as assessed by startle eye-blink response and self-report. *Journal of Personality and Social Psychology, 84*(4), 738–753.

Anderson, E. (2011). *The cosmopolitan canopy: Race and civility in everyday life.* New York, NY: W. W. Norton.

Apfelbaum, E. P., Pauker, K., Ambady, N., Sommers, S. R., & Norton, M. I. (2008). Learning (not) to talk about race: When older children underperform in social categorization. *Developmental Psychology, 44*(5), 1513–1518.

Apfelbaum, E. P., Sommers, S. R., & Norton, M. I. (2008). Seeing race and seeming racist? Evaluating strategic colorblindness in social interaction. *Journal of Personality and Social Psychology, 95*(4), 918–932.

Arrington, E. G., Hall, D. M., & Stevenson, H. C. (2003, Summer). The success of African-American students in independent schools. *Independent School, 62,* 10–21.

Asante, M. K. (1987). *The Afrocentric idea.* Philadelphia, PA: Temple University Press.

Avery, D. R., Hebl, M. R., Richeson, J. A., & Ambady, N. (2009). It does not have to be uncomfortable: The role of behavioral scripts in Black–White interracial interactions. *Journal of Applied Psychology, 94*(6), 1382–1393.

Azibo, D.A.Y. (2003). *African-centered psychology: Culture-focusing for multicultural competence*. Durham, NC: Carolina Academic Press.

Babad, E. Y., Bernieri, F., & Rosenthal, R. (1989). Nonverbal communication and leakage in the behavior of biased and unbiased teachers. *Journal of Personality and Social Psychology, 56,* 89–94.

Baldwin, J. (1985). Introduction: The price of the ticket. In *The price of the ticket: Collected nonfiction 1948–1985*. New York, NY: St. Martin's Press.

Barnes, L. L., Mendes de Leon, C. F., Lewis, T. T., Bienias, J. L., Wilson, R. S., & Evans, D. A. (2008). Perceived discrimination and mortality in a population-based study of older adults. *American Journal of Public Health, 98(7),* 1241–1247. doi: 10.2105/AJPH.2007.114397

Barnes, L. L., Mendes De Leon, C. F., Wilson, R. S., Bienias, J. L., Bennett, D. A., & Evans, D. A. (2004). Racial differences in perceived discrimination in a community population of older Blacks and Whites. *Journal of Aging Health, 16(3),* 315–337.

Bartoli, E., Michael, A., Bentley-Edwards, K., Stevenson, H. C., Shor, R. E., & McClain, S. E. (2013). *Chasing colorblindness: White family racial socialization* (technical paper). Philadelphia, PA: University of Pennsylvania.

Beals, M. P. (2011). *Warriors don't cry: A searing memoir of the battle to integrate Little Rock's Central High School*. Tantor eBooks. Retrieved from www.tantor.com/BookDetail.asp?Product=B0494_WarriorsDont

Bell, D. (1992). *Faces at the bottom of the well: The permanence of racism*. New York, NY: Basic Books.

Benjamin, L. T. (2006). *A history of psychology in letters*. New York, NY: Wiley & Sons.

Bennett, C. (1976). Student's race, social class, and academic history as determinants of teacher expectation of student performance. *Journal of Black Psychology, 3(1),* 71–86.

Bentley, K. L., Thomas, D. E., & Stevenson, H. C. (2013). Raising consciousness: Promoting healthy coping among African American boys at school. In C. Clauss-Ehlers, Z. Serpell & M. Weist (Eds.), *Handbook of culturally responsive school mental health: Advancing research, training, practice, and policy* (pp. 121–133). New York, NY: Springer.

Bertrand, M., & Mullainathan, S. (2003). Are Emily and Greg more employable than Lakisha and Jamal? A field experiment on labor market discrimination (NBER working paper series no. 9873). Cambridge, MA: National Bureau of Economic Research. Retrieved from www.nber.org/papers/W9873

Blascovich, J., Mendes, W. B., Hunter, S. B., & Lickel, B. (2000). Stigma, threat, and social interaction. In T. F. Heatherton, M. R. Hebl, & J. G. Hull (Eds.), *The social psychology of stigma* (pp. 307–333). New York, NY: Guilford Press.

Blascovich, J., Mendes, W. B., Hunter, S. B., Lickel, B., & Kowai-Bell, N. (2001). Perceiver threat in social interactions with stigmatized others. *Journal of Personality and Social Psychology, 80,* 253–267.

Blascovich, J., Spencer, S. J., Quinn, D., & Steele, C. (2001). African-Americans and high blood pressure: The role of stereotype threat. *Psychological Science, 12,* 225–229.

Blascovich, J., & Tomaka, J. (1996). The biopsychosocial model of arousal regulation. *Advances in Experimental Social Psychology, 28,* 1–51.

Bonilla-Silva, E. (2001). *White supremacy and racism in the post–civil rights era.* Boulder, CO: Lynne Rienner.

Bonilla-Silva, E. (2003). *Racism without racists: Color-blind racism and the persistence of racial inequality in the United States.* New York, NY: Rowman & Littlefield.

Bourdieu, P. (1990). Structures, habitus, practices. In *The logic of practice* (pp. 52–65). Cambridge, MA: Polity.

Brody, G. H., Chen, Y., Murry, V. B., Ge, X., Simons, R. L., Gibbons, F. X., Gerrard, M., & Cutrona, C. E. (2006). Perceived discrimination and the adjustment of African American youths: A five-year longitudinal analysis with contextual moderation effects. *Child Development, 77(5),* 1170–1189.

Bulkley, K. (2005). Losing voice? Educational management organizations and charter schools' educational programs. *Education and Urban Society, 37(2),* 204–234.

Cafferty, J. (2012). How racially divided is the United States today? Retrieved from http://caffertyfile.blogs.cnn.com/2012/04/09/how-racially-divided-is-the-united-sates-today/

Cassidy, E. F., Davis, G. Y., & Stevenson, H. C., Jr. (2003). "If we must die": CPR for managing Catch-33, cultural alienation, and hypervulnerability. In H. C. Stevenson (Ed.), *Playing with anger: Teaching coping skills to African American boys through athletics and culture* (pp. 89–114). Westport, CT: Greenwood Praeger.

Casteel, C. A. (1998). Teacher-student interactions and race in integrated classrooms. *Journal of Educational Research, 92(2),* 115–120.

Chang, D. F., & Sue, S. (2003). The effects of race and problem type on teachers' assessments of student behavior. *Journal of Consulting and Clinical Psychology, 71(2),* 235–242.

Clark, K. (1965). *Dark ghetto: Dilemmas of social power.* New York, NY: Harper & Row.

Coates, B. (1972). White adult behavior toward Black and White children. *Child Development, 43(1),* 143–154. doi:10.2307/1127878

Cohen, G. L., & Garcia, J. (2005). I am us: Negative stereotypes as collective threats. *Journal of Personality and Social Psychology, 89,* 566–582.

Cohen, G. L., Garcia, J., Apfel, N., & Master, A. (2006). Reducing the racial achievement gap: A social-psychological intervention. *Science, 313,* 1307–1310.

Cohen, G. L., Garcia, J., Purdie-Vaughns, V., Apfel, N., & Brzustoski, P. (2009). Raising minority performance with a values-affirmation intervention: A two-year follow-up. *Science, 324,* 400–403.

Coleman, S., & Stevenson, H. C. (2013). The racial stress of membership: Development of the faculty inventory of racialized experiences in independent schools. *Psychology in the Schools, 50(6),* 548–566.

Combs, G. S., & Griffith, J. (2007). An examination of interracial contact: The influence of cross-race interpersonal efficacy and affect regulation. *Human Resource Development Review, 6,* 222–244.

Comer, J. P., & Emmons, C. (2006). The research program of the Yale Child Study Center School Development Program, *Journal of Negro Education, 75*(3), 353–372.

Cooper, D. C., Mills, P. J., Bardwell, W. A., Ziegler, M. G., & Dimsdale, J. E. (2009). The effects of ethnic discrimination and socioeconomic status on endothelin-1 among Blacks and Whites. *American Journal of Hypertension, 22*(7), 698–704. doi: 10.1038/ajh.2009.72

Cooper, H. M., Baron, R. M., & Lowe, C. A. (1975). The importance of race and social class information in the formation of expectancies about academic performance. *Journal of Educational Psychology, 67*(2), 312–319.

Cooper, R. (2012). Enhancing the schooling experiences of African American students in predominantly White independent schools: Conceptual and strategic considerations to developing a critical third space. In D. Slaughter-Defoe, H. Stevenson, E. Arrington, & D. Johnson (Eds.), *Black educational choice in a climate of school reform: Assessing the private and public alternatives to traditional K–12 public schools* (pp. 205–216). Santa Barbara, CA: Praeger, ABC-Clio.

Crenshaw, K., Gotanda, N., Peller, G., & Thomas, K. (1995). *Critical race theory: The key writings that formed the movement.* New York, NY: New Press.

Cress Welsing, F. (1990). *The Isis papers: The keys to the colors.* Chicago, IL: Third World Press.

Crocker, J., Major, B., & Steele, C. (1998). Social stigma. In D. T. Gilbert, S. T. Fiske, & G. Lindzey (Eds.), *The handbook of social psychology* (Vols. 1 and 2, 4th ed., pp. 504–553). New York, NY: McGraw-Hill.

Cross, W. E. (1991). *Shades of Black: Diversity in African American identity.* Philadelphia, PA: Temple University Press.

Cross, W. E., & Vandiver, B. J. (2001). Nigrescence theory and measurement: Introducing the Cross Racial Identity Scale. In J. G. Ponterotto, J. M. Casas, L. A. Suzuki, & C. M. Alexander (Eds.), *Handbook of multicultural counseling* (2nd ed., pp. 371–393). Los Angeles, CA: Sage.

Daniels, J., & Schulz, A.J. (2006). Constructing whiteness in health disparities research. In A. J. Schulz & L. Mullings, (Eds.), *Gender, race, class, and health* (pp. 89–127). San Francisco, CA: Jossey-Bass.

Datnow A., & Cooper, R. (2000). *Creating a climate for diversity? The institutional response of predominantly White independent schools to African-American students.* Baltimore, MD: Johns Hopkins University.

Davis, L. W., & Bangs, R. (2010). *Race in America: Restructuring inequality.* Pittsburgh, PA: University of Pittsburgh.

Dee, T. (2004). Teachers, race, and student achievement in a randomized experiment. *Review of Economics and Statistics, 86,* 195–210.

DeGruy-Leary, J. (2005). *Post-traumatic slave syndrome: America's legacy of enduring injury and healing.* Baltimore, MD: Uptone Press.

Devine, P. G., Evett, S. R., & Vasquez-Suson, K. A. (1996). Exploring the interpersonal dynamics of intergroup contact. In R. M. Sorrentino & E. T. Higgins (Eds.), *Handbook of motivation and cognition: The interpersonal context* (Vol. 3, pp. 423–464). New York, NY: Guilford Press.

Devine, P. G., & Vasquez, K. A. (1998). The rocky road to positive intergroup relations. In J. L. Eberhardt & S. T. Fiske (Eds.), *Confronting racism: The problem and the response* (pp. 234–262). Thousand Oaks, CA: Sage.

Dobbs, M. (2005, May 17). Youngest students most likely to be expelled. *Washington Post*. Retrieved from www.washingtonpost.com/wp-dyn/content/article/2005/05/16/AR2005051601201.html

Douglass, F. (1857). *Two speeches, by Frederick Douglass: One on West India emancipation, delivered at Canandaigua, Aug. 4th, and the other on the Dred Scott decision, delivered in New York, on the occasion of the anniversary of of the American Abolition Society, May, 1857*. Ithaca, NY: Cornell University Library Digital Collections.

Douglass, F. (2000). Speech at the American and Foreign Anti-Slavery Society annual meeting, New York City, May, 1853. In P. S. Foner (Ed.), *Frederick Douglass: Selected speeches and writings* (pp. 250–259). Chicago, IL: Chicago Review Press.

DuBois, W. E. B. (1903). *The souls of Black folk*. New York, NY: Bantam Classic.

DuBois, W. E. B. (1935). Does the Negro need separate schools? *Journal of Negro Education, 4*(3), 328–329.

Duckworth, A., Quinn, P., & Tsukayama, E. (2011). What *No Child Left Behind* leaves behind: The roles of IQ and self-control in predicting standardized achievement test scores and report card grades. *Journal of Educational Psychology*. Retrieved from www.sas.upenn.edu/~duckwort/images/publications/DuckworthQuinnTsukayama_2012_WhatNoChildLeftBehindLeavesBehind.pdf

Dunton, B. C., & Fazio, R. H. (1997). An individual difference measure of motivation to control prejudiced reactions. *Personality and Social Psychology Bulletin, 23*, 316–326.

Eberhardt, J. L. (2005). Imaging race. *American Psychologist, 60 (2)*, 181–190.

Eberhardt, J. L., Goff, P. A., Purdie, V. J., & Davies, P. G. (2004). Seeing Black: Race, crime, and visual processing. *Journal of Personality and Social Psychology, 87*(6), 876–893.

Education Week. (2011, July). Achievement gap. Retrieved from http://www.edweek.org/ew/issues/achievement-gap

Essed, P. (1999): Ethnicity and diversity in Dutch academia, social identities: *Journal for the Study of Race, Nation, and Culture, 5*(2), 211–225. Retrieved from dx.doi.org/10.1080/13504639951563

Fanon, F. (1967). *Black skins, white masks* (C. L. Markmann, Trans.). New York, NY: Grove Press.

Fantuzzo, J., LeBoeuf, W., & Rouse, H. (2012). Academic achievement of African American boys: A city-wide, community-based investigation of risk and resilience. *Journal of School Psychology, 50*(5), 559–579.

Feagin, J. R. (2009). *The White racial frame: Centuries of racial framing and counter framing*. New York, NY: Routledge.

Fine, M., Weis, L., Powell, M., & Wong, F. (1997). *Off-White: Readings on race, power, and society*. New York, NY: Routledge.

Fordham, S. (1988). Racelessness as a strategy in Black students' school success: Pragmatic strategy or pyrrhic victory? *Harvard Educational Review, 58*, 54–84.

Fordham, S. (1991). Racelessness in private schools: Should we deconstruct the racial and cultural identity of African-American adolescents? *Teachers College Record, 92*(3), 470–484.

Foster, K. C. (2008). The transformative potential of teacher care as described by students in a higher education access initiative. *Education and Urban Society, 41*, 104.

Frankenberg, R. (1993). *The social construction of Whiteness: White women, race matters.* Minneapolis, MN: University of Minnesota Press.

Garcia, D. R., & Stigler, M. L. (2011). Closed: Competition, segregation, and the Black student experience in charter schools. In D. T. Slaughter-Defoe, H. Stevenson, E. Arrington, & D. Johnson (Eds.), *Black educational choice in a climate of school reform: Assessing the private and public alternatives to traditional K–12 public schools* (pp. 205–216). Santa Barbara, CA: Praeger ABC-Clio Publishers.

Garrett, M. (2010, October 29). Top GOP priority: Make Obama a one-term president. Senate minority leader Mitch McConnell on working with Obama—and then ending his presidency. *National Journal.* Retrieved from http://www.nationaljournal.com/member/magazine/top-gop-priority-make-obama-a-one-term-president-20101023

Gibson, M. A. (2007). Keepin' it real: School success beyond Black and White [Review]. *Social Forces, 86*(2), 869–871.

Gilliam, W. S. (2005). *Prekindergarteners left behind: Expulsion rates in state prekindergarten programs.* Available at www.fcd-us.org/usr_doc/Expulsion-Complete Report.pdf

Giuliano, L. D., Levine, D., & Leonard, J. (2006). Manager race and the race of new hires. *Journal of Labor Economics, 27*(4), 589–631.

Good, C., Rattan, A., & Dweck, C. S. (2012). Why do women opt out? Sense of belonging and women's representation in mathematics. *Journal of Personality and Social Psychology, 102*, 700–717. doi:10.1037/a0026659

Gordon, E. W., & Bridglall, B. L. (2007). *Affirmative development: The cultivation of academic ability.* Lanham, MD: Rowman and Littlefield.

Greene, M. L., Way, N., & Pahl, K. (2006). Trajectories of perceived adult and peer discrimination among Black, Latino, and Asian American adolescents: Patterns and psychological correlates. *Developmental Psychology, 42*, 218–238. doi:10.1037/0012-1649 .42.2.218

Gregory, A., Cornell, D., & Fan, X. (2011). The relationship of school structure and support to suspension rates for Black and White high school students. *American Educational Research Journal, 48*, 904–934.

Grier, W. H., & Cobbs, P. M. (1968). *Black rage.* New York, NY: Basic Books.

Gudykunst, W. B. (1995). Anxiety/uncertainty management (AUM) theory: Current status. In R. Wiseman (Ed.), *Intercultural communication theory* (pp. 8–58). Thousand Oaks, CA: Sage.

Gudykunst, W. B. (2005). *Theorizing about intercultural communication.* Thousand Oaks, CA: Sage.

Gudykunst, W. B., & Shapiro, R. B. (1996). Communication in everyday interpersonal and intergroup encounters. *Journal of Intercultural Relations, 20*, 19–45.

Guess, T. J. (2006). The social construction of Whiteness: Racism by intent; racism by consequence. *Critical Sociology, 32*(4), 649–673.

Guinier, L. (2004). From racial liberalism to racial literacy: *Brown v. Board of Education* and the interest-divergence dilemma. *Journal of American History, 91*(1), 92–118.

Guinier, L., & Torres, G. (2003). *The miner's canary: Enlisting race, resisting power, transforming democracy.* Cambridge, MA: Harvard University Press.

Hacker, A. (1995). *Two nations: Black and White, separate, hostile, unequal.* New York, NY: Ballantine.

Hall, D. M., & Stevenson, H. C. (2007). Double jeopardy: Being African American and "doing diversity" in independent schools. *Teachers College Record, 109* (1), 1–23.

Hamm, J. V. (2001). Barriers and bridges to positive cross-ethnic relations: African American and White parent socialization beliefs and practices. *Youth and Society, 33,* 62–98.

Harrell, S. P. (2000). A multidimensional conceptualization of racism-related stress: Implications for the well-being of people of color. *American Journal of Orthopsychiatry, 70*(1), 42–57.

Harris, M. A., & Wallace, D. (2008). What's so critical about critical race theory? *Contemporary Justice Review, 11*(1), 7–10.

Hebl, M. R., Tickle, J., & Heatherton, T. F. (2000). Awkward moments in interactions between nonstigmatized and stigmatized individuals. In T. F. Heatherton, R. E. Kleck, M. R. Hebl, & J. G. Hull (Eds.), *The social psychology of stigma* (pp. 273–306). New York, NY: Guilford.

Heuer, R., & Stullich, S. (2011). *Comparability of state and local expenditures among schools within districts : A report from the study of school-level expenditures.* Washington, DC: U.S. Department of Education, Office of Planning, Evaluation and Policy Development, Policy and Program Studies Service. Retrieved from www2.ed.gov/rschstat/eval/title-i/school-level-expenditures/school-level-expenditures.pdf

Hileman, J., & Clark, J. J. (2012, July). *Educating Black and Latino males: Striving for educational excellence and equity.* Retrieved from www.americanreading.com/documents/educating-males-of-color.pdf

Hilton, A., & MacDonald, K. (2008, December 9). Race as a social construct—no—and yes!" *The Occidental Observer.* Retrieved from www.theoccidentalobserver.net/articles/CollectiveEditorial-Race.html

Howard, G. R. (2006). *We can't teach what we don't know.* New York, NY: Teachers College Press.

Howard, J. (2010). *On the social construction of race.* Available at www.togonline.com/blog/on-the-social-construction-of-race-2/

Huber, R. (2013, March). Being White in Philly. *Philadelphia Magazine.* Retrieved from www.phillymag.com/articles/white-philly/

Hughes, D. L., Johnson, D., Smith, E., Rodriguez, J., Stevenson, H. C., & Spicer, P. (2006). Parents' ethnic/racial socialization practices: A review of research and directions for future study. *Developmental Psychology, 42* (5), 747–770.

Hughey, M. W. (2010). The (dis)similarities of White racial identities: The conceptual framework of "hegemonic whiteness." *Ethnic and Racial Studies, 33*(8), 1289–1309.

Hyers, L. L., & Swim, J. K. (1998). A comparison of the experiences of dominant and minority group members during an intergroup encounter. *Group Processes and Intergroup Relations, 1,* 143–163.

Jackson, J. L. (2008). *Racial paranoia: The unintended consequences of political correctness.* New York, NY: Basic Civitas Books.

Johnson, D., Slaughter-Defoe, D. T., & Bannerjee, M. (2012). The influence of private and public school contexts on the development of children's racial coping. In D. T. Slaughter-Defoe, H. Stevenson, E. Arrington, & D. Johnson (Eds.), *Black educational choice in a climate of school reform: Assessing the private and public alternatives to traditional K–12 public schools* (pp. 106–122). Santa Barbara, CA: Praeger, ABC-Clio.

Katznelson, I. (2005). *When affirmative action was White: An untold history of racial inequality in twentieth-century America.* New York, NY: W. W. Norton.

Killen, M., Lee-Kim, J., McGlothlin, H., & Stangor, C. (2002). *How children and adolescents evaluate gender and racial exclusion. Monographs of the Society for Research in Child Development, 67*(4) (Serial No. 27). Boston, MA: Blackwell.

King, D. S., & Smith, R. M. (2005). Racial orders in American political development. *American Political Science Review, 99*(1), 75–92.

King, M. L. (1963). Letter from a Birmingham jail. Retrieved from http://www.africa.upenn.edu/Articles_Gen/Letter_Birmingham.html

Kuriloff, P., Soto, A. C., & Garver, R. (2012). The Black-White achievement gap in highly selective independent schools: Towards a model explaining emergent racial differences. In D. T. Slaughter-Defoe, H. Stevenson, E. Arrington, & D. Johnson (Eds.), *Black educational choice in a climate of school reform: Assessing the private and public alternatives to traditional K–12 public schools* (pp. 91–105). Santa Barbara, CA: Praeger, ABC-Clio.

Ladson-Billings, G., & Tate, W. (1995) Toward a critical race theory of education. *Teachers College Record, 97*(1), 47–68.

Lazarus, R. S., & Folkman, S. (1984). *Stress, appraisal, coping.* New York, NY: Springer.

Lesane-Brown, C. L. (2006). A review of race socialization within Black families. *Developmental Review, 26,* 400–426.

Lewin, T. (2012, March 6). Black students face more discipline, data suggests. *New York Times.* Retrieved from www.nytimes.com/2012/03/06/education/black-students-face-more-harsh-discipline-data-shows.html

Lewis, A. (2004). "What group?" Studying Whites and Whiteness in the era of colorblindness. *Sociological Theory 22*(4), 623–646.

Linn, R. L., & Welner, K. G. (Eds.) (2007). *Race-conscious policies for assigning students to schools: Social science research and the Supreme Court cases.* National Academy of Education Committee on Social Science Research Evidence on Racial Diversity in Schools. Retrieved from nepc.colorado.edu/files/Brief-NAE.pdf

Lopez, I.F.H. (2000). The social construction of race. In R. Del Gado & J. Stefancic (Eds.), *Critical race theory: The cutting edge* (pp. 163–175). Philadelphia, PA: Temple University Press.

Loury, G. C. (2005). Racial stigma and its consequences. *Focus, 24*(1), 1–6.

Lovelace, V., Scheiner, S., Dollberg, S., Segui, I., & Black, T. (1994). Making a neighborhood the Sesame Street way. Developing a methodology to evaluate children's understanding of race. *Journal of Educational Television, 20,* 69–77.

Macedo, D. (1995). *Literacies of power: What Americans are not allowed to know.* Boulder, CO: Westview Press.

Maisonet, E., III. (2012, January 16). Jackie Robinson, Martin Luther King, and the stress of revolution. *The Sports Fan Journal.* Retrieved from www.thesportsfanjournal.com/columns/ed-the-sports-fan/jackie-robinson-martin-luther-king-and-the-stress-of-revolution/

Martinot, S., & Sexton, J. (2003). The avant-garde of White supremacy. *Social Identities: The Journal of Race, Nation, and Culture, 9*(2), 169–181. Retrieved from www.ocf.berkeley.edu/%7Emarto/avantguard.htm

Massey, D. S. (2007). *Categorically unequal: The American stratification system.* New York, NY: Russell Sage Foundation.

Mattison, E., & Aber, M. S. (2007). Closing the achievement gap: The association of racial climate with achievement and behavioral outcomes. *American Journal of Community Psychology, 40*(1–2), 1–12.

Mays, V. M., Cochran, S. D., & Barnes, N. W. (2007). Race, race-based discrimination, and health outcomes among African Americans. *Annual Review of Psychology, 58*, 201–225.

McConnell, M. (2010). Mitch McConnell: Top priority, make Obama a one term president. http://www.youtube.com/watch?v=W-A09a_gHJc

McDermott, R. P. (1987). The explanation of minority school failure, again. *Anthropology and Education Quarterly, 361*–364. Retrieved from www.jstor.org/stable/3216663

McDonald, K. B., Harvey, A. M., & Brown, S. (2005). *Visibility/invisibility blues: The marginalization of minority faculty at independent schools.* Paper presented at the annual meeting of the American Sociological Association, Philadelphia, PA. Retrieved from www.allacademic.com/meta/p18286_index.html

McDonald, S., Lin, N., & Ao, D. (2009), Networks of opportunity: Gender, race, and job leads. *Social Problems, 56*(3), 385–402.

Milner, H. R. (2003). Reflection, racial competence, and critical pedagogy: How do we prepare preservice teachers to pose tough questions? *Race, Ethnicity, and Education, 6*(2), 193–208.

Moses, R. P., & Cobb, C. E. (2002). *Radical equations: Civil rights from Mississippi to the Algebra Project.* Boston, MA: Beacon Press.

Murray, C. B. (1996). Estimating achievement performance: A confirmation bias. *Journal of Black Psychology, 22*(1), 67–85. doi: 10.1177/00957984960221006.

Nauert, R. (2011). "Racial battle fatigue" seems to fuel anxiety disorder among African Americans. Retrieved from psychcentral.com/news/2011/03/04/racial-battle-fatigue-seems-to-fuel-anxiety-disorder-amongafrican-americans/24132.html

Neal, L.V.I., McCray, A. D., Webb-Johnson, G., & Bridgest, S. T. (2003). The effects of African American movement styles on teachers' perceptions and reactions. *Journal of Special Education, 37*(1), 49–57.

Neville, H. A., Tynes, B. M., & Utsey, S. O. (2010). *Handbook of African American psychology.* Thousand Oaks, CA.: Sage Press.

Nobles, W. W. (2006). *Seeking the Sakhu: Foundation writings for an African psychology.* Chicago, IL: Third World Press.

Noddings, N. (1988). An ethic of caring and its implications for instructional arrangements. *American Journal of Education, 96*, 215–230.

Noddings, N. (2007). *When school reform goes wrong.* New York, NY: Teachers College Press.

Nyborg, V. M., & Curry, J. F. (2003). The impact of perceived racism: Psychological symptoms of African American boys. *Journal of Clinical Child and Adolescent Psychology, 32,* 258–266.

Oates, G.L.S.C. (2003). Teacher-student racial congruence, teacher perceptions, and test performance. *Social Science Quarterly, 84*(3), 508–525.

Omi, M., & Winant, H. (1994). *Racial formation in the United States.* New York, NY: Routledge.

Orfield, G. (2008, Spring). *Race and schools: The need for action.* Civil Rights Project/Proyecto Derechos Civiles, University of California–Los Angeles, NEA Research Visiting Scholars Series, Vol. 1b.

Orfield, G. (2009). *Reviving the goal of an integrated society: A 21st century challenge.* Los Angeles, CA: The Civil Rights Project/Proyecto Derechos Civiles at UCLA.

Orfield, G., & Frankenberg, E. (2013). *Educational delusions? Why choice can deepen inequality and how to make schools.* Berkeley, CA: University of California Press.

Orfield, G., Kucsera, J., & Siegel-Hawley, G. (2012). *E Pluribus . . . separation. Deepening double segregation for more students.* The Civil Rights Project/ Proyecto Derechos Civiles at UCLA, Los Angeles, CA.

Ott, T. (2013, January 25). Long forgotten, 16th Street Baptist Church bombing survivor speaks out. Retrieved from www.npr.org/2013/01/25/170279226/long-forgotten-16th-street-baptist-church-bombing-survivor-speaks-out

Ozer, E. J., Wolf, J. P., & Kong, C. (2008). Sources of perceived school connections among ethnically-diverse urban adolescents. *Journal of Adolescent Research, 23,* 438.

Parker, L., & Lynn, M. (2002). What's race got to do with it? Critical race theory's conflicts with and connections to qualitative research and epistemology. Qualitative research and epistemology. *Qualitative Inquiry, 8*(1), 7–22.

Parker, L., & Villalpando, O. (2007). A racialized perspective on education leadership: Critical race theory in educational administration. *Education Administration Quarterly, 43*(5), 519–524. doi: 10.1177/0013161x07307795

Parsons, E. C. (2005): From caring as a relation to culturally relevant caring: A White teacher's bridge to Black students. *Equity and Excellence in Education, 38*(1), 25–34. Retrieved from dx.doi.org/10.1080/10665680390907884

Perry, P. (2001). White means never having to say you're ethnic: White youth and the construction of "cultureless" identities. *Journal of Contemporary Ethnography 30*(1), 56–91.

Plant, E. A., & Devine, P. G. (1998). Internal and external motivation to respond without prejudice. *Journal of Personality and Social Psychology, 75,* 811–832.

Pollock, M. (2004). *Colormute: Race talk dilemmas in an American school.* Princeton, NJ: Princeton University Press.

Purdie-Vaughns, V., Cohen, G. L., Garcia, J., Sumner, R., Cook, J. C., & Apfel, N. H. (2009, September 23). Improving minority academic performance: How a values-affirmation intervention works. *Teachers College Record.* Retrieved from www.tcrecord.org ID Number: 15774.

Rattan, A., & Dweck, C.S. (2010). Who confronts prejudice? The role of implicit theories in the motivation to confront prejudice. *Psychological Science, 21,* 952–959. doi: 10.1177/0956797610374740

Rattan, A., & Eberhardt, J. L. (2010). The role of social meaning in inattentional blindness: When the gorillas in our midst do not go unseen. *Journal of Experimental Social Psychology, 46,* 1085–1088. doi: 10.1016/j.jesp.2010.06.010

Rattan, A., Levine, C. S., Dweck, C. S., & Eberhardt, J. L. (2012). Race and the fragility of the legal distinction between juveniles and adults. *Public Library of Science, 7*(5). doi:10.1371/journal.pone.0036680

Rattan, A., Savani, K., Naidu, N.V.R., & Dweck, C. S. (2012). Can everyone be highly intelligent: Cultural differences in and societal experiences of beliefs about the universal potential for intelligence. *Journal of Personality and Social Psychology, 103*(5), 787–803.

Richeson, J. A., & Trawalter, S. (2005). Why do interracial interactions impair executive function? A resource depletion account. *Journal of Personality and Social Psychology, 88*(6), 934–947.

Richman, C. L., Bovelsky, S., Kroovand, N., Vacca, J., & West, T. (1997). Racism 102: The classroom. *Journal of Black Psychology, 23*(4), 378–387.

Rist, R. (1970). Student social class and teacher expectations: The self-fulfilling prophecy in ghetto education. *Harvard Educational Review, 40*(3), 411–451.

Rockquemore, K. A., Laszloffy, T., & Noveske, J. (2006). It all starts at home: Racial socialization in multi-racial families. In D. L. Brunsma (Ed.), *Mixed messages: Multiracial identities in the "color-blind" era* (pp. 203–216). Boulder, CO: Lynne Rienner.

Rodgers, W. (2010, January 5). A year into Obama's presidency, is America postracial? *The Christian Science Monitor.* Retrieved from www.csmonitor.com/Commentary/Walter-Rodgers/2010/0105/A-year-into-Obama-s-presidency-is-America-postracial

Romer, D., Duckworth, A. L., Sznitman, S., & Park, S. (2010). Can adolescents learn self-control? Delay of gratification in the development of control over risk taking. *Prevention Science, 11*(3), 319–330.

Schofield, J. W. (2007). Racial diversity in the classroom. *Congressional Quarterly Researcher, 17*(32), 761.

Schofield, J. W., & Hausmann, L.R.M. (2004). The conundrum of school desegregation: Positive student outcomes and waning support. *University of Pittsburgh Law Review, 66*(1), 83–111.

Schomberg, S. (2013). The enduring world of Dr. Schultz: James Baldwin, *Django Unchained,* and the crisis of Whiteness. Retrieved from theotherjournal.com/2013/09/12/the-enduring-world-of-dr-schultz-james-baldwin-django-unchained-and-the-crisis-of-whiteness/

Scott, J. T. (2011). When community control meets privatization: The search for empowerment in African American charter schools. In D. T. Slaughter-Defoe, H. Stevenson, E. Arrington, & D. Johnson (Eds.), *Black educational choice in a climate of school reform: Assessing the private and public alternatives to traditional K-12 public schools* (pp. 191–204). Santa Barbara, CA: Praeger, ABC-Clio.

Scott, L. D., & House, L. E. (2005). Relationship of distress and perceived control to coping with perceived racial discrimination among Black youth. *Journal of Black Psychology, 31,* 254–272.

Searle, J. (1995). *The social construction of social reality*. New York, NY: Free Press.

Seaton, E. K., & Yip, S. (2009). School and neighborhood contexts, perceptions of racial discrimination, and psychological well-being among African American adolescents. *Journal of Youth and Adolescence, 38,* 153–163. doi: 10.1007/s10964-008-9356-x

Sentencing Project Newsletter, Race and Justice News. (2012, September 25). Justice Department finds Meridian, Mississippi's school-to-prison-pipeline violates students' constitutional rights. Retrieved fromorg2.democracyinaction.org/o/5269/blastContent.jsp?email_blast_KEY=1219599

Shelton, J. N. (2003). Interpersonal concerns in social encounters between majority and minority group members. *Group Processes and Intergroup Relations, 6,* 171–186.

Shelton, J. N., Richeson, J. A., Salvatore, J., & Hill, D. M. (2006). Silence is not golden: The intrapersonal consequences of not confronting prejudice. In S. Levin & C. Van Laar (Eds.), *Stigma and group inequality: Social psychological perspectives* (pp. 65–82). Mahwah, NJ: Erlbaum.

Shelton, J. N., & Stewart, R. E. (2004). Confront perpetrators of prejudice: The inhibitory effects of social costs. *Psychology of Women Quarterly, 28,* 215–223.

Skiba, R. J., Horner, R. H., Chung, C-G., Rausch, M. K., May, S. L., & Tobin, T. (2011). Race is not neutral: A national investigation of African American and Latino disproportionality in school discipline. *School Psychology Review, 40*(1), 85–107.

Skiba, R. J., Michael, R. S., Nardo, A. C., & Peterson, R. L. (2002). The color of discipline: Sources of racial and gender disproportionality in school punishment. *Urban Review, 34*(4), 317–342.

Skiba, R. J., & Rausch, M. K. (2006). Zero tolerance, suspension, and expulsion: Questions of equity and effectiveness. In C. M. Evertson & C. S. Weinstein (Eds.), *Handbook of classroom management: Research, practice, and contemporary issues* (pp. 1063–1089). Mahwah, NJ: Lawrence Erlbaum Associates.

Slaughter-Defoe, D. T. (2012). *Racial stereotyping and child development. Contributions to human development.* New York, NY: Karger. doi: 10.1159/000336272

Slaughter-Defoe, D. T., Stevenson, H. C., Arrington, E. G., & Johnson, D. J. (2012). *Black educational choice in a climate of school reform: Assessing the private and public alternatives to traditional K–12 public schools.* Santa Barbara, CA: Praeger, ABC-Clio.

Soto, J. A, Dawson-Andoh, N. A., & BeLue, R. (2011). The relationship between perceived discrimination and generalized anxiety disorder among African Americans, Afro-Caribbeans, and non-Hispanic Whites. *Journal of Anxiety Disorders, 25,* 258–265.

Spillius, A. (2009). Jimmy Carter: Attacks on Barack Obama fuelled by racism. Retrieved from www.telegraph.co.uk/news/worldnews/barackobama/6198519/Jimmy-Carter-attacks-on-Barack-Obama-fuelled-by-racism.html

Steele, C. M. (2010). *Whistling Vivaldi and other clues as to how stereotypes affect us.* New York, NY: W. W. Norton.

Steele, C. M., & Aronson, J. (1995). Stereotype threat and the intellectual test performance of African Americans. *Journal of Personality and Social Psychology, 69,* 797–811.

Stephan, W. G., & Stephan, C. W. (1985). Intergroup anxiety. *Journal of Social Issues, 41,* 157–175.

Stephan, W. G., & Stephan, C. W. (2001). *Improving intergroup relations.* Thousand Oaks, CA: Sage.

Stevenson, H. C. (1998). Theoretical considerations in measuring racial identity and socialization: Extending the self further. In R. Jones (Ed.), *African American identity development: Theory, research, and intervention* (pp. 227–263). Hampton, VA: Cobb & Henry.

Stevenson, H. C. (2002). Wrestling with destiny: Cultural socialization of anger and healing for African American males. *Journal of Psychology and Christianity, 21,* 357–364.

Stevenson, H. C. (2003). *Playing with anger: Teaching coping skills to African American boys through athletics and culture.* Westport, CT: Greenwood Press.

Stevenson, H. C. (2011). The politeness of whiteness. *The Teachers Voice, 3*(3). Retrieved from www.the-teachers-voice.org/howard_stevenson.html

Stevenson, H. C. (2012). *Elephant attention.* In H. C. Stevenson, *Finding Mojo, a collection of poems.* Unpublished manuscript, University of Pennsylvania, Philadelphia, PA.

Stevenson, H. C. (2013). *What if Trayvon made it home? Giving the stalking talk to Black males.* Unpublished essay, University of Pennsylvania, Philadelphia, PA.

Stevenson, H. C., & Arrington, E. G. (2009). Racial/ethnic socialization mediates perceived racism, and identity experiences of African American students. *Cultural Diversity and Ethnic Mental Health, 15*(2), 125–136.

Stevenson, H. C., & Arrington, E. G. (2012). "There is a subliminal attitude": African American parental perspectives on independent schooling. In D. T. Slaughter-Defoe, H. C. Stevenson, E. G. Arrington, & D. J. Johnson, (Eds.), *Black educational choice in a climate of school reform: Assessing the private and public alternatives to traditional K–12 public schools* (pp. 64–77). Santa Barbara, CA: Praeger, ABC-Clio.

Stevenson, H. C., Davis, G. Y., & Abdul-Kabir, S. (2001). *Stickin' to, watchin' over, and gettin' with: An African American parent's guide to discipline.* San Francisco, CA: Jossey-Bass.

Stevenson, H. C., Davis, G. Y., Carter, R., & Elliott, S. (2003). Why black males need cultural socialization. In H. C. Stevenson (Ed.), *Playing with anger: Teaching coping skills to African American boys through athletics and culture* (pp. 89–114). Westport, CT: Greenwood Praeger.

Stevenson, H. C., McNeil, J. D., Herrero-Taylor, T., & Davis, G. Y. (2005). Influence of neighborhood cultural diversity on the racial socialization experiences of Black youth. *Journal of Black Psychology, 31*(3), 273–290.

Stevenson, H. C., Slaughter-Defoe, D. T., Arrington, E. G., & Johnson, D. J. (2012). Visible now? Black educational choices for the few, the desperate, and the far between. In D. T. Slaughter-Defoe, H. C. Stevenson, E. G. Arrington, & D. J. Johnson (Eds.), *Black educational choice in a climate of school reform: Assessing the private and public alternatives to traditional K–12 public schools* (pp. 268–274). Santa Barbara, CA: Praeger, ABC-Clio.

Stinson, D. A., Logel, C., Shepherd, S., & Zanna, M. P. (2011). Rewriting the self-fulfilling prophecy of social rejection: Self-affirmation improves relational security and social behavior up to 2 months later. *Psychological Science, 22*(9), 1145–1149.

Sue, D. W. (2010). *Microaggressions in everyday life: Race, gender, and sexual orientation.* New York, NY: Wiley.

Sue, D. W., Capodilupo, C. M., Torino, G. C., Bucceri, J. M., Holder, A.M.B., Nadal, K. L. et al. (2007). Racial microaggressions in everyday life: Implications for clinical practice. *American Psychologist, 62,* 271–286.

Sue, D. W., Lin, A. I., Torino, G. C., Capodilupo, C. M., & Rivera, D. P. (2009). Racial microaggressions and difficult dialogues on race in the classroom. *Cultural Diversity and Ethnic Minority Psychology, 15*(2), 183–190.

Tack, M. W., & Patitu, C. L. (1992). *Faculty job satisfaction: Women and minorities in peril.* (ASHE-ERIC Higher Education Report no. 4). Washington, DC: The George Washington University, School of Education and Human Development.

Tatum, B. D. (2003). *"Why are all the Black kids sitting together in the cafeteria?": A psychologist explains the development of racial identity.* New York, NY: Basic Books.

Taylor, T. R., Williams, C. D., Makambi, K. H., Mouton, C., Harrell, J. P., Cozier, Y., Palmer, J. R., Rosenberg, L., & Adams-Campbell, L. L. (2007). Racial discrimination and breast cancer incidence in U.S. Black women: The Black Women's health study. *American Journal of Epidemiology, 166*(1), 46–54.

Thompson, M., & Schultz, K. (2003). The psychological experiences of students of color. *Independent School Magazine 62*(4). Retrieved from www.nais.org/publications/ismagazinearticle.cfm?

Torres, K. C., & Charles, C. Z. (2004). Metastereotypes and the Black-White divide: A qualitative view of race on an elite college campus. *Du Bois Review, 1*(1), 115–149.

Towles-Schwen, T., & Fazio, R. H. (2003). Choosing social situations: The relation between automatically-activated racial attitudes and anticipated comfort interacting with African Americans. *Personality & Social Psychology Bulletin, 29,* 170–182.

Trawalter, S., Todd, A. R., Baird, A. A., & Richeson, J. A. (2008). Attending to threat: Race-based patterns of selective attention. *Journal of Experimental Social Psychology, 44*(5), 1322–1327.

Twine, F. W. (2003). Racial literary in Britain: Antiracist projects, Black children and white parents. *Contours: A Journal of the African Diaspora, 1*(2), 129–153.

Twine, F. W. (2004). A White side of Black Britain: The concept of racial literacy. *Ethnic and Racial Studies* (a special issue on racial hierarchy), 27(6), 1–30.

Twine, F. W. (2011). *A White side of Black Britain: Interracial intimacy and racial literacy.* Durham, NC: Duke University Press.

Twine, F. W., & Gallagher, C. (2008). The future of Whiteness: A map of the "third wave." *Ethnic and Racial Studies, 31*(1), 4–24.

USA Today. (2012, October 27). U.S. majority have prejudice against Blacks. Retrieved from www.usatoday.com/story/news/politics/2012/10/27/poll-black-prejudice-america/1662067/

Ward, J. V. (1996). Raising resisters: The role of truth telling in the psychological development of African American girls. In B. Ross & N. Way (Eds.), *Urban girls: Resisting stereotypes, creating identities* (pp. 85–99). New York, NY: New York University Press.

Webb-Johnson, G. (2002). Are schools ready for Joshua? Dimensions of African-American culture among students identified as having behavioral/emotional disorders. *Qualitative Studies in Education, 15*(6), 653–671.

Weinstein, R. S. (2002). *Reaching higher: The power of expectations in schooling.* Cambridge, MA: Harvard University Press.

West, C. (1994). *Race matters.* Boston, MA: Beacon Press.

Whaley, A. L., & Davis, K. E. (2007). Cultural competence and evidence-based practice in mental health services: A complementary perspective. *American Psychologist, 62*(6), 563–574.

Wilson, W. J. (1996). *When work disappears: The world of the new urban poor.* New York: Knopf.

Wingfield, A. H., & Feagin, J. R. (2009). *Yes we can? White racial framing and the 2008 presidential campaign.* New York, NY: Routledge.

Wong, C. A., Eccles, J. S., & Sameroff, A. (2003). The influence of ethnic discrimination and ethnic identification on African American adolescents' school and socioemotional adjustment. *Journal of Personality, 7,* 1197–1232.

Woodson, C. G. (1990). *The Mis-education of the Negro.* Trenton, NJ: Africa World Press.

Word, C. O., Zanna, M. P., & Cooper, J. (1974). The nonverbal mediation of self-fulfilling prophecies in interracial interaction. *Journal of Experimental Social Psychology, 10*(2), 109–120.

Zirkel, S. (2005). Ongoing issues of racial and ethnic stigma in education 50 years after *Brown v. Board. The Urban Review, 37*(2), 107–126.

Index

About the Author

Dr. Howard C. Stevenson is professor of Education and Africana Studies and former chair of the Applied Psychology and Human Development Division in the Graduate School of Education at the University of Pennsylvania. Dr. Stevenson has served for 28 years as a clinical and consulting psychologist working in poor rural and urban neighborhoods in Pasadena, California, rural Delaware, and New York City with families in crisis.

His research and clinical work involves developing culturally relevant in-the-moment (ITM) therapeutic play interventions for families and youth to improve their emotional and academic achievement psychological adjustment and racial literacy in stressful school and neighborhood situations. This work has been funded by the W. T. Grant Foundation, National Institutes of Mental Health and Child Health and Human Development. The *PLAAY (Preventing Long-Term Anger and Aggression in Youth)* Project uses basketball and racial socialization to help Black youth and parents cope with face-to-face violence, social rejection, and stress from peers, family, schools, and society. With Penn professors Loretta and John Jemmott, Dr. Stevenson co-leads the SHAPE-UP: Barbers Building Better Brothers Project, which trains Black barbers as health educators to provide risk reduction and negotiation skills to prevent retaliation violence and HIV/STDs for Black heterosexual 18- to 24-year-old males during haircut appointments.

He has written numerous articles and three books, including *Playing with Anger: Teaching Coping Skills to African American Boys Through Athletics and Culture; Stickin' To, Watchin' Over, and Gettin' With: An African American Parent's Guide to Discipline;* and *Black Educational Choice in a Climate of School Reform: Assessing the Private and Public Alternatives to Traditional K–12 Public Schools.*